Profits, Security, and Human Rights in Developing Countries

The extractive sector is a particular area of expertise for Canada and more than half of Canada's mining assets abroad are located in Latin America, specifically in Brazil, Peru, Chile, and Colombia. The Canada–Colombia accord was the first free-trade agreement in the world to include annual Human Rights Impact Assessments (HRIA), and also includes a labour side accord where abuse complaints can be formally registered. Using Colombia as a case study, James Rochlin and his international and multidisciplinary line up of Canadian and Colombian scholars, and activists working in the area of human rights, and the judiciary explore:

- What is the best way to identify and operationalize for mutual benefit the concentric space between the interests of extractive corporations in profit and security, on the one hand, and the interests of the host communities in the promotion of human rights and human security, on the other?
- What can the four emblematic and diverse cases in Colombia (Meta, Segovia, Marmato, and Bolivar/La Guajira) tell us about how to fine tune and improve a newly implemented governmental HRIA to render it an increasingly useful global instrument to promote simultaneously corporate security and human security for host communities?
- What is the most efficient and effective way to design and implement Corporate Social Responsibility Programs in a manner that promotes simultaneously corporate security and community human security?

Written in a clear and accessible style, *Profits, Security, and Human Rights* presents practical lessons on how to promote both corporate security and human security in communities where the extractive sector operates in the Global South.

James Rochlin is Professor of Political Science at the University of British Columbia – Okanagan. He has published widely in the areas of Latin American Politics, Global Theory, and Critical Security.

Routledge advances in international relations and global politics

Profits, Security, and Human Rights in Developing Countries

Global Lessons from Canada's Extractive Sector in Colombia

Edited by James Rochlin

Routledge
Taylor & Francis Group

LONDON AND NEW YORK

First published 2015 by Routledge

2 Park Square, Milton Park, Abingdon, Oxon OX14 4RN
711 Third Avenue, New York, NY 10017, USA

Routledge is an imprint of the Taylor & Francis Group, an informa business

First issued in paperback 2017

Library of Congress Cataloging in Publication Data
Profits, security and human rights in developing countries: global lessons from Canada's extractive sector in Colombia / edited by James Rochlin.
    pages cm. – (Routledge advances in international relations and global politics; 122)
    Includes bibliographical references and index.
    1. Mineral industries–Moral and ethical aspects–Colombia. 2. Mineral industries–Moral and ethical aspects–Canada. 3. Human rights–Colombia. 4. Human rights–Canada. 5. Canada–Foreign economic relations–Colombia. 6. Colombia–Foreign economic relations–Canada. I. Rochlin, James Francis, 1956–
    HD9506.C66P76 2015
    338.20971–dc23   2014048866

ISBN: 978-1-138-77621-0 (hbk)
ISBN: 978-1-138-06670-0 (pbk)

Typeset in Times New Roman
by Wearset Ltd., Boldon, Tyne and Wear

Contents

Tables

Contributors

Jairo Agudelo Taborda is a Professor of Relaciones Internacionales at the Universidad del Norte, Barranquilla, Colombia. He directs the PhD program there. He was recently the Director of the Escuela Latinoamericana de Cooperación y Desarrollo at the Universidad San Buenaventura, Cartagena, Colombia. He specializes in Latin American Development.

Ibelis Blanco Rangel has a degree in sociology from the Universidad Catolica Andres Bello (Caracas), and is a Masters student and researcher at the Escuela Latinoamericana de Cooperacion y Desarrollo, Universidad de San Buenaventura, Cartagena.

Claudia Donoso is a PhD candidate in Political Science and Latin American Studies at the University of British Columbia – Okanagan, in Kelowna, BC, Canada. Her publications have focused on feminism and human security in Ecuador and elsewhere. She has a Masters Degree in International Relations from FLACSO, Ecuador.

Gustavo Gallón is Director, Comisión Colombiana de Juristas (CCJ), in Bogotá, Colombia. The CCJ is a non-governmental organization run by lawyers and dedicated to social justice in Colombia and elsewhere. He has also been active as an academic, teaching at the Kellogg Institute at Notre Dame University in 1998 and 1999, as well at a variety of Colombian universities.

Wilmar Martínez Márquez is a Professor at the Instituto de Estudios Políticos at the Universidad de Antioquia, Medellín, Colombia. He specializes in philosophy and is coordinator of a research group at his university on Hegemony, War, and Conflict. He has many publications in the area of contemporary Colombian domestic and international politics.

Juan José Moncada Carvajal specializes in both politics and anthropology. He is a researcher at the Instituto de Estudios Políticos at the Universidad de Antioquia, Medellín, Colombia. His research focuses on human rights, human security, and free trade agreements.

Ana María Muñoz Segura has a Masters in Law from the University of the Andes and PhD in Law from the Pontificia Universidad Javeriana, both in Colombia. She is a Fellow at the International Labour Organization in partnership with the University of Bologna and Castile – La Mancha. She is Associate Professor and Director of the area of Labour Law at the Law Faculty of the University of the Andes. Her interests are in the areas of social security, pension systems, pensions, and gender harassment.

Adrián Restrepo Parra is a Professor at the Instituto de Estudios Políticos at the Universidad de Antioquia, Medellín, Colombia. He is the coordinator of Political Studies research there. He has published various books, chapters, and articles on contemporary aspects of politics in Colombia.

James Rochlin is Professor of Political Science at the University of British Columbia – Okanagan. He has numerous books, academic articles, and policy papers in the areas of Latin American politics and security. Dr. Rochlin is the principal researcher for the academic grant that funded this book from the Social Sciences and Humanities Research Council of Canada.

Gustavo Rodríguez Albor is an economist and has a PhD in Social Sciences. He is a Professor and researcher at the Faculty of Management, Economics and Financial Sciences at the Universidad del Caribe, Barranquilla (Colombia). His publications have been especially about institutions, development, and economy.

Sebastián Rubiano Galvis has a JD and MA in Geography from the University of the Andes (Bogotá, Colombia). He is a researcher at the Centre for Socio-Legal Research (CIJUS) and coordinator of the Public Interest Law Clinic. He has consulted for organizations such as the Alexander von Humboldt Research Institute for Biological Resources, the Ministry of Environment, and the National Environmental Forum. He is the author of several publications on environmental legal issues. His areas of interest are conservation and land use policies, environmental law, human rights, and extractive industries.

Beatriz Eugenia Sánchez Mojica is an International Law Lecturer at the Law Faculty of Los Andes University, Colombia. She is a lawyer and holds a Master degree in European Social Action and International Cooperation awarded by Carlos III University, Spain. She also holds a PhD in Human Rights from Carlos III University. She is a research fellow at the Instituto Universitario de Migraciones at Pontificia Universidad de Comillas, Madrid. Her research is focused on human rights, protection of internally displaced persons, refugees, and migrants. Her work has been published in books, academic journals, and research reports.

Gus Van Harten is a Professor at Osgoode Hall Law School, at York University in Toronto, Canada. He previously taught at the law department of the London School of Economics. He is author of *Investment Treaty Arbitration and Public Law* (Oxford University Press, 2007) and *Sovereign Choice and Sovereign Constraints: Judicial Restraint in Investment Treaty Arbitration* (Oxford University Press, 2014). He has authored numerous academic and popular articles.

Marco Alberto Velásquez Ruiz is a Colombian lawyer (Javeriana University, Bogotá) with graduate studies in International Law (IHEID, Geneva). Currently, he is a PhD candidate at Osgoode Hall Law School – York University. He has extensive experience as a lecturer and researcher in legal theory, migration studies, human rights, and international investment law. Additionally, he has worked as a consultant to various national and international organizations (Human Rights Bureau Colombia, IOM, UNHCR, and Saclabrini International Migration Network) in projects related to the rule of law, transitional justice, and development issues.

Foreword

Gustavo Gallón

Social justice is a crucial yet sometimes elusive goal in Colombia. Nowhere is this clearer than in the extractive sector. In many ways, Colombia represents a microcosm for the panorama of human rights threats that exist in the oil and mining industry throughout the Global South. These include threats to workers' rights, ethnic rights, and gender rights. They also entail epistemic clashes, the proliferation of violence, and threats to environmental sustainability.

The case studies in this volume are analyzed through the lens of Critical Human Security. This framework addresses social justice through a focus on the synergy between security, development and human rights. It is a highly practical approach for identifying key problems and for providing workable mechanisms for their resolution.

The aim of this project is to promote social harmony by empowering host communities of foreign investment in the extractive sector, and to do so in a manner that benefits corporations through the provision of a more secure and stable environment in which to operate. Solutions depend on rising above polemics by defining the common space between the interests of host communities, foreign corporations, and government. Further, interdisciplinary approaches can be helpful to address complex social problems. This project benefits from the contributions of experts from non-governmental organizations and from academics. Its members specialize in the fields of law, politics, development, philosophy, labour relations, economics, and Latin American studies.

The case of Canadian corporations is particularly significant. Because Canada is a dominant player in the extractive sector of Colombia, and more generally in the Global South, investments by Canadian corporations can represent important case studies from which to draw global implications. I shall proceed to provide some brief contextual information in the realms of Colombian history, human rights, and Canada–Colombia relations.

Historical Context of the Extractive Sector in Colombia

Since pre-colonial times Colombia has had a strong reliance upon non-renewable natural resources such as gold, coal, and petroleum. Prior to the Conquest, the Indigenous cosmogony assigned a prominent place to gold as a cultural value that represented them as population. The arrival of colonizers substantially altered the symbolic value given to gold by Indigenous peoples. It suddenly adopted a primarily economic value. And to realize that value, Spanish colonizers exploited Indigenous peoples and newly imported African slaves to work in gold mines.

In the late eighteenth century, the reign of Charles III of Bourbon improved the technology for the extraction of gold and silver in Colombia. German engineers were hired to achieve higher productivity in the extraction process. That trend was maintained following the country's independence in 1821. The Republican governments embraced new technology and saw an opportunity to achieve wealth, free of the colonial tax. In 1825, many contractors from Germany and England arrived to Marmato and Supía in the department of Caldas, and to Santa Ana de Lajas in Tolima. The aim of these foreigners was not only to advise the government and the emerging mining business class in extracting precious metals, but also to make significant capital investments regarding the exploitation of resources. In 1886, with the promulgation of the Constitution of Núñez, the government adopted the Mining Code of the former Sovereign State of Antioquia, with the firm intention of harmonizing and promoting extractive activities throughout Colombia. As a result, in 1920 the first oil drilling took place in Barrancabermeja, and in 1941 a new peak in gold production was reached.

In 1950, the mining sector began to yield to other industries, such as manufacturing, agriculture, and cattle. The importance of the mining sector in the economy reappeared in mid-1980s when coal mining commenced in the Cerrejón in the department of La Guajira. This involved the establishment of the largest open pit coal mine in the world. During the 2000s, massive mining concessions in Colombia proliferated alongside rising commodity prices and a government that rendered the extractive sector to be the country's engine of development. The Mining Code of 2001 and the National Mining Development Plan of 2006 made clear the government's intention of promoting Colombia's extractive sector through foreign investment. This was accompanied by Colombia's engagement in multiple international economic agreements designed to expedite the flow of investment and trade. In this context, Colombia has signed 12 such agreements,[1] including one with Canada.

Social Justice, the Extractive Sector, and Free Trade Regimes

In the new millennium the human rights movement has drawn attention to threats to human security associated with the sudden expansion of extractive industries in Latin America. There are two broad impediments to the achievement of human security in the extractive sector. First is the persistence among many Latin American governments of weak regulatory frameworks, and the absence of effective judicial remedies to prevent or compensate for the damage caused during the exploitation of non-renewable natural resources. A second challenge is the lack of sufficient support from the home State of investors, which typically promote extractive investment in the Global South without doing enough to protect host communities from real and potential threats to human security posed by such projects.

The case of the Free Trade Agreement (FTA) between Colombia and Canada takes into account that the implementation of such agreements can generate tensions between the guarantee of human rights and the promotion of trade and investment. The governments of Colombia and Canada are obliged to submit Annual Reports on Human Rights to their respective legislatures. This is something of a novelty because it reinforces international engagement on the crucial matters of human security and social justice.

While the principle of linking bilateral economic agreements with human rights is a sound and praiseworthy idea, in practice the Annual Reports associated with the FTA have been quite weak. Both the Colombian and Canadian governments appear to view the Annual Report as a rote formality. These Human Rights Impact Assessments (HRIAs) are revivable. But to be meaningful they require a government with the vision to empower host communities in a manner that also benefits business and the State. Governmental HRIAs represent a powerful and practical tool for a State that is equipped to use one with sincerity. Corporate HRIAs are also highly significant in this regard. These ideas are developed throughout the volume.

This book empirically and theoretically unveils the complex relationships that exist between host communities, TNCs in the extractive sector, and the Colombian State. The cases in this volume are well chosen to explore a wide variety of themes related to human security and the extractive sector. They vary in geographical location, and examine the three key commodities of petroleum, coal, and gold. While the cases share common threats to social justice and human security, there are also crucial problems that are peculiar to each case. Altogether, they make an excellent platform from which to consider the array of challenges and opportunities for the achievement of human security in the extractive sector.

Note

1 These Free Trade Agreements include: Tratado de Libre Comercio entre los Estados Unidos Mexicanos y la República de Colombia; Tratado de Libre Comercio entre la República de Colombia y las Repúblicas de el Salvador, Guatemala y Honduras; Acuerdo de la Comunidad Andina de Naciones; Acuerdo principal sobre comercio y cooperación económica y técnica entre la República de Colombia y la Comunidad del Caribe (CARICOM); Acuerdo de Complementación Económica N° 59 (ACE 59) CAN – MERCOSUR; Tratado de Libre Comercio entre la República de Colombia y la República de Chile; Acuerdo de Libre Comercio entre la República de Colombia y los Estados EFTA (Suiza, Liechtenstein, Noruega e Islandia); Acuerdo de Promoción Comercial entre la República de Colombia y Estados Unidos de América; Acuerdo de Alcance Parcial de Naturaleza Comercial AAP.C N° 28 entre la República de Colombia y la República Bolivariana de Venezuela; Acuerdo de Alcance Parcial de Naturaleza Comercial AAP.C N° 28 entre la República de Colombia y la República Bolivariana de Venezuela; Acuerdo de alcance parcial suscrito entre la República de Colombia y la República de Nicaragua; Acuerdo Comercial entre la Unión Europea, Colombia y Perú.

Acknowledgments

James Rochlin

As the editor of this volume, I would like thank my colleagues for their wonderful efforts and insights over the three-year period it took to write this book. I am especially grateful to the Social Sciences and Humanities Research Council of Canada for its generous Partnership Development Grant that funded the research for this project. I am also very grateful to the University of British Columbia – Okanagan (UBCO) for its internal grants that have been essential to the book's publication, especially funding for translation services and for work study projects that have subsidized student research.

I would especially like to thank Barbara Sobol, a member of our wider project regarding human security and extraction in Colombia. She has been the information manager for the project, and has provided research assistance and direction that is above and beyond. I am also grateful for the strong support we received from Melody Burton, Deputy University Librarian at University of British Columbia.

I am highly appreciative of the support we received from Colombia's Escuela Nacional Sindical (ENS), an NGO that is on the front lines of labour rights in the country. The ENS is a partner in our larger project, and has provided valuable research for this book.

A number of students at UBCO have been essential for their contributions to this book. Claudia Donoso, a PhD candidate at UBCO, has provided excellent research for the book, and has helped coordinate the book's team of contributors. She and I translated Chapters 2, 4, and 5, as well as the Foreword, from Spanish to English. Elise Hjalmarson, a Masters Student at UBCO, has offered truly outstanding research and support throughout the project. I am also extremely grateful to a former PhD student, Julian Torres, for his superb research and technical abilities that helped this project get off the ground. Mitch Young, a fourth-year student in International Relations at UBCO, provided very helpful research on the issue of Corporate Social Responsibility.

Most of all, I thank Ruth for everything.

1 Introduction

James Rochlin and Gustavo Gallón

In the early twenty-first century the extractive sector has emerged as the face of Canada in the resource rich Andean region of South America. The same is true with regard to Mexico, key Central American countries, as well as many African nations. In so many ways, Colombia represents a crucial microcosm regarding the presence of transnational extractive corporations in the Global South. This is especially the case with regard to the wide assortment of problems that can occur within the nexus of development, security and human rights – a triad of themes to which we shall refer under the rubric of Critical Human Security (CHS).

This volume addresses the following central research questions. First, what is the best way to identify and operationalize for mutual benefit the concentric space between the interests of host communities in the promotion of human rights, development and security, on the one hand, and the interests of extractive corporations in profit and stability, on the other? Second, what can the four emblematic and diverse cases in Colombia tell us about how to refine and improve a newly implemented governmental Human Rights Impact Assessment (HRIA) in tandem with individual corporate HRIAs? Finally, what global lessons can be gleaned from the Colombian cases regarding the promotion of human security in the extractive sector of the Global South?

There are three central arguments to emerge from the analyses in this volume. First, tripartite negotiation between the State, business, and the community historically has been rare in Colombia, but it is crucial to achieve conflict resolution. Of the four cases treated here, this occurred in a major way only in the case involving Pacific Rubiales Energy Corporation. The creation of programs for State capacity building, and for confidence building mechanisms among key actors, is required to facilitate tripartite negotiation. This necessitates both international guidance and financial assistance. Rather than the prevailing tendency in Colombia of relying on violence and imposition to settle scores, conflict resolution needs to be institutionalized, inclusive, transparent, and secure.

Second, HRIAs, in both their corporate and government versions, can be a highly useful instrument that benefits both communities and Transnational Corporations (TNCs). They can help promote a more secure, stable, and predictable environment that respects human rights. But these need to be developed and conducted with sincerity and great care, rather than as a ploy to placate human rights critics, as Canada's Harper Administration has done with regard to the world's first governmental HRIA that is attached to the Canada–Colombia Free Trade Agreement (CCFTA).

Finally, the Colombian State needs to adopt a medium- and long-term vision of sustainable development and political harmony. By relying on a myopic policy designed to please the short-term financial interests of TNCs, the State has perpetuated an insecure and volatile environment that harms both business and host communities. This is especially true in relation to the boom and bust cycles inherent in the extractive sector, and the recent collapse of commodity prices.

The volume celebrates an interdisciplinary and collaborative perspective. It includes contributions from academics in the fields of law, political science, economics, development, philosophy, and Latin American Studies. It also provides insights from the Comisión Colombiana de Juristas – a globally respected non-governmental organization (NGO) in Colombia that focuses on legal aspects of social justice. The project has benefited from the research of one of our key partners, the Escuela Nacional Sindical in Medellín, the country's leading NGO in the area of labour relations. Rather than a collection of disparate essays from autonomous researchers, the volume is integrated since its various authors are part of a larger collaborative project regarding social justice, the extractive sector, and the Global South. For three years, we have had team meetings in Colombia to plan the volume, and then to present our work to one another for comments and suggestions.

The volume affords vast liberty to the contributors with regard to conceptualization and the incorporation of their particular areas of specialization. At the same time, for the sake of coherency, each of the case studies follows a similar structural format that provides historical context, as well as a discussion of the triangular relationship between the State, the corporation, and the community. The case studies also raise suggestions for conflict resolution, and analyze the prospects for further development and improvement of Human Rights Impact Assessments. Each of the cases touches on specific aspects of the Critical Human Security framework in relation to development, security, and human rights.

Chapter 2 concerns the case of the Pacific Rubiales Energy Corporation in Puerto Gaitán, Meta. This large company is responsible for about a quarter of the petroleum produced in the country. The chapter is written by Colombian academic experts in the field of international law. There are numerous issues at play here, such as allegations of serious violations of labour rights and the host community's struggle for empowerment. All of this has occurred within an often chaotic and violent scenario involving a complex array of actors, including two left-wing rebel groups, right-wing paramilitaries, military forces, and competing unions. This case features a rare example of State-led tripartite negotiation to resolve conflict.

Chapter 3 addresses the case of Gran Colombia Gold Corporation (GCG) in Marmato, Caldas. It is written by a Canadian political scientist who focuses on Latin American political economy and security. The community of Marmato has been mining gold since long before the arrival of Spanish colonists, and in many ways, represents a world of its own. In a very unique way, Marmato does not host the illegal armed groups that plague so many other regions of the country.

Although its project of an open pit mine appears to be arrested as of this writing, when the project was alive GCG had pressed to relocate this historic community apparently against its will – hence the issue of displacement. Ethnicity is a key factor in this case, given that over 50 percent of the community are Afro-Colombians and almost 20 percent are Indigenous. There exists an epistemological clash between the community and the TNC. Marmato residents value a spiritual relationship to territory. They prefer a slow extraction of gold to last another eight centuries, and are adamant about the preservation of their unique culture. The corporation, on the other hand, moves to the postmodern rhythm of ultra-speed, celebrates monetary value, and embraces a de-territorialized approach to globalization whereby a particular piece of land is of fleeting value.

In sharp contrast to the situation in Marmato, Chapter 4 analyses the case of Gran Colombia Gold Corporation in the communities of Segovia and Remedios, Antioquia. It is written by Colombian academics in the fields of politics, philosophy and economics. This region is plagued by pronounced and systemic violence, and involves a wide array of criminal organizations, ex-paramilitary groups, left-wing guerrillas, private security corporations, and a community struggling to survive. Segovia and Remedios host the worst mercury pollution on the planet due to gold extraction. As is the case throughout the country's mining industry, a major problem concerns artisanal or non-traditional miners without legal title to their mines. As we shall see, the vast majority of gold extracted in Colombia is done by traditional miners that the Colombian government has recently deemed to be illegal.

Chapter 5 involves the La Caypa Mine in La Guajira, and concerns Pacific Coal Resources Ltd. It is written by Colombian political scientists and specialists in the field of development. Here the commodity extracted is coal, and in contrast to the larger and more organized communities examined in the other cases, this one is unique due to the smallness of the community. This micro-study examines the various effects of the coal mine on a community that is tiny, relatively unorganized, and isolated. Key issues here include workers' rights, health issues allegedly related to the mine, sustainable development, and the sinking of the community's recent economy that focused on subsistence agriculture.

Chapter 6 provides a legal analysis of the Canada–Colombia Free Trade Agreement (CCFTA), and its related side agreements on Labour and the Environment, in relation to the extractive sector. It is written by a Canadian law professor, and focuses on the social power behind trade agreements. It examines the legal rights and responsibilities of Canadian investors in Colombia's extractive sector. The chapter also provides an in-depth legal analysis of the Annual Report on Human Rights attached to the CCFTA. This chapter draws from the report's case studies to examine their broader legal implications. Finally, Chapter 7 will draw broad analytical conclusions from the variety of cases presented throughout the book.

This introductory chapter will set the stage for the case studies and analyses that follow. Because the cases are diverse and they are covered from a variety of academic disciplines, a wide assortment of essential themes will be addressed here. First, we shall trace the development of the concept of human security to that of the Critical Human Security approach used in this book. Next, there will be a brief examination of Colombia's historical context in relation to the current situation of the country's extractive sector. Third, we shall provide a summary of the historical development of Canada's role in Latin America, and then shift to an analysis of the evolution of the Canada–Colombia Free Trade Agreement. Fourth, the role of corporate and governmental Human Rights Impact Assessments will be discussed. Overall, while one could write book-length volumes on each of those themes, our task here is to provide a succinct contextual basis from which to situate the ensuing case studies.

Finally, the research and writing for this volume occurred when a boom in the extractive industry appeared to veer into an abrupt and calamitous bust. This has raised profound questions regarding Colombia's model of development that has relied so heavily on the extractive sector. Colombian leaders appeared to believe that the good times would never end for the mining and petroleum industries, despite the long historical record of their cyclical and volatile trajectories. We shall explore the implications of this in Chapter 7.

The Development of the Concept of Human Security: a Critique

The pursuit of wealth on the part of Canadian firms in Colombia's extractive sector needs to be placed against the backdrop of the intersection of security, development and human rights. Canadian firms abroad operate within a particular model of development embraced by the host country. Transnational corporations (TNCs) must also navigate the security context of the country and community in which they operate. The workers of TNCs, and the community members that host them, are guaranteed human rights by various international charters that in principle should be enforced by the host State. This dynamic nexus of development, security and human rights is particularly complicated in the Colombian case, with its sad but improving record of social violence and human rights abuse.

That nexus, in its ideal form, represents the foundation of the human security approach.[1] It emerged in 1994 out of the United Nations Developmental Program (UNDP). The context was the end of the Cold War, the hegemony of transnational capitalism, and the proliferation of transnational NGOs that attempted to fill the welfare and developmental gaps created by the neoliberal State. It was conceived with an appreciation for newly defined security threats in the form of environmental concerns, identity politics (ethnicity, religion, gender), and transnational criminal organizations such as narcotraffickers. The seminal UNDP document argued that:

> For too long, the concept of security has been shaped by the potential for conflict between states ... security has been equated with threats to a country's borders.... Future conflict may often be within nations rather than between them.... The search for security in such a milieu lies in development, not arms.[2]

As opposed to the neo-realist concept of national security, human security avoided a focus on the nation state and instead emphasized that "...human security is people centered."[3] The two primary points of reference for human security are, firstly, "the security of the individuals" with an emphasis on "their protection and empowerment."[4] Second is the notion that "most people derive security from their membership in a group – a family, a community, an organization, a racial or ethnic group that can provide cultural identity and a reassuring sense of values."[5] Human security, then, has been conceived for a globalized world with a fresh landscape of actors and interests.

In 1994, this newfangled approach suggested that at least some mainstream political actors were amenable to a vast reinterpretation of security. The concept of human security found expression in the foreign policy of Canada during the last couple of years of the 1990s and in Japan for a few years during the new millennium.[6] In 2006, the United Nations refined and further developed the concept of human security – but continued to emphasize the foundational nexus of development, security and human rights. Rather than ignoring or refuting the concept of national security, as it seemed to in 1994, the UN in 2006 indicated that "Human security is needed in response to the complexity and the interrelatedness of both old and new security threats."[7] Beyond complexity and contingency, human security embraced "transnational" aspects of security.[8]

Most importantly in a conceptual sense, the 2006 rethinking of human security by the UN links a "top down" or State-centered approach with a "bottom up" perspective that empowers the marginalized through inclusive and participatory mechanisms.[9] It is this aspect that affords the concept of human security with the potential for sweeping and emancipatory change – a point to which we shall return. Significantly, the 2006 document emphasizes that the looseness of the concept is practical and helpful, since its basic elements can be adapted and altered to the particular context of the case at hand. Thus, a contextual application of human security provides the concept with a practical specificity. Refreshingly, it also emphasizes transnational partnership, collaboration and synergy. Further, it underscores the combined focus of the individual and the community as referents for security.[10] With regard to the Colombian case in particular, the 2006 document helpfully acknowledges some salient security problems such as war economies, embedded war, rampant impunity, and illegal networks of economy and security.[11]

Setting in Motion a Critical Human Security Framework

While United Nations agencies developed and gradually honed the concept of human security between 1994 and 2006, academics of various stripes have offered insightful critiques of the concept. Let us begin with a consideration of some of the weaknesses identified by critics of human security, and then suggest how these can be addressed so the concept can be successfully employed. The key question that defines how to operationalize human security in its most emancipatory sense is "Security, development, and rights for whom?" Issues that emerge in relation to this question help situate the concept of human security within the school of Critical Theory. That is, they shift the focus from how to tinker in a minor way with the existing system in order to preserve it, to focus instead on systemic change that affords real power to the marginalized.

First, some critics have argued that the concept of human security is much too loose to be employed successfully. One scholar, in 2004, suggested that it "is ultimately nothing more than a shopping list; it involves slapping the label of human security on a wide range of issues that have no necessary link..."[12] It is certainly true, especially with regard to the debut of the concept in 1994, that human security entailed an enormous breadth of issues with no clear relation between them other than their threat to the well-being of individuals and communities. These issues ranged from economic security, community security, ethnic and gender rights, and health security, to environmental security and other concepts.[13]

Second, other scholars have criticized what they view as human security's conservative agenda and its preservation of a global system whereby the North dominates the South. For example, some have observed a conservative bias apparent in human security's focus on the individual, its struggle to fight "poverty" without focusing on economic inequity, and its willingness to accept and work within a system of economic globalization.[14] Thus, for some human security is one component of a larger neoliberal package, featuring the hegemony of transnational capital, the proliferation of NGOs to perform social welfare roles formerly done by an ever-weaker State, and the promotion of an atomized populace unable to launch an organized challenge to basic systemic problems.

Thirdly, some scholars within the Critical School of security have found other problems with the concept of human security. From the postmodern perspective, one academic has argued that human security can be deployed by the North to utilize Foucauldean "biopolitics" as an instrument of control vis-à-vis the South.[15] For other thinkers in this camp, "human security has taken on the image of the velvet glove on the iron hand of power."[16] On the left-leaning flank of Critical Security Studies, human security has been cast as part of what Robert Cox called "problem-solving theory," that is, it addresses relatively minor problems to perpetuate a system based largely on the power of transnational capital.[17]

Finally, human security has faced other, more general complaints. A human rights scholar argues that the concept pays insufficient homage to a wide berth of human rights regimes beginning with the 1948 Universal Declaration of Human Rights, and that these regimes subsume the elements contained in the human security approach.[18] More broadly, it has been argued that the concept is no longer relevant, that it has not succeeded in promoting any significantly positive change in the realm of security.[19] Let us proceed to address these concerns.

The approach to human security utilized here is sympathetic to the field of Critical Security Studies, and advocates bridging elements of these perspectives for the creation of what may be called Critical Human Security.[20] We shall make eight points in this regard. First, Critical Human Security should not be regarded as a framework whose parameters are set in stone. It is a concept that is under construction. It can be assembled in a progressive and critical way to allay the important doubts raised above.

Second, rather than a disparate array of unrelated issues, human security can be developed and applied in a coherent manner, and this was the clear intent of the 2006 review of the concept by the United Nations. While the approach can potentially address a huge range of issues, it is the specificity of the particular *context* in which human security is constructed and applied that provides it with both precision and adaptability. Critical Human Security highlights neglected but important themes, especially for the Global South, and these need to be fine-tuned in a coherent way to suit the particular case at hand.

Third, human security is people centered, but which people are the focus of the framework? If the approach is used to embrace the concerns of the marginalized and those who lack political power relative to northern States and TNCs, then we are constructing an approach from a critical perspective that seeks sweeping and democratic change to current power relations. If human security is combined with elements of post-development along the lines suggested by Arturo Escobar,[21] it can provide a liberating construction of development models and security regimes through the celebration of localized knowledge and culture. As we saw above, human security claims an allegiance to strong community participation and engagement. A sturdy platform of development and security can be attained by operationalizing views on these themes that emerge from within local communities, and by respecting their epistemological foundations. The Critical Human Security perspective promotes systemic change by empowering localized communities in the Global South.

Fourth, power relations do not have to be a zero-sum affair, they can be a win–win situation. The empowerment of the South, for example, can yield obvious benefits for Northern business interests. First and foremost, these include the provision of a stable and secure environment in which to invest. This stands in contrast to the expensive and dangerous security nightmares that can occur when operating in a context of imposed authority, profound inequity, political exclusion, social violence, widespread human rights abuses, insurgencies and so on.

Fifth, Critical Human Security appreciates the integrity of the realms of security, development and human rights, but recognizes that in practice they are closely linked. Improvements or problems in each of these realms can have synergetic results throughout the circuit of the three. Security is borne of an environment where development plays out in a democratic and empowering manner and where human rights are recognized and protected. In so many ways, security/human rights/development is a package deal. A Critical Human Security approach builds on the synergy of that package.

Sixth, the Critical Human Security perspective bridges individual and community rights. Enshrined human rights are by definition rights for every human being. They are clearly defined by the Universal Declaration and other seminal documents, such as the International Covenant on Civil and Political Rights and the International Covenant on Economic, Social and Cultural Rights. These underpin the notion of social justice at both the individual and community levels. This is foundational for the Critical Human Security approach. The CHS framework underscores the link between security, development and human rights within a localized community. This occurs within the broader context of national and transnational spheres. The focus is not only upon territorial community, but also upon ethnic, racial, gendered, epistemological and other communities. Power, security and development are all relational concepts – they do not appear in a vacuum at the individual level. It is at the community level that these three concepts intersect, and this is an important and highly practical focus for the Critical Human Security perspective. While a more conservative view of human security might focus solely upon the individual, Critical Human Security focuses on the interplay of social power between the community, the State, and transnational corporations.

A seventh point is that Critical Human Security is oriented toward practical policy matters. It relies on neo-Gramscian "critical realism," blending Machiavellian practicality with the critical objective of empowering the marginalized and subaltern.[22] That is, its praxis is informed by the tenets of classical realism[23] with the goal of empowering those without political voice in a manner that promotes security, development and respect for human rights.

Finally, the Critical Human Security framework utilized here appreciates the epistemic jump from Modernity to the postmodern condition. It embraces complexity, rather than relying strictly on the binary causality associated with Modernity. CHS contends with the realities of globalization, transnational actors, cyber-connectivity and deterritorialization. In contrast to Modernity's focus on universalization, homogenization and assimilation, Critical Human Security appreciates diversity and celebrates difference to achieve security and development. CHS respects diverse epistemes, and this represents a primary consideration regarding the construction of models of development. Rather than Modernity's promotion of "man's conquest over mother nature," CHS abandons tired constructions of gender and also appreciates the importance of sustainability. It strives to adapt to non-linear change. One could go on. In short, Critical Human Security represents a practical approach to achieve development, security and human rights in a postmodern world.

Now let us turn to a brief consideration of Colombia's colourful historical trajectory. This will provide the context from which to apply the Critical Human Security perspective to the recent role of the extractive sector in the country. It will also offer a basis for the construction of conflict resolution mechanisms.

Colombia's Historical Context

The 1800s

Colombia's history of almost incessant violence and its pronounced political fragmentation represent a crucial backdrop for its current political landscape. Colombia is the only country in the world to host the academic discipline of "Violentology." Historians have pointed to the virtually interminable warfare between the indigenous populations of what is now Colombia during the pre-conquest period.[24] After the initial carnage associated with the Spanish invasion, colonial rule generally minimized violence in what today is Colombia.

Following independence, almost constant civil war between the Liberals and Conservatives led to the death of 35,000 Colombians during 1820–1879, a figure that would equate proportionately to about five to 10 million deaths during the last 50 years of the twentieth century.[25] Colombia's Liberals represented agro-export and mercantile interests, while the Conservatives comprised the local agrarian and landed elite. Conservatives predominated in former colonial centers, while Liberals represented the upstarts from the peripheral regions that grew in economic significance during the post-colonial period.

The culmination of violent feuds and civil wars between the Liberals and Conservatives during much of the 1800s was the renowned Thousand Day War from 1899 to 1902, which marked the largest civil war in Latin America during the nineteenth century. Somewhere between 80,000 and 200,000 Colombians lost their lives during that imbroglio. The fact that neither party was able to defeat the other decisively was one of the factors that contributed to pronounced political fragmentation and endless violence. Rather than working to create a centralized State, the Liberals and Conservatives behaved as competing and exclusive governments, hoping in vein that the next civil war would provide them with a conclusive victory over the other.

Geographical barriers underpinned political fragmentation. Three ranges of the steep Andes Mountains presented huge obstacles for travel. This retarded the construction of roads and railways that could otherwise have assisted in connecting and uniting the country. Riverine travel was highly hazardous. Such geographical obstacles encouraged Colombia's towns to be largely self-sufficient, and stifled trade between regions. Within the predicament of necessary self-sufficiency, each town often produced similar things, further reducing prospects for trade.[26] Rather than uniting into a modern nation-state, Colombia's rival towns remained dispersed and isolated.

Epistemological factors also contributed to Colombia's notorious fragmentation. Spanish colonialism introduced a pre-modern system of thought. This meant, among other features, a fusion between the Church and State, political space conceived in terms of rival city-states, and feudal economic relations as manifested through the *encomienda* system. It was not until well into the twentieth century that modern ideas began to appear in Colombia with any semblance of vitality, such as the notions of progress, secular politics, institutionalized conflict resolution, and the importance of an industrialized economy.

The amplified fragmentation of Colombian politics has resulted in some noteworthy effects. First, violence has been rife in the absence of a centralized State with a monopoly on the use of force – or a Leviathan in the words of Hobbes. Second, this has meant that in Colombia, security historically has been privatized and dispersed. Examples include the private armies of *encomiendas* that were used to settle local accounts and that were also employed in inter-party warfare, the development of peasant and community defense organizations, the proliferation of private forces hired to protect a wide assortment of economic enterprises, the private forces of criminal syndicates, as well as a slew of other manifestations. Third, in the context of a State that has been historically weak, illegitimate, or even completely absent in many regions, economic enterprise has often operated totally outside government structures – a phenomenon that would otherwise count as contraband trade in a strong and functional nation state.

The Twentieth Century

By the dawn of the twentieth century, Colombia remained relatively isolated. It slowly came into the fold of global affairs beginning in 1915 and into the 1920s. US interest grew in Colombia's small oil sector and larger mining industry. The country also rode a boom of the coffee export market during this period. Colombia's astonishing entrepreneurial talent was obvious and began to grow in strides as the country faced the international market and made inroads towards industrialization. Global influences and ideas – particularly those associated with Western Modernity – grew considerably during this epoch of increased global contact.

Amidst heavy pressure from the United States, the ever-feuding Liberals and Conservatives finally agreed to negotiate in Spain beginning in 1956 to reach a power-sharing agreement deemed as the National Front. Implemented in 1958, it meant a consociational democracy whereby the Liberals would rule for four years, the Conservatives for the next four, over a 16-year period. While this meant a relative increase in State stability, there was a continuation of the political dynamic of exclusion, violence and a notoriously weak State. Inter-capitalist rivalry ended with the National Front, and immediately shifted to a new battlefield populated by the Left and Right.

1958–1989: Elusive Modernity – Colombia, Subversive Forces, and Illicit Drugs

According to its own literature, key components of the Fuerzas Armadas Revolucionarias de Colombia (FARC) emerged in 1950 – during La Violencia – with a merging of Liberal guerrillas and communist "self-defense" units.[27] In 1964, Jacobo Arenas of Colombia's Communist Party joined with "resistance" forces, which included former Liberal guerrilla Manuel Marulanda. The group existed in form in 1964, and conducted its first Guerrilla Conference in that year. But it did not officially assume its name until 1966 when it had approximately 350 armed recruits.[28] At this point Colombia's imbroglio rather belatedly shifted to a class war in the context of the global Cold War, and was steeped in the influence of the 1959 Cuban Revolution.

The FARC represented agrarian farmers, or peasants, and placed land reform and a redistribution of national wealth at the center of its political agenda. Between the 1960s and 1980s meager government attempts at land reform had failed. When the government attempted to implement such policies, they were typically resisted by big landowners.

Within a few years after the Liberals and Conservatives stopped fighting one another, under the direction of the United States they began to fight the FARC. The centerpiece of Washington's intervention in Colombia during the 1960s was Plan Laso, which aimed to reorganize the Colombian military in order to fight the guerrillas. It is worth emphasizing that Plan Laso was the biggest US military aid package in Latin America until the Reagan Administration's intervention in Central America during the 1980s. Of huge significance is that by the late 1970s, the FARC had been pushed militarily to concentrate its forces in the remote interior jungles of Guaviara, Caquetá and Putumayo. These were exactly the regions that would serve in the 1980s and beyond as its lucrative base for coca growth and for its role in the enormous narcotrafficking industry. The FARC entered an entirely new era in the 1980s, when it transformed from the classic Latin American peasant guerrilla group influenced by Fidel Castro and Che Guevara to a highly sophisticated belligerent force propelled from the bonanza it reaped from participating in narcotrafficking, extortion, and kidnapping.

Right-wing paramilitaries emerged as a dominant player by the mid-1980s, as they became the major security wing of the country's burgeoning narcotraffickers – thereby replacing components of the FARC in this role. Their allegiance remained with defending the interests of the agricultural elite, but now ranching and traditional agriculture took a back seat to narcotrafficking. The paramilitaries described themselves as defenders of capitalism in a country where the State was weak and there was no Leviathan.[29] At times they have represented the interests of illicit national capital and of extractive corporations. Often their interests have paralleled those of the Colombian and US governments through their combat with leftist guerrillas.

A major watershed began in 1984 when the FARC launched a program of political development, with the creation of its political unit the Unión Patriótica (UP) in 1984. The UP ran candidates in local and national elections, with its members winning 14 congressional seats and numerous local positions in 1986. It was hoped that an atmosphere of political inclusion would cement peace in the country, and would signify the elusive achievement of the institutionalization of conflict resolution. But that hope was ruptured completely with the assassination by paramilitary forces of some 3,000 to 4,000 UP members and candidates between 1986 and 1992, including the 1990 murder of the UP's popular presidential candidate, Carlos Pizarro Leóngómez.

Overall, we observe an interrelated set of historical problems whereby political violence became socially entrenched, where exclusionary politics were the norm, and where space was conceived not in national terms but through fragmented regions or city states. This basis for this was epistemological. Colombia did not play by Modern assumptions. It did not embrace the notion of institutionalizing conflict resolution through the State. In the main, Colombia continued to rely on violence to deal with conflict. Only the actors changed, not the game. Political time was conceived as a nearly unending war in the country, weaving within the population bitter historical memories and unsettled scores.

Colombia – the 1990s

With the failure of the UP experiment Colombia sank into darkest decade since La Violencia. In the wake of the assassinations of thousands of leftists who had attempted to work through the ballot box rather than through guerrilla movements, the message derived by the FARC was that there was no way to work with or through the State. By 1996 it launched devastating attacks against the country's armed forces that were poorly trained and organized. To the astonishment of outside observers, President Pastrana granted to the FARC a parcel in the jungle the size of Switzerland that the rebels insisted they needed to enter into serious peace negotiations with the government. Armed confrontations between the FARC and the military grew from an average of about 150 annually during 1985–1990, to about 400 annually for most of the 1990s.[30] By the late 1990s the FARC had an estimated 17,000 troops organized into over 60 fronts. It had the political support of coca growers, of peasants, radical students, and so on. This was the high point of the FARC's trajectory.

Right-wing paramilitaries witnessed an even stronger arc of growth than the FARC during the 1990s. According to Colombia's Ministry of Defense, they ballooned from 93 soldiers in 1986 (the beginning of the UP) to 8,150 in 2000.[31] They grew from disparate armed groups into a major political force with the formation in 1994 of the Autodefensas Unidas de Colombia (AUC). They worked at the behest of politically conservative narcotraffickers and had as their strategic enemies leftist guerrillas – the same enemies as the United States and the Colombia government. The growth of paramilitary forces over the 1990s correlated with a sharp uptick in violent human rights abuses. US data shows, for example, that human rights violations attributed to the paramilitaries grew 100 percent between 1995 and 1996. In 1997 they were responsible for 69 percent of assassinations in Colombia, and by 2000 caused about one-third of the country's population displacement.[32]

The rise of guerrilla and paramilitary warfare, the expansion of the illicit economy and the vacuous nature of the Colombian State combined to take a vast toll on Colombia's economy in the 1990s. Capital investment as a percentage of GDP declined from about 26 percent in 1993 to just under 13 percent by 1999. During those same years GDP went from nearly 6 percent growth to a steep decline of more than 4 percent.[33] Net external debt jumped from about US$10 billion in 1990 to near US$25 billion a decade later.[34]

Colombia in the New Millennium

There have been five noteworthy trends regarding Colombia in the new millennium. First, there has been the shift from the relative chaos of the 1990s to a more ordered environment that began to take shape in the year 2000 through the implementation of Plan Colombia. Second, the country emerged as Washington's key South American ally and the major site of US militarization in the region. Third, crime rates in Colombia have improved substantially. Fourth, until 2014 the economy grew vigorously against the backdrop of growing foreign interest in Colombia's extractive sector, and Colombia's newfound reputation for TNC-friendly policies. Importantly, this boom appeared to go bust by 2014. Fifth, levels of poverty and economic inequity have improved significantly through 2014. But major challenges remain in this regard, not the least of which is an economy that may be on the verge of collapse in the context of crashing commodity prices. Let us proceed to develop these points.

Plan Colombia (PC) was approved by US Congress in July 2000, and was formulated shortly after Washington woke up to the implications of Colombia's descent in the 1990s. At the outset, PC involved the planned provision of US$7 billion in mostly military assistance to Colombia between 2000 and 2006, though only about US$4.7 billion was allotted during that period. The country was the third largest recipient of US military aid until the costly US invasion of Iraq.

Plan Colombia sharply diminished the relative power of the FARC. The Colombian government estimated in 2010 that FARC military members decreased from around 20,000 in the year 2000 to about 8,000 in 2010. While those numbers are debatable, most experts agree their numbers have diminished markedly. About 22,000 members of the FARC and other leftist groups have demobilized during that period.[35] Further, the bombing in Ecuador in March 2008 of a FARC camp that killed second in command Raul Reyes, and the death by natural causes of FARC leader Manuel Marulanda in that same year, dealt severe blows to the rebel organization. So, too, did the death of FARC leader Alfonso Cano during combat with the Colombian military in 2011. Rather than the power vacuum of the 1990s when the FARC and other rebel groups appeared to be on the ascendant, the new millennium saw the wilting of leftist insurgencies.

By 2015, the FARC was weakened severely in a number of senses. Certainly the number of its rank and file diminished largely as a result of Plan Colombia, as we observed. Perhaps most importantly, during the first 15 years of the twenty-first century the rebel group had transformed into an ideologically bankrupt dinosaur. With its involvement in global narcotrafficking, or transnational illicit capitalism, it has been difficult for rebel leaders to legitimize their allegiance to leftist ideology. Its use of landmines that have maimed and killed civilians and military members alike, and its reliance on crimes such as extortion and kidnapping, eroded its already withering public support.[36] So has its escalated engagement in ecocide, a point to which we shall return. Perhaps most importantly, the Left in other Latin American countries came to power through peaceful democratic means that won massive popular support – as the cases of Venezuela, Bolivia, Ecuador, Uruguay, Argentina, El Salvador, and others demonstrate. Rather than the creative power of democratic popularity, the FARC had only to rely on its diminished but still formidable power of military destruction. Against this backdrop, the FARC chose to enter peace talks with the Santos Government in the fall of 2012, and although it was initially expected to take two years, this process has continued as of this writing.[37] But unlike the three previous peace negotiations in which it participated, the latest one has the most chance of success because the future prospects of the FARC appear so dim.

In many ways, the peace negotiations have provided a positive backdrop for foreign investors, given the prospects of terminating a war that has lasted more than half a century. However, it is important to keep in mind that most of the country's homicides are not a result of the armed conflict between the military and leftist guerrilla forces. A study released in 2014 indicated that during the period of 2011–2012, 75 percent of homicides in the country were committed by other actors: 36 percent by an unidentified attacker; 27 percent by common criminals; and 12 percent by right-wing armed groups.[38]

It is also important to underscore that the FARC and the Colombian military have remained in active combat throughout the peace negotiations. The FARC has attempted to increase its bargaining power with the Colombian government during the peace talks through escalating attacks on the country's oil pipelines. Not only has this stymied Colombia's oil export capacity, the many hundreds of such attacks have resulted in ecological disaster. There were 259 bombings of oil pipelines in 2013, the highest in a decade.[39] In the first 7.5 months of 2014 there were 97 attacks that tended to be more damaging than the ones in 2013, and which the Colombia Oil Association estimates to have cost them US$521 million in profits.[40] Not all of those attacks were launched by the FARC. The country's second largest leftist guerrilla group, the Ejército de Liberación Nacional (ELN), officially declared war against the country's oil industry in November 2013, and along with pipeline bombings, have engaged in the kidnapping of oil company workers.[41]

Overall, the process of peace negotiations has represented a mixed bag with regard to implications for the extractive industry in Colombia. The achievement of peace between the government and leftist rebels would represent a milestone on the country's path to security and development, but other important and violent actors remain, especially the rightist armed groups. That is, in contrast to the generally fading power of leftist insurgents, illegal armed groups and the remnants of former right-wing paramilitaries demonstrate significant and growing strength in the country. These groups include Los Rastrojos, Los Urabeños, Las Águilas Negras, and an assortment of others.

Crime

During the new millennium there have been notable improvements with regard to the reduction in crime. For example, kidnappings fell from a high of 3,572 in 2000 to 213 in 2009 near the end of the second Uribe Administration, and to 292 in 2013 during the Santos government.[42] Further, basic travel along the country's highways became safer, permitting people to travel by land in a way they had not been able to for years. Homicides dropped by half between Uribe's inaugural year of 2002 of 29,000 murders to 15,817 in 2009, and to 14,782 in 2013 during the Santos government. While this drop is substantial, murder rates in the country have remained alarmingly high in a global sense, with the country's assassination rate at the tenth highest in the world by 2012.[43]

Moreover, the electoral system has become more secure, as evidenced by the leftist Polo Party's successful participation in both the 2006 and 2010 federal elections without the array of carnage that characterized the Union Patriótica's experience in the late 1980s and early 1990s. Colombia's Ministry of Defense deemed the re-election of President Santos in 2014 to represent the safest presidential electoral period in the country's history.[44] As with the mellowing of the armed conflict, the reduction in crime and a safer voting environment has had a cross-class appeal.

But serious problems continue to plague the country, especially in relation to labour. A total of 498 unionists were murdered during Uribe's tenure from 2002–2009. There has been at least a 95 percent impunity rate regarding the assassination of union members in the twenty-first century. While murders of trade unionists declined from 101 in 2003 to the sharply lower rates of 17 in 2009 and to 26 in 2013, others kinds of crimes against labour increased. For example, between 2007 and 2008 there was a 97.1 percent increase in death threats and a 52.4 percent increase in forced displacements of union members.[45] Moreover, in 2013 there were 149 death threats against members of trade unions, which has a very similar political effect as an assassination.[46] In other words, while it is certainly a good thing that murders are down, the same political game continues of fear, stigmatization, and intimidation to exclude the political role of unions.[47] The case studies in this volume will offer a vivid illustration of this theme.

Political Economy

In many ways, Colombia has emerged as one of the last bastions of neoliberal economics in South America in the twenty-first century. This business friendly environment has yielded a number of effects. Foreign investment in Colombia increased from US$2.1 billion in 2002 to a decade high of US$10.6 billion in 2008. It rose to a record level of US$16.8 billion in 2013, with an astonishing 81.6 percent of this in the country's extractive sector.[48]

Colombia's economy has done well in the new millennium, at least until the crash of the extractive sector that became very apparent in late 2014. Generally, the economy grew during much of President Uribe's tenure, though the post-2007 crisis deeply affected Colombia for a limited period of time. GPD growth rose from 2.5 percent in 2002 to a decade high of 7.5 percent in 2007, but shrank 0.4 percent in 2009. Under President Juan Santos, annual GDP growth rose from 4.0 percent in 2010 to 4.3 percent in 2013.[49] The level of poverty fell from 53.7 percent of the population in 2002 to 46 percent in 2008, and to 30.6 percent by 2013. The level living in extreme poverty rose from 15.6 percent to 17.8 percent in 2008, but fell significantly to 9.1 percent by 2013. Here it is important to emphasize that the Santos government introduced a new methodology for measuring poverty that effectively decreased poverty levels. According to a government report on the new methodology, "...the rates in the new series differ from previous ones. Poverty and extreme poverty achieve lower levels."[50] In 2013, the government indicated that the official poverty line was about US$3.80 a day in urban centers, and about US$2.30 in rural areas. For anyone who is familiar with the major cities of Bogotá , Medellin, and Cartagena, the figure of US$3.80 is jaw dropping. If the authors of the report had to live on that amount, perhaps the figures would be revised. At any rate, even critics agree that there is significantly less poverty in 2014 than at the beginning of the millennium.[51]

Regarding inequity, the United Nations Habitat organization indicated that Gini coefficients rose from 0.58 to 0.59 between 2005 and 2008, making Colombia the second most inequitable country in Latin America.[52] But the Gini dropped to 0.539 in both of 2012 and 2013.[53] Overall, during the first 14 years of the twenty-first century Colombia's economy has grown substantially, and the levels of both poverty and inequity have improved. However, a significant challenge remains with regard to the gap between the improving economic scenario for Colombia's bustling urban centers versus the stagnation, poverty and inequity that persists in the countryside. Given Colombia's reliance on the extractive sector, clearly the biggest challenge to the country's economy is the drastic decline in commodity prices apparent by 2014. We shall develop that crucial point in Chapter 7. Let us now turn to a consideration of some other themes in Colombia during the new millennium that are relevant to our investigation of foreign investment in the extractive sector.

Displacement

The Inter-American Commission on Human Rights noted in 2013 that "Colombia [is] the country with the largest number of internally displaced people in the world, between 4.9 and 5.5 million people have been internally displaced."[54] Some of this, according to the Commission, "is also linked to the development of mining and large infrastructure projects, through relocation processes, massive sales of territories due to lack of opportunities, and concessions of territories by the State without complying with the requirements of the Law."[55] In fact, this broad issue remains at the heart of the cases dealt with in Chapters 3 and 4, regarding Marmato as well as the communities of Segovia and Remedios.

In particular, Indigenous and Afro-descendant communities have been severely affected by recent economic development policies that favor investment in the sectors of mining, oil and hydrocarbons, and agro-industry. The development of mega infrastructure projects can violate the constitutional rights of the local population, both at the individual and the collective level.[56] Such projects can clash with the international legal framework and the special regime of protection for Indigenous peoples and Afro-descendant communities. One of these rights includes the requirement of prior and informed consent regarding proposed mega projects in accordance with the parameters established in Convention No. 169 of the International Labour Organization on Indigenous and Tribal Peoples. Prior consultation allows the community to shape policy and programs that directly affect its interests in order to ensure the preservation of its cultural, social and economic identity. The violation of the right to prior consultation is one of the main concerns of Colombian Indigenous peoples. The Inter-American Commission of Human Rights has found that "many Indigenous communities and organizations have denounced the presence of activities related to mining, oil and extractivism in their territories. Sometimes officials from corporations are accompanied by members of the military or the police to conduct exploration or exploitation tasks, and this is done without complying with the requirements of consultation and prior informed consent in accordance with the obligations of Colombia in the international field."[57]

Overall, Colombia has become an increasingly attractive target for extractive industries in the twenty-first century. Security has improved, crime rates are down, and the government has implemented business-friendly policies. But some important problems remain, including persistent inequity, displacement, rural poverty and political alienation, as well as the proliferation of illicit armed groups. A heavy reliance on the notoriously cyclical extractive sector has left the country particularly vulnerable to a commodity crash that emerged by late 2014. While these are crucial themes that each merit expansive attention, our purpose here has been to provide a brief context from which to consider the cases studies in this volume. Let us shift now to a consideration of another important dimension to the cases at hand, namely Canada's relations with the region and the development of the free trade agreement between Canada and Colombia.

The Historical Context of Canada's Relations with Latin America

Canada had important and growing economic interests in Latin America near the turn of the twentieth century, but Ottawa's relations with the region were constrained. Part of this had to do with the fact that Canada lacked autonomy from England in the foreign policy realm until the 1926–1931 period and the culmination of the Statute of Westminster. Its foreign policy matured after World War II. Instead of blaming Soviet and later Soviet–Cuban subversion for strategic troubles in the hemisphere, which underpinned Washington's approach, Ottawa maintained throughout the Cold War that an inequitable distribution of wealth combined with pronounced social injustice were the bases of strategic problems in the Americas. While Canada pursued growing economic interests in the Americas during this period, it never fully engaged politically in Latin America.[58]

A major shift occurred in Canada, and at the level of the world order, beginning in the late 1960s and stretching into the next decade. With the lost war in Vietnam, growing global economic competition, and the termination of the Bretton Woods system, as well as the Soviet achievement of nuclear parity with the US, among other issues, the government of Pierre Trudeau attempted to craft a foreign policy for Canada that was decidedly independent from American policy. The result was the so-called "Third Option," whereby Canada placed Latin America among the top targets for the enhancement of Canadian foreign policy and trade diversification. Although the Third Option did not succeed as a general global policy for Canada, clearly this was a turning point for the country and thrust it into Latin American affairs like never before.

Although the context changed significantly in the 1980s, this period hosted another incremental jump that deepened Canada's role in the hemisphere. This decade witnessed the dawn of neoliberalism.[59] The general effect was that Canadian economic links to the region were fortified as Canada underwent its own period of neoliberal transformation beginning with the Progressive Conservative government of Brian Mulroney. This marked the beginning of an ideological convergence in the Americas that was underpinned by prevailing neoliberal structures and that would last until the new millennium. This restructuring paved the way for the North American Free Trade Agreement (NAFTA) and for a series of bilateral trade agreements pursued by Canada in Latin America.

Although there were a couple of potholes in the road during the 1990s, the political atmosphere of Latin America during this era was just what Ottawa hoped it would be when Canada decided to join the Organization of American States (OAS) in 1990. Ottawa had been reluctant to join the OAS during the Cold War because it preferred not to get involved in feuds between the US and various factions of Latin America. But that scenario evaporated in the 1990s. It was a relatively short-lived period of perceived nirvana in the story of Canada's relations with the Americas. Within such a context, Ottawa sought to entrench its ties to the United States first through the US–Canada Free Trade Agreement and then through NAFTA. And given that the world seemed to be tilting to three economic regions, Canada's growing role in the Americas seemed more important than ever.[60]

As we saw, Ottawa enjoyed the ideological homogeneity of the 1990s and presumably projected that this trend would spill into the new decade. That view propelled Canada's support for democratic structures, as it hosted the 2001 Summit of the Americas in Quebec City, where Peruvian politicians pressed for the establishment of the Inter-American Democratic Charter that was signed in Lima in September 2001.[61] The charter celebrated "respect for human rights ... periodic, free, and fair elections ... and the separation of powers and independence of the branches of government."[62] Despite the election of Hugo Chávez in Venezuela and Nestor Kirchner in Argentina, signatories to the Charter did not anticipate that radical revolutions would transpire not through guerrilla movements – as they had in the twentieth century in Cuba and Nicaragua – but through the ballot box as the decade progressed. Examples include not only subsequent re-elections of Chávez and the Kirchners, but the election of Bolivia's Evo Morales, Nicaragua's Daniel Ortega, Ecuador's Rafael Correa, Uruguay's Jose Mujica, El Salvador's Mauricio Funes, Peru's Ollanta Humala, and so on. Democracy, as it turned out, had triggered the emergence of a New Left in the Americas.

The widening ideological gulf in the Americas created pressure· for the Stephen Harper Government. While Ottawa noted that the Prime Minister's truncated 2007 tour of the Caribbean and South America "launched a new beginning for Canada's engagement of the western hemisphere,"[63] it seemed more like a blast from the Cold War past that Ottawa had hoped it would never have to revisit when it entrenched its interests in the Americas during the 1990s. During his visit to Chile in 2007 to celebrate the tenth anniversary of Canada's free trade agreement with the country, Harper was interpreted by the media and an assortment of academics to utter a thinly veiled attack on Hugo Chávez when he criticized those who wished "to return to the syndrome of economic nationalism, political authoritarianism and class warfare."[64] The Harper Government failed to build bridges or to promote conflict resolution with Venezuela or other Latin American countries that had moved to the hard Left. The Canadian government seemed to adopt a polarized position that toed the US line not only with respect to its scathing reference to Venezuela, but with regard to Harper's visit to just one other South American country besides Chile during his trip – America's strongest ally in the region, Colombia.

Canada and Colombia in the Twenty-First Century

As noted in the discussion of Critical Human Security, development occurs within a context involving security structures and human rights. Plan Colombia provided the strategic backdrop to introduce a new security regime that would weaken leftist insurgencies, bolster the repressive apparatus of the State, and render Colombia as the US conduit for strategic power in South America. At the same time, Colombia's economy was being restructured to promote the country's promising extractive sector – especially oil, gold, silver, and coal. An executive for a Canadian junior mining company indicated that during the late 1990s, he was with a unit of the Canadian military that scouted Colombia's countryside in order to discern security implications for prospective mining sites.[65] From 1997 to 2001, the Canadian International Development Agency (CIDA) funded a CAD$11.3 million project in Colombia whereby its staff as well as members of the University of Calgary's Canadian Energy Research Institute (CERI) assisted the Colombian government while it vastly revised its mining laws. According to CERI's website at the time, the program with CIDA would offer "advice, training and institutional strengthening in the environment, hydrocarbons and mining sectors" during this period.[66] A third and crucial player in the project was the Colombian law firm Martínez Córdoba and Associates, which provided legal advice to about half of mining firms in Colombia at the time.[67] Dodging allegations that CIDA, CERI and the law firm were the dominant players behind the revised mining laws, an anonymous CIDA spokesperson indicated that CIDA's role was "relatively minor" and that "[t]he project itself did not draft the mining-related legislation, which was of course the purview of the Government of Colombia."[68]

What is clear is that the mining laws changed dramatically after the CIDA project, significantly dropping the Colombian "government take" – the final amount accruing to the government through royalties and taxes on minerals and petroleum. After the law's enactment in 2001, about 40 percent of Colombian land opened up to mineral and petroleum exploration. Over half of new mining contracts went to Canadian firms,[69] and an estimated 73 percent of new oil contracts went to Canadian companies.[70] A study by the Colombian Government's Contraloría General in 2013 indicated that Colombia had the second lowest "government take" in South America's resource sector.[71]

During the period in which the new law was being created, critics warned Canadian politicians of the pernicious nexus between security problems, human rights abuses and Colombia's extractive sector. Speaking before a parliamentary Subcommittee on Human Rights and International Development in Ottawa, a renowned Colombian activist, Emmanuel Rosental, told Canadian politicians:

> This is the process of violence in Colombia. First, there are economic resources in the region. Second, armed actors come into the region to create space for those resources by getting rid of the only obstacle – organized people defending their rights. Thirdly, the resources are open for international legal and illegal interests...

His compatriot, Pablo Leal, echoed that concern and added that:

> If this is a territory that's under dispute, and then somebody says there's oil under there, let's put that up for sale, you know that something is going to happen. You know there's going to be that kind of displacement. And this is the kind of analysis that needs to take place before the investment takes place.[72]

That is a sound suggestion, though it was ignored at the time. As we shall see, suggestions such as those represent a key component for a proper Human Rights Impact Assessment – whether performed by a government or a corporation.

More generally, it is important to emphasize that in key areas of the Global South the extractive industry is the clearest reflection of Canada's foreign presence. For many parts of Latin America, Africa and Asia, it is the extractive sector, and not so much the maple leaf, that represents Canada. Natural Resources Canada indicates that by 2008 three-quarters of the world's mining companies were headquartered in Canada.[73] In 2013, Canada's extractive industry had about CAD$138.5 billion invested abroad.[74]

Canada, Colombia, and the Free Trade Agreement

We observed that Prime Minister Harper's policy toward Latin America, as with the rest of the world, has tended to echo that of the United States. That approach was expressed again in 2007, when Canada indicated it was in discussions with Colombia regarding a Free Trade Agreement a year after Washington announced its interest in an FTA with the country. When the US initially expressed its intentions, immediately there was a loud rebuttal from labour activists and some Democratic Congressional members regarding the poor human rights record in Colombia, especially with regard to the labour sector. Colombia cherished the notion of a potential free trade deal with the US, and President Uribe may have calculated that concluding a free trade agreement with Canada would entice the Americans to reach a pact with Colombia.

There were other factors that underpinned Ottawa's interest in an FTA with Colombia. Both countries were avid embracers of neoliberalism. Economically, Canada's expertise in the extractive sector was valued by Colombia, and the reshaping of the Colombian mining law in 2001 made Colombia's resources even more attractive to Canada as the global extractive sector boomed after 2006. Canadian investment in Colombia increased from about CAD$740 million in 2007 when FTA talks began, to CAD$1.7 billion in 2011, the year the FTA commenced. Investment rose to CAD$1.8 billion by the end of 2012.[75] Most of that investment occurred in the extractive sector.

There was considerable protest in Canada regarding the proposed FTA with Colombia given the record of human rights abuses in the country. In March 2010 the Liberal Party of Canada insisted on an attempt to improve the human rights situation in Colombia through an attachment to the FTA that annually evaluated human rights. The idea was to create a win-win situation for Canadian companies

Table 1.1 Canada's trade with Colombia, 2010–2013, millions US

	2010	2011	2012	2013
Exports	642.3	760.9	828.2	716.9
Imports	717.3	799.4	664.7	691.3

Source: Government of Colombia, *Segundo Informe Anual del Acuerdo en material de Informes Anuales Sobre Derechos Humanos y Libre Comercio Entre la República de Colombia y Canada*, May 2013, p. 6 and Government of Canada, "Annual Report Pursuant to the Agreement concerning Annual Reports on Human Rights and Free Trade between Canada and the Republic of Colombia," Ottawa, May 2014, p. 8.

investing in Colombia, especially in the extractive sector, and for communities in Colombia that hosted them. After a protracted struggle with the governing Conservative Party, the Liberals finally bragged that the inclusion of the Party's amendment to the CCFTA sets a "Gold Standard" for human rights reporting and renders the deal to be the first in the world that requires annual Human Rights Impact Assessments.[76] The Liberal amendment succeeded due to tireless pressure not only from party members, but from a variety of well-informed NGOs in Canada such as the Canadian Labour Congress and the Canadian Council for International Co-operation. While there is no standard definition of a governmental HRIA, functionally these assessments are designed to measure concrete human rights impacts associated with the FTA in order to improve the human rights landscape in the future.[77]

The agreement on the HRIA, concluded in May 2010, stipulated only that:

> Each Party shall provide a report to its national legislature by May 15 in the year after the entry into force of the Free Trade Agreement between Canada and the Republic of Colombia and annually thereafter. These reports will be on the effect of the measures taken under the Free Trade Agreement between Canada and the Republic of Colombia on human rights in the territories of both Canada and the Republic of Colombia.[78]

But what effects, and what measures in particular? What methodology would be implemented to determine those effects? In practice, the HRIA has proven to be quite weak due to the failure of the governments in Canada and Colombia to treat them seriously. Along with well-intentioned leaders, to be successful this governmental HRIA requires a serious revision, or perhaps even a complete rewriting. We shall develop those points and provide a thorough critique of this particular HRIA in Chapters 6 and 7. For now, in an introductory way, let us step back a bit to trace the evolution of corporate HRIAs to governmental HRIAs.[79] Let us also consider what an ideal HRIA might look like.

Corporate Human Rights Impact Assessments

Two general types of HRIAs emerged after 2000, the more common corporate version and the governmental HRIA. Some key features mentioned in corporate

HRIAs are highly relevant for inclusion into governmental HRIAs, such as the one attached to the Canada–Colombia Free Trade Agreement. A good example of a thorough, business-oriented impact assessment is the Human Rights Compliance Assessment Quick Check, produced in 2006 by the Danish Institute for Human Rights. It provides 350 questions for businesses regarding their operations, and also includes 1,000 corresponding human rights indicators. It addresses issues such as forced labour, fair contracts that are understood by labour, appropriate procedures for workers leaving a position, and the importance of providing workers with a living wage and salary advancements. It also covers freedom of association vis-à-vis unions, sanitary and appropriate working and living facilities for workers, the avoidance of relying on part-time labour to depress wages, and the absence of coercion or intimidation vis-à-vis workers.[80]

Because TNC's are naturally drawn to a business-friendly approach, a popular and accessible source of information is the World Bank's 2011 "Guide to Human Rights Impact Assessment and Management." The Guide notes that human rights violations may be a particularly important concern for TNCs investing in areas where there is a weak governance zone, a prevalence of conflict, and where the political elite has little regard for human rights. Other red flags include the presence of significant environmental sensitivities and socially vulnerable groups.[81] The Guide outlines the significance of creating careful baseline data, so that future progress or weaknesses can be documented.[82] It emphasizes important factors to set a HRIA in motion. These include the creation of clear human rights performance indicators, community engagement, a transparent and fair grievance mechanism, mitigation and improvement plans, and management adaptability.[83] It emphasizes that TNCs must also assume full responsibility for the human rights actions of its contractors,[84] which is a significant concern in the Global South and particularly in Colombia. This highly useful and compact guide concludes with a long list of basic workers rights with which TNCs must be familiar.[85]

The "Ruggie Report" has emerged as the global benchmark for human rights in relation to transnational corporations. John Ruggie notes that the evolution of the reports[86] was simulated by the obvious impact of transnational corporations on human rights within the context of escalating globalization. The Report also underscored that powerful corporate interests resisted the legislation of binding human rights obligations through international law. Hence the Report represents a voluntary approach to a "common global platform for action."[87] Three pillars are emphasized: the State's duty to *protect* against human rights abuses from third parties (e.g., TNCs); corporate responsibility to *respect* human rights; and greater access for victims of human rights abuses to effective *remedies*. These principles underscore the Ruggie Report's chief emphasis on the concept of human rights due diligence, whereby both the State and corporations are responsible for monitoring and promoting human rights.

Based on the International Bill of Human Rights and the International Labour Organization's Declaration on Fundamental Rights at Work, the Ruggie Report emphasizes cooperation between the State, TNCs and the communities in which they operate. The Report recommends that the State provide all relevant information for TNCs investing in particular regions. This includes highlighting areas of conflict where human rights abuses are most likely to occur, as well as assisting businesses to identify, prevent and mitigate such risks. TNCs are recommended to develop a clear policy toward human rights, to account for how human rights are addressed, and to provide quick and effective remediation when problems occur.[88] The reports emphasize that stock exchanges where TNCs raise capital can be sites to help promote human rights, especially through the creation of a socially responsible investment index.[89] It points out that the private security arrangements of a corporation, as well as the behaviour of its various contractors, must also be considered part of the human rights promotion policy of TNCs.[90] The Ruggie Report underscores that not just the host States, but the home State of a TNC, need to provide adequate information and support regarding human rights and foreign investment.[91] This is particularly salient regarding Canada's HRIA in relation to its free trade agreement with Colombia.

Governmental HRIAs

Governmental HRIAs are a work in progress.[92] A seminar of experts summarily observed that "HRIAs should not have a one-size-fits-all approach. They should be flexible and adapted to different national contexts and to address priority issues."[93] Harrison and Goller emphasize the important distinctions between corporate and governmental HRIAs. Corporate HRIAs focus on the human rights effects of a particular business or sector. By contrast, governmental HRIAs – and more specifically any HRIA that examines the effect of a trade agreement on human rights – explore:

> ...the impact of international legal obligations and how they are implemented at the national level.... Complex issues such as causality, attribution or responsibility and the difficulty of data collection benefit greatly from in-depth consideration in the specific context of international trade agreements.[94]

For governmental HRIAs that examine the effects of FTAs, the key issue is how the trade and investment agreement affects human rights in the target country. For example, if it can be shown that an FTA has increased or helped sustain investment in a particular country, the next step would be to determine how the sustenance or increase of investment affects human rights. For the purposes at hand, there are two causal links to be established. First, can a case be made that the Canada–Colombia FTA helped sustain or increase Canadian investment in the extractive sector? Second, can a link be established between that investment and human rights issues? We shall return to those points later in the volume.

United Nations human rights standards are key for governmental HRIAs.[95] They provide a globally accepted standard upon which to base human rights reports. These impact assessments should examine "not only State obligations but also the corporate duty to respect rights."[96] Additionally, they should help build the capacity of the target country to better monitor and promote such rights.

One expert suggests five steps for the HRIA process. The first is preparation, which entails establishing baseline data, identifying key stakeholders, as well as setting the general parameters and focus of the impact assessment.[97] The second component concerns screening. This involves the identification of existing stresses on human rights, a determination of whether human rights are improving or not, as well as an examination of the institutional capacity to improve the situation. Very important is the third aspect of scoping, which necessitates the development of clear human rights indicators, both quantitative and qualitative. Scoping addresses the question of what to assess and how. The final two steps include the analysis of data collected and then the drafting of specific recommendations to improve human rights.[98]

An ideal HRIA should include participatory case studies. Case studies bring the HRIA alive with concrete examples and unanticipated nuances. Such cases need be carefully chosen to focus on key sectors affected by the trade and investment agreement, and to highlight key communities where human rights have been problematic. In short, the case studies should be emblematic of the intersection between human rights and effects emanating from the international economic agreement.[99] It is in this context that the case studies have been selected for this volume.

A seminal contribution regarding governmental HRIAs is the United Nations' De Schutter Report – "Guiding Principles on Human Rights Impact Assessment of Trade and Investment Agreements." De Schutter reinforces the point that despite the proliferation of important political actors beyond the State in a globalized world, it is ultimately the State that bears the responsibility for respecting, protecting and fulfilling human rights.[100] De Schutter emphasizes that it is best for the HRIA to be conducted by an independent, multidisciplinary body.[101] That is, the State by itself might not produce a worthwhile HRIA, due to a possible reticence by a government to criticize itself or to find fault with corporations with which it may be aligned. An ideal team to carry out such an HRIA would be non-governmental and interdisciplinary in nature, and would include economists, developmental specialists, legal and political scholars, historians, etc. It would also involve a mix of academics and experts from NGOs that specialize in human rights.

With respect to the development of human rights indicators, the Report points out that these should refer to specific human rights norms and standards. It also underscores the significance of providing data on the basis of gender, age, ethnicity, region, and so on.[102] The Report alludes to some possible nuances, noting, for example, that on the positive side of things an FTA may promote economic growth that in turn can provide funding for institutions to improve human rights.[103] Overall, there exists a rich literature from which to construct highly useful HRIAs for use by governments and corporations.

Concluding Thoughts

This wide-ranging chapter has provided the context from which to situate the following interdisciplinary case studies and analyses. We have traced the historical trajectory of Colombia, noting the persistent weakness of the State and the prevalence of violence as a means to settle conflict. We then took a look at Canada's role in the region, and observed that the extractive sector is the face of the country in much of the Global South. One instrument that has great potential to promote a more harmonious environment in communities that host TNCs in the extractive sector is a Human Rights Impact Assessment. With that backdrop, the rest of the book addresses prospects for the achievement of a form of human security that is beneficial for communities, corporations, and the State.

Notes

1 Human Security Unit, Office for the Coordination of Humanitarian Affairs, United Nations, *Human Security in Theory and Practice* (New York: United Nations, 2006), p. 7.
2 United Nations Development Program, *United Nations Human Development Report* (New York: United Nations Development Program, 1994), pp. 1 and 3.
3 Ibid., p. 23.
4 Human Security Unit, *Human Security in Theory and Practice*, op. cit., p. 6.
5 United Nations Development Program, *United Nations Human Development Report*, op. cit., p. 31.
6 See, for example, Lloyd Axworthy, "Human Security: Individuals' Security in a Changing World," Politique Etrangere, vol. 64, #2, 1999, pp. 333–343 and "Human Security as Global Governance," *Global Governance*, vol. 7, #1, 2001, pp. 19–23.
7 Human Security Unit, *Human Security in Theory and Practice*, op. cit., p. 6.
8 Ibid.
9 Ibid., pp. 8 and 12.
10 Ibid., pp. 11 and 30.
11 Ibid., pp. 32 and 36.
12 Keith Krasue, "Is Human Security 'More than Just a Good Idea?" in M. Brozoska and P Croll, eds., *Promoting Security: Contributions to BICC's Ten-year Anniversary Conference*, BICC Brief 30, 2004, p. 44.
13 United Nations Development Program, *UN Human Development Report*, op. cit., pp. 24–28.
14 See, for example, Ryerson Christie, "Critical Voices and Human Security: To Endure, To Engage, or To Critique?" *Security Dialogue*, vol. 41, pp. 169–190, especially pages 176–177.
15 See Mark Duffield, *Development, Security and Unending War*, (Cambridge: Politic Press, 2007).
16 Ken Booth, *Theory of World Security* (Cambridge: Cambridge University Press, 2007), p. 324.
17 Robert Cox introduced this duality in his seminal article, "Social Forces, States, and World Orders: Beyond International Relations Theory," *Millennium: Journal of International Studies*, vol. 10, #2, pp. 126–155. For a broader discussion of this, see, for example: Edward Newman, "Critical Human Security Studies," *Review of International Studies*, vol. 36, 2010, pp. 77–94.
18 See R.E. Howard-Hassmann, "Human Security: Undermining Human Rights?" *Human Rights Quarterly*, vol. 34, 2012, pp. 88–112, see especially pp. 93–94 and 111.
19 See R. Christie, op. cit., pp. 186–187.
20 Edward Newman has done an excellent job of initiating discussion of the bridging of human and critical security in his "Critical human security studies," op. cit.
21 See Arturo Escobar, *Encountering Development: The Making and Unmaking of the Third World* (Princeton: Princeton University Press, 1994).
22 See Antonio Gramsci, *Selections from the Prison Notebooks* (New York: International Press, 1971), especially his discussion of the Modern Prince.

23 These include writers such as Thucydides, Machiavelli, and non-Western writers such as Sun Tzu.

24 For an excellent discussion of Colombia's historical violence see: Malcolm Deas and Fernando Gaitán Daza, *Dos ensayos especulativos sobre la violencia en Colombia* (Bogotá: Tercer Mundo, 1985) and Paul H. Oquist, *Violence, Conflict and Politics in Colombia* (New York: Academic Press, 1980). Even cannibalism was apparent in the region of present day Cali and northward. See Frank Safford and Marco Palacios, *Colombia: Fragmented Land, Divided Society* (New York: Oxford University Press, 2002), p. 21.

25 See John Coatsworth, "Colombia: Roots of Violence in Colombia," *Revista: Harvard Report on the Americas*, vol. 2, #3, Spring 2003, p. 8.

26 See Safford and Palacios, op. cit., pp. 10 and 161, and David Sowell, *The Early Colombian Labor Movement* (Philadelphia: Temple University Press, 1992), pp. 2 and 17.

27 Fuerzas Armadas Revolucionarias de Colombia (FARC), "Nuestra Historia," 2004, www.farc-ep.org/aniversario/especial40aniv/textcrono.html. Accessed May 2, 2005.

28 See Eduardo Pizarro Leongómez, *Las Farc 1949–1966* (Bogotá: Tercer Mundo, 1991), pp. 198–199.

29 Autodefensas Unidas de Colombia, "Discurso del Jefe del Estado Mayor de las AUC, Comandante Salvatore Mancuso, en el acto de Instalación Oficial del Proceso de Negociación entre el Gobierno Nacional y las Autodefensas Unidas de Colombia," July 2004, www.colombialibre.org/ver_imp.php?Varid=6425. Accessed October 18, 2005.

30 Alfredo Rangel, "El Repliegue de las FARC: Derrota o Estrátegia," Fundación Seguridad y Democracia, 2004, p. 13, www.seguridadydemocracia.org. Accessed March 26, 2005.

31 Government of Colombia, Ejército Nacional, Ministerio de Defensa, "Los Grupos Ilegales de Autodefensa de Colombia," Colombia (Bogotá: Éjercito Nacional, December 2000).

32 See James Rochlin, *Vanguard Revolutionaries*, p. 167.

33 Departamento Administrativo Nacional de Estadísticas (DANE), Indicatores Económicos, various years, www.dane.gov.co. Accessed June 7, 2010.

34 Paper by Sergio Clavijo, member of the Board of Directors of the Central Bank of Colombia, mimeograph, August 2001, "Viability of the External Debt: the Case of Colombia over the 2000s," p. 7, statistics from Central Bank of Colombia.

35 See *El Tiempo*, July 24, 2010.

36 See James Rochlin, "Plan Colombia and the Revolution in Military Affairs," *Review of International Affairs*, March 2011, #37, pp. 715–740.

37 For an excellent timeline of the peace negotiations between the FARC and the Colombian Government, which are held in Havana, Cuba, see the website www. Colombiapeace.org/timeline2013. Accessed November 10, 2014.

38 Edwin Hernández and Paola Chaparro, "Negociación de paz no termina con todas las violencias," Instituto de Estudios Políticos y Relaciones Internacionales," Universidad Nacional de Colombia, *UN Periódico*, # 181, September 2014.

39 See Reuters, Colombia oil pipeline paralyzed by rebel attacks, 12 July 2014, no author, www.reuters.com/article/2014/07/12/us-colombia-oil-attack-idUSKBN0FH0 U020140712. Accessed September 10, 2014.

40 David Gagne, "Losses of $521 Mn Show Guerrilla Impact on Colombia Oil Industry," 21 August 2014, www.insightcrime.org/news-briefs/colombia-oil-industry-500-mn-losses-guerrilla-attacks. Accessed September 10, 2014.

41 See "ELN declares war on oil companies," November 5, 2013, *Colombia Reports.*

42 United States Department of State, "Colombia 2014 Crime and Safety Report," www. osac.gov/pages/ContentReportDetails.aspx?cid=15445. Accessed September 3, 2014.

43 *Colombia Reports*, "Colombia has 10th Largest Crime Rate in World – UN," no author, 14 April 2014. http://colombiareports.co/colombia-10th-highest-homicide-rate-world-un/ Accessed May 20, 2014.

44 *Colombia Report*, "Colombia's Election Most Quiet and Safe in Country's History," no author, 15 June 2014. http://colombiareports.co/colombias-election-quiet-safe-recent-history-govt/. Accessed August 20, 2014.

45 See Escuela Nacional Sindical, "Una Política de Exclusión Sistemática," May 2009, pamphlet, available for download on group's website, www.ens.org.

46 Escuela Nacional Sindical, "En 2013 aumento la violencia contra el movimiento sindical Colombiano," December 11, 2013, www.ens.org.co/index.shtml?apc=Na–; 1;-;-;&x=20168317, accessed January 20, 2014.

47 Interview by J. Rochlin with: Jose Luis Sanin, Director, Escuela Nacional Sindical, Medellín, 12 August 2010; and Unión Sindical Obrera (USO) Cartagena, group meeting with: Julio Carrascal, Fiscal Director; Carlos Franco, Human Rights; Enrique Marcias, Popular Education; Jorge Manjarres, Popular Education; May 5, 2009, Cartagena, Colombia.

48 Government of Colombia, Banco de la República, "Flujos de Invesión Directa," www.banrep.gov.co/es/info-temas-a/2297, accessed August 20, 2014.

49 World Bank, "GDP Growth by Country," www.data.worldbank.org. Accessed September 3, 2014.

50 Government of Colombia, National Administrative Department of Statistics and National Planning Department (DANE), "Monetary Poverty in Colombia: New Methodology and 2002–2010 figures," (Bogota: DANE, February 2012) p. 8.

51 Interview by J. Rochlin, Senator Jorge Robledo, Polo Democrático Alternativo, Bogotá, September 15, 2014.

52 United Nations Habitat figures as published by Escuela Nacional Sindical, "Informe nacional de coyuntura económica, laboral y sindical en 2009 – Balance de los 8 años del gobierno Uribe," 2009. www.ens.org.co/index.shtml?apc=Na–;27;-;-;&x=20155 546. Accessed February 3, 2012.

53 "La Pobreza en Colombia se Redujo en el 2013," 21 March 2014, no author, www.portafolio.co/economia/pobreza-colombia-el-2013. Accessed March 22, 2014.

54 Comisión Interamericana de Derechos Humanos – Organización de los Estados Americanos, *Verdad, justicia y reparación: Cuarto informe sobre la situación de derechos humanos en Colombia*, 2013, párr. 545, pág. 227. http://justiciaviva.org.pe/webpanel/doc_int/doc28082014–181944.pdf. Accessed September 20, 2014.

55 Comisión Interamericana de Derechos Humanos – Organización de los Estados Americanos, op. cit., párr.551, p. 229.

56 Comisión Colombiana de Juristas (CCJ), "Despojo de Tierras Campesinas y vulneración de los territorios ancestrales", (Bogotá: CCJ, 2013), pp. 131–132.

57 Comisión Interamericana de Derechos Humanos – Organización de los Estados Americanos, op. cit., párr. 832, pág. 333.

58 For an extended view of Canada's history in Latin America, see James Rochlin, *Discovering the Americas: the Evolution of Canadian Foreign Policy to Latin America* (Vancouver: UBC Press, 1993).

59 Arguably the best definition and analysis of neoliberalism is provided in David Harvey's *A Brief History of Neoliberalism* (London: Oxford, 2005). A brief definition is provided on page 2, with the historical context found throughout the book. He notes on page 2:

> Neoliberalism is in the first instance a theory of political economic practices that proposes that human well-being can best be advanced by liberating individual entrepreneurial freedoms and skills within an institutional framework characterized by strong private property rights, free markets, and free trade. The role of the state is to create and preserve an institutional framework appropriate to such practices. The state has to guarantee, for example, the quality and integrity of money. It must also set up those military, defence, police, and legal structures and functions required to secure private property rights and to guarantee, if forces if need be, the proper functioning of the markets…

60 For a discussion of Canada's economic relations with the region during the late 1990s, see Peter McKenna, "Canada's Southern Exposure," *Hemisphere: A Magazine of the Americas*, vol. 8, #3, Fall 1998, pp. 26–29.

61 Max Cameron has done much important work in the area of Canada and democracy in Latin America. See, for example, Max Cameron and Catherine Hecht, "Canada's Engagement with Democracies in the Americas," *Canadian Foreign Policy*, vol. 14, #3, Fall 2008, pp. 11–28.

62 Organization of American States, 11 September 2001, *Inter-American Democratic Charter*. Lima, Peru. www.oas.org/charter/docs/resolution1_en_p4.htm. Accessed December 2, 2009.

63 Government of Canada, *Canada and the Americas – Priorities and Progress* (Ottawa, 2009) p. 1.

64 As reported by *National Post*, no author, "Harper Steers into Unchartered Waters," 17 June 2007. www.nationalpost.com/news/story.html?id=afaf7cd2–194f–4033–98f4–2b8af1b19404#__federated=1. Accessed September 10, 2007.

65 Interview by J. Rochlin with person who wishes anonymity. August 5, 2014.

66 The website is not available as of this writing. The quote is taken from Scott Pearce, "Fueling War: The Impact of Canadian Oil Investment on the Conflict in Colombia," CERLAC Working Paper, November 2002, York University, Toronto, p. 27.

67 See Francisco Ramirez Cuellar, *Profits of Extermination: Big Mining in Colombia* (Monroe, Maine: Common Courage, 2005), p. 55.

68 *Macleans*, no author, "New CIDA code Provokes Controversy," July 1, 2006, reprinted in The Canadian Encyclopedia, www.thecanadianencyclopedia.ca/en/article/new-cida-code-provokes-controversy/. Accessed August 20, 2014.

69 See Thomas Abbot, "Pressing Gold Mining Reform in Colombia," *Washington Report on the Hemisphere*, vol. 33., #16, September 13, 2013, p. 2.

70 See Francisco Ramirez Cuellar, *Profits of Extermination* op. cit., p. 41.

71 The lowest was Peru. See Luis Garay, et al., *Minería en Colombia* (Bogota: Contraloría General de la Republica, 2013). See page 144, and more generally, pp. 140–155.

72 Canadian Parliament, "Sub Committee on Human Rights and International Development of the Standing Committee on Foreign Affairs and International Trade," May 3, 2001, from interventions beginning at 17:05pm and 17:25pm,www.parl.gc.ca/HousePublications/Publication.aspx?DocId=1040878&Mode=1&Parl=37&Ses=1&Language=E. Accessed August 15, 2015.

73 Natural Resources Canada, "Evaluation of the Minerals and Metals Markets, 2012," www.nrcan.gc.ca/evaluation/reports/2012/802. Accessed October 19, 2014.

74 Government of Canada, Foreign Affairs, Trade and Development, "Canada's State of Trade, 2014," www.international.gc.ca/economist-economiste/performance/state-point/state_2014_point/index.aspx?lang=eng#6.0. Accessed 19 October 2014.

75 Canadian Trade Commissioner Service, January 2013, www.tradecommissioner.gc.ca/eng/office.jsp?oid=62. Accessed September 4, 2014.

76 The announcement was posed on its website, www.liberal.ca on March 25, 2010. Link no longer active.

77 See James Harrison and Alessa Goller, "Trade and Human Rights: What Does 'Impact Assessment' Have to Offer?" *Human Rights Law Review*, vol. 8, #4, 2008, pp. 5–7.

78 Canada Colombia Free Trade Agreement, "Agreement Concerning Annual Reports on Human Rights and Free Trade Between Canada and the Republic of Colombia," 27 May 2010. www.treaty-accord.gc.ca/text-texte.aspx?id=105278. Accessed October 2, 2014.

79 For a broader discussion of this, see James Rochlin, "A Golden Opportunity Lost: Canada's Human Rights Impact Assessment and the Free Trade Agreement with Colombia," *International Journal of Human Rights*, vol. 18, Issue 4–5, 2014, pp. 545–566.

80 See Danish Institute for Human Rights, *Human Rights Compliance Assessment Quick Check*, 2006, pp. 4, 12, 13, 14, 27, 32, 39, and 55. https://hrca2.humanrights-business.org/. Accessed August 10, 2014.
81 World Bank, "Guide to Human Rights Impact Assessment and Management," 2011, accessed June 2013, www.guidetohriam.org, p. 8. Accessed June 15, 2014.
82 Ibid., p. 12.
83 Ibid., p. 62.
84 Ibid., p. 63.
85 Ibid., see pages 67–167.
86 The Ruggie Report is actually a series of documents.
87 *Report of the Special Representative of the Secretary General on the Issue of Human Rights and Transnational Corporations and other Business Enterprises, John Ruggie – Guiding Principles on Business and Human Rights: Implementing United Nations 'Protect, Respect and Remedy' Framework*, March 2011, pp. 3, 5. www.ohchr.org/documents/issues/business/A.HRC.17.31.pdf. Accessed September 4, 2013.
88 Ibid., pp. 7 and 13–15.
89 *Report of the Special Representative…, Human Rights and Corporate Law; Trends and Observations from a Cross-National Study Conducted by the Special Representative,"* May 23, 2011, p. 13. www.ohchr.org/documents/issues/business/a-hrc-17–31-add2.pdf. Accessed 13 September 2013.
90 *Special Report…. Principles for Responsible Contracts: Integrating the Management of Human Rights Risks into State-Investor Contract Negotiations – Guidance for Negotiators,"* May 25, 2011, pp. 15–19.www.ohchr.org/documents/issues/business/a.hrc.17.31.add.3.pdf. Accessed 12 June 2013. Accessed September 3, 2014.
91 *Special Report…. Business and Human Rights in Conflict Affected Regions: Challenges and Options Towards State Responses*, May 27, 2011. www.ohchr.org/Documents/Issues/TransCorporations/A.HRC.17.32.pdf. Accessed September 3, 2014.
92 For a broader discussion of this, see James Rochlin, "A Golden Opportunity Lost: Canada's Human Rights Impact Assessment and the Free Trade Agreement with Colombia," *International Journal of Human Rights*, vol. 18, Issue 4–5, 2014, pp. 545–566.
93 See 'Report of the Expert Seminar, 23–24 June 2010, Geneva, "Human Rights Impact Assessments for Trade and Investment Agreements, p. 3. www.ccic.ca/what_we_do/Report_HRIA-seminar_2010_eng%5B1%5D.pdf. Accessed June 15, 2012.
94 James Harrison and Alessa Goller, "Trade and Human Rights: What does impact assessment have to offer?" *Human Rights Law Review*, vol. 8, #4, 2008, p. 594.
95 Ibid., p. 14.
96 Ibid, pp. 26. 10.
97 Ibid., pp. 45–6.
98 See pages 89–100.
99 Ibid., p. 114.
100 De Schutter Report, United Nations General Assembly, Human Rights Council, "Report of the Special Rapporteur on the Right to Food, Olivier de Schutter: Guiding Principles on Human Rights Impact Assessments of Trade and Investment Agreements," December 19, 2011, pp. 6–7. www.ohchr.org/Documents/HRBodies/HRCouncil/RegularSession/Session19/A-HRC-19–59-Add5_en.pdf. Accessed 12 June 2013.
101 Ibid., p. 10.
102 Ibid., p. 12.
103 Ibid., p. 12.

Bibliography

Abbot, Thomas. "Pressing Gold Mining Reform in Colombia." *Washington Report on the Hemisphere* 33, no. 16 (September 13, 2013): 1–3.

Arsenault, Chris. "COLOMBIA: Foreign Firms Cash in on Generous Mining Code." *IPSNews.net*, October 22, 2007. Accessed August 20, 2014. www.ipsnews.net/2007/10/colombia-foreign-firms-cash-in-on-generous-mining-code/.

Autodefensas Unidas de Colombia. "Discurso del Jefe del Estado Myor de ls AUC, Comandante Salvatore Mancuse, en el acto de Instalcion Oficial del Proceso de Negociación entre el Gobierno Nacional y las Autodefensas Unidas de Colombia." July 2004. Accessed October 18, 2005. Link no longer active. www.colombialibre.org/ver_imp.php?Varid=6425.

Axworthy, Lloyd. "Human Security: Individuals' Security in a Changing World." *Politique Étrangère* 64, no. 2 (1999): 333–343.

Axworthy, Lloyd. "Human Security as Global Governance." *Global Governance* 7, no. 1 (2001): 19–23.

Berne Declaration, the Canadian Council for International Cooperation, and Misereor. *Human Rights Impact Assessments for Trade and Investment Agreements: Report of the Expert Seminar June 22–23, 2010, Geneva, Switzerland.* Accessed September 4, 2014. www.ccic.ca/what_we_do/Report_HRIA-seminar_2010_eng%5B1%5D.pdf.

Booth, Ken. *Theory of World Security.* Cambridge: Cambridge University Press, 2007.

Cameron, Max, and Catherine Hecht. "Canada's Engagement with Democracies in the Americas." *Canadian Foreign Policy* 14, no. 3 (Fall 2008): 11–28.

Canada Treaty Information. *Agreement Concerning Annual Reports on Human Rights and Free Trade Between Canada and the Republic of Colombia.* 2011. Accessed October 2, 2014. www.treaty-accord.gc.ca/text-texte.aspx?id=105278.

Canadian Trade Commissioner Service. "Trade Commissioner Service – Colombia." January 2013. Accessed September 4, 2014. www.tradecommissioner.gc.ca/eng/office.jsp?oid=62.

Coatsworth, John H. "Roots of Violence in Colombia: Armed Actors and Beyond." *ReVista: Harvard Review of Latin America* 2, no. 3 (Spring 2003).

Clavijo, Sergio, Member of the Board of Directors of the Central Bank of Colombia. "Viability of the External Debt: the Case of Colombia over the 2000s." Statistics from the Central Bank of Colombia. Mimeograph, August 2001.

Comisión Colombiana de Juristas. *Despojo de tierras campesinas y vulneración de los territorios ancestrales.* Bogota, June 2011. Accessed September 5, 2012. http://servindi.org/pdf/despojo_de_tierras_campesinas.pdf.

Comisión Interamericana de Derechos Humanos – Organización de los Estados Americanos. *Verdad, justicia y reparación: Cuarto informe sobre la situación de derechos humanos en Colombia.* December 31, 2013. Accessed June 16, 2014. http://justiciaviva.org.pe/webpanel/doc_int/doc28082014-181944.pdf.

Cox, Robert. "Social Forces, States, and World Orders: Beyond International Relations Theory." *Millennium: Journal of International Studies* 10, no. 2 (1981): 126–155.

Damsgaard, Nina. "Colombia's Election Most Quiet and Safe in Recent History: Govt." *ColombiaReports.co*, June 15, 2014. Accessed September 10, 2014. http://colombiareports.co/colombias-election-quiet-safe-recent-history-govt/.

Danish Institute for Human Rights. Human Rights Compliance Quick Check. 2006. Accessed December 20, 2013. https://hrca2.humanrightsbusiness.org/.

Deas, Malcolm, and Fernando Gaitán Daza. *Dos ensayos especulativos sobre la violencia en Colombia.* Bogotá: Tercer Mundo, 1985.

Departamento Administrativo Nacional de Estadísticas (DANE). "Indicatores económicos." Various years. Accessed June 7, 2010. www.dane.gov.co.

Duffield, Mark. *Development, Security and Unending War.* Cambridge: Polity Press, 2007.

Escobar, Arturo. *Encountering Development: The Making and Unmaking of the Third World.* Princeton: Princeton University Press, 1994.

Escuela Nacional Sindical. "En 2013 aumento la violencia contrac el movimiento syndical Colombiano." December 11, 2013. Accessed January 20, 2014. www.ens.org.co/index.shtml?apc=Na-;1;-;-;&x=20168317.

Escuela Nacional Sindical. "Informe nacional de coyuntura económica, laboral y sindical en 2009—Incluye balance de los 8 años del gobierno Uribe." 2009. Accessed September 3, 2014. www.ens.org.co/index.shtml?apc=Na-;27;-;-;&x=20155546.

Escuela Nacional Sindical. "Una política de exclusión sistemática." May 2009. Accessed January 20, 2014. www.ens.org.co/index.shtml?s=e&m=c&als%5BMENU___%5D=Documentos&v=008&cmd%5B22%5D=c-1-008-c-2-Documentos.

Foreign Affairs, Trade and Development. "Canada's State of Trade, 2014." Accessed October 19, 2014. www.international.gc.ca/economist-economiste/performance/state-point/state_2014_point/index.aspx?lang=eng#6.0.

Fuerzas Armadas Revolucionarias de Colombia (FARC). "Nuestra historia." 2004. Accessed May 2, 2005. www.farc-ep.org/aniversario/especial40aniv/textcrono.html.

Gagne, David. "Losses of $521 Mn Show Guerrilla Impact on Colombia Oil Industry," *InSightCrime.org.* August 21, 2014. Accessed September 10, 2014. www.insightcrime.org/news-briefs/colombia-oil-industry-500-mn-losses-guerrilla-attacks.

Gramsci, Antonio. *Selections from the Prison Notebooks.* New York: International Press, 1971.

Government of Canada. *Annual Report Pursuant to the Agreement Concerning Annual Reports on Human Rights and Free Trade between Canada and the Republic of Colombia.* Ottawa, May 15, 2014. Accessed May 30, 2014. www.canadainternational.gc.ca/colombia-colombie/bilateral_relations_bilaterales/AnnualReport_RapportAnnuel-2013.aspx?lang=eng.

Government of Canada, Foreign Affairs and International Trade. *Canada and the Americas – Priorities and Progress.* Ottawa, 2009. Accessed February 10, 2010. http://publications.gc.ca/site/eng/357143/publication.html.

Government of Colombia, Banco de la República. "Flujos de invesión directa." Accessed August 20, 2014. www.banrep.gov.co/es/info-temas-a/2297.

Government of Colombia, Ejército Nacional, Ministerio de Defensa. "Los grupos ilegales de autodefensa de Colombia." (Bogotá: Éjercito Nacional, December 2000).

Government of Colombia, National Administrative Department of Statistics and National Planning Department. *Monetary Poverty in Colombia: New Methodology and 2002–2010 figures.* Mission for the Splicing of Employment, Poverty and Inequality Series: Bogota, February 2012. Accessed March 1, 2013. www.dane.gov.co/files/investigaciones/condiciones_vida/pobreza/ingles/Monetary%20Poverty%20in%20Colombia.pdf.

Government of Colombia. *Segundo informe anual del acuerdo en material de informes anuales sobre derechos humanos y libre comercio entre la república de Colombia y Canada.* (Bogotá: Departamento de Relaciones Exteriores, May 2013).

Harrison, James, and Alessa Goller. "Trade and Human Rights: What Does 'Impact Assessment' Have to Offer?" *Human Rights Law Review* 8, no. 4 (2008): 587–615.

Harvey, David. *A Brief History of Neoliberalism.* London: Oxford, 2005.

Hernández, Edwin, and Paola Chaparro. "Negociación de paz no termina con todas las violencias." *UN Periódico* (Instituto de Estudios Políticos y Relaciones Internacionales, Universidad Nacional de Colombia) 181 (September 2014).

Howard-Hassmann, Rhoda E. "Human Security: Undermining Human Rights?" *Human Rights Quarterly* 34 (2012): 88–112.

Krause, Keith. "Is Human Security 'More than Just a Good Idea?" In *Brief 30: Promoting Security: But How and for Whom?: Contributions to BICC's Ten-year Anniversary Conference*, edited by M. Brozoska and P. Croll, 43–46. Bonn: BICC's International Conference, 2004.

Liberal Party of Canada. www.liberal.ca.

Macleans. "New CIDA Code Provokes Controversy." Reprinted in *The Canadian Encyclopedia* and available online. July 1, 2006. Accessed August 20, 2014. www.thecanadianencyclopedia.ca/en/article/new-cida-code-provokes-controversy/.

McKenna, Peter. "Canada's Southern Exposure." *Hemisphere: A Magazine of the Americas* 8, no. 3 (Fall 1998): 26–29.

Natural Resources Canada. "Evaluation of the Minerals and Metals Markets, 2012." Accessed October 19, 2014. www.nrcan.gc.ca/evaluation/reports/2012/802.

Newman, Edward. "Critical Human Security Studies." *Review of International Studies* 36, no. 1 (2010): 77–94.

Oquist, Paul Herbert. *Violence, Conflict and Politics in Colombia*. New York: Academic Press, 1980.

Organization of American States. *Inter-American Democratic Charter*. Lima, Peru, September 11, 2001. Accessed December 2, 2009. www.oas.org/charter/docs/resolution1_en_p4.htm.

Parliament of Canada. "Sub-Committee on Human Rights and International Development of the Standing Committee on Foreign Affairs and International Trade." May 30, 2001. Accessed August 15, 2014. www.parl.gc.ca/HousePublications/Publication.aspx?DocId=1040878&Mode=1&Parl=37&Ses=1&Language=E.

Pearce, Scott. "Fueling War: The Impact of Canadian Oil Investment on the Conflict in Colombia." *CERLAC Working Paper Series* (York University, Toronto), November 2002. Accessed April 12, 2014. www.yorku.ca/cerlac/documents/Pearce.pdf.

Pizarro Leongómez, Eduardo. *Las Farc 1949–1966.* Bogotá: Tercer Mundo, 1991.

Portafolio.co. "La pobreza en Colombia se redujo en el 2013." March 21, 2014. Accessed September 15, 2014. www.portafolio.co/economia/pobreza-colombia-el-2013.

Ramirez Cuellar, Francisco. *The Profits of Extermination: Big Mining in Colombia.* Monroe, Maine: Common Courage, 2005.

Rangel, Alfredo. "El repliegue de las FARC: Derrota o estratégia." *Fundación Seguridad y Democracia*, (2004). Accessed March 26, 2005. www.seguridadydemocracia.org.

Reuters. "Colombia Oil Pipeline Paralyzed by Rebel Attacks." July 12, 2014. Accessed September 10, 2014. www.reuters.com/article/2014/07/12/us-colombia-oil-attack-id USKBN0FH0U020140712.

Rochlin, James. *Discovering the Americas: the Evolution of Canadian Foreign Policy to Latin America.* Vancouver: UBC Press, 1993.

Rochlin, James. "Plan Colombia and the Revolution in Military Affairs." *Review of International Affairs* 37 (2011): 715–740.

Rochlin, James. *Vanguard Revolutionaries in Latin America: Peru, Colombia, Mexico.* Boulder: Lynne Rienner Publishers, 2002.

Ryerson, Christie. "Critical Voices and Human Security: To Endure, To Engage, or To Critique?" *Security Dialogue* 41 (2010): 169–190.

Safford, Frank, and Marco Palacios. *Colombia: Fragmented Land, Divided Society.* New York: Oxford University Press, 2002.

Sheldon, Oliver. "Colombia Has 10th Highest Homicide Rate in World: UN." *Colombi-aReports.co*, April 14, 2014. Accessed September 10, 2014. http://colombiareports.co/colombia-10th-highest-homicide-rate-world-un/.

Sowell, David. *The Early Colombian Labor Movement: Artisans and Politics in Bogota, 1832–1919*. Philadelphia: Temple University Press, 1992.

United Nations, General Assembly, Human Rights Council. "Business and Human Rights in Conflict-Affected Regions: Challenges and Options Towards State Responses." 27 May 2011. *Report of the Special Representative of the Secretary-General on the Issue of Human Rights and Transnational Corporations and Other Business Enterprises, John Ruggie*, A/HRC/17/32. United Nations, May 27, 2011. Accessed September 3, 2014. www.ohchr.org/Documents/Issues/TransCorporations/A.HRC.17.32.pdf.

United Nations, General Assembly, Human Rights Council. "Guiding Principles on Business and Human Rights: Implementing the United Nations "Protect, Respect and Remedy" Framework." *Report of the Special Representative of the Secretary-General on the Issue of Human Rights and Transnational Corporations and Other Business Enterprises, John Ruggie*, A/HRC/17/31. United Nations, March 21, 2011. Accessed September 4, 2013. www.ohchr.org/documents/issues/business/A.HRC.17.31.pdf.

United Nations, General Assembly, Human Rights Council. "Guiding Principles on Human Rights Impact Assessments of Trade and Investment Agreements." *Report of the Special Rapporteur on the Right to Food, Olivier De Schutter*, A/HRC/19/59/Add.5. December 19, 2011. Accessed September 4, 2014. www.srfood.org/images/stories/pdf/officialreports/20120306_hria_en.pdf.

United Nations, General Assembly, Human Rights Council. "Human Rights and Corporate Law: Trends and Observations from a Cross-National Study Conducted by the Special Representative." *Report of the Special Representative of the Secretary-General on the Issue of Human Rights and Transnational Corporations and Other Business Enterprises, John Ruggie*, A/HRC/17/31/Add.2. United Nations, May 23, 2011. Accessed September 4, 2013. www.ohchr.org/documents/issues/business/a-hrc-17-31-add2.pdf.

United Nations, General Assembly, Human Rights Council. "Principles for Responsible Contracts: Integrating the Management of Human Rights Risks into State-Investor Contract Negotiations: Guidance for Negotiators." *Report of the Special Representative of the Secretary-General on the Issue of Human Rights and Transnational Corporations and Other Business Enterprises, John Ruggie*, A/HRC/17/31/Add.3. United Nations, May 25, 2011. Accessed September 3, 2014. www.ohchr.org/documents/issues/business/a.hrc.17.31.add.3.pdf.

United Nations Human Security Unit, Office for the Coordination of Humanitarian Affairs. *Human Security in Theory and Practice: Application of the Human Security Concept and the United Nations' Trust Fund for Human Security*. United Nations, 2006. Accessed May 1, 2013. https://docs.unocha.org/sites/dms/HSU/Publications%20and%20Products/Human%20Security%20Tools/Human%20Security%20in%20Theory%20and%20Practice%20English.pdf.

United Nations. *United Nations Human Development Report.* New York: United Nations Development Program, 1994.

United States Department of State. *Colombia 2014 Crime and Safety Report: Bogotá.* Accessed September 3, 2014. www.osac.gov/pages/ContentReportDetails.aspx?cid=15445.

Washington Office on Latin America. "Peace Timeline 2013." *ColombiaPeace.org.* Accessed August 15, 2014. www.Colombiapeace.org/timeline2013.

Wight, Andrew. "ELN Declares War on Oil Companies." *ColombiaReports.co*, November 5, 2013. Accessed September 10, 2014. http://colombiareports.co/guerilla-group-declares-war-oil-companies/.

World Bank Group. "GDP Growth by Country." Accessed September 3, 2014. http://data.worldbank.org.

World Bank Group. International Finance Corporation. "Guide to Human Rights Impact Assessment and Management." 2011. Accessed June 15, 2013. www.guidetohriam.org.

2 Foreign Investment, Oil, and Human Security

The Case of Pacific Rubiales Energy Corporation in Puerto Gaitán

Beatriz Eugenia Sánchez Mojica,
Marco Alberto Velásquez Ruiz,
Sebastián Rubiano Galvis, and
Ana María Muñoz Segura

The central argument of this case study is that soft law and Corporate Social Responsibility programs may be the most effective way to promote critical human security in Colombia's extractive sector, despite their voluntary and non-binding nature. From a legal perspective we examine a case that focuses on a violent struggle between workers and community members, on the one hand, and Pacific Rubiales Energy Corporation and its various contractors, on the other. The rights of trade unions are featured. The case is especially signficant since the corporation produces about one-quarter of all the oil pumped in Colombia, and is relatively unique because of its resolution-entailed tripartite negotiation and an unusual degree of participation by the State. Various aspects of human security are addressed, especially regarding workers rights, but also with regard to themes involving the environment, Indigenous groups, and the community. The case demonstrates the triangular relation between security, development, and human rights that underpins the Critical Human Security perspective. We shall begin with a brief background to the case, procede to a discussion of the actors involved, and conclude with an analysis of the utility of various regimes of law in relation to conflict resolution and the promotion of human security.

Background

On July 19, 2011, violent clashes between a group of workers and the police were taking place in the Rubiales camp, an oil exploration field located in the east of the country and operated by the Canadian company Pacific Rubiales Energy Corporation (PREC).[1] This was the first episode of a conflict that drew nationwide attention and would develop for the rest of the year.

The protests were motivated due to the circumstances in which workers were linked to several contractors used by the multinational. Workers claimed to be forced to accept very short contracts, to be underpaid, to endure long hours of work, and to be subject to the whim of the foremen. Moreover, they complained that the conditions for housing were inhumane. These complaints soon compounded those of the inhabitants of the municipality of Puerto Gaitán where the oil field is located. The community demanded a greater State presence, and greater involvement of the oil company in terms of the community's human security. The company was accused of enriching itself from community land without giving back anything in return.

This situation became even more complex with the involvement of one of the country's main unions, the Workers' Trade Union (USO). The combative stance of USO soon created friction with other actors, leading to serious allegations of violations of trade union rights and threats to members of the union by the multinational and its contractors. Months later, a new union, supported by the company, claimed the affiliation of nearly half of those workers directly related to Pacific Rubiales. Further, complaints related to union member persecution persisted.

The Colombian government, through the Vice Presidency, quickly became involved in mediating the conflict. By the end of 2011, it had reached two agreements by which the multinational assumed commitments to the community, such as the improvement of conditions for hiring local labour. The company also improved the conditions of its employees and took steps to monitor the performance of their contractors. However, the company was very clear to point out that its legal obligations were related only to its own employees, a position endorsed by the national government.[2] The contractors, meanwhile, pledged to substantially improve the working conditions of their employees.

Campo Rubiales has stopped appearing in the media, at least as it relates to labour conflict, and social tensions have been reduced considerably. Despite the apparent success of the agreements reached, two general themes arise from this conflict. First, it is debatable as to whether it is possible to make a multinational company responsible for acts committed by its contractors with regard to elements of human rights and human security. Second, what legal commitment should the company have to the community in which it operates?

This chapter addresses the relationship between the investing companies, workers, trade unions and communities in the context of the Free Trade Agreement between Colombia and Canada (hereafter TLC). The case study is presented not as a purely local problem, but as a matter that involves local and global actors, whose behaviour is governed by domestic and international legal frameworks that intersect to form a complex scenario. Hence, the case study has global implications.

The chapter is divided into five sections. The first section examines the profile of the actors involved in the conflict. The second explains the conflict. The third analyzes the legal frameworks that are intertwined in this situation. The fourth presents paths to conflict resolution. Finally, in the fifth section, global lessons learned are presented and some conclusions are formulated. This chapter is the result of the work of four lawyers.

The Actors

The Colombian State

The role of the Colombian State is crucial in the conflicts arising between the multinational, its contractors, unions, workers, and the community. An analysis of the role of the State must start by recognizing its complexity. It is an integrated, multi-agency body that sometimes pursues clashing goals. This is especially the case here, where the State promotes a neoliberal economic model that is friendly to transnational corporations. But the State is also responsible for the protection of human rights and human security in communities throughout the country.

The economic model, which is the first axis of State action, has been constructed gradually by successive governments that the country has had since the 1990s. The roots of this model were established during the administration of President César Gaviria (1994–1998),[3] and were consolidated under the command of Alvaro Uribe (2002–2010) and Juan Manuel Santos (2010–2018). This economic model rests on two pillars: the extractive natural resource industries and foreign investment.[4] This framework has been presented to Colombian society by the national government as the most suitable route for growth. It is argued that the application of this model will generate jobs and growth to all economic sectors. Likewise, it is argued that this approach will provide the public coffers with needed resources for social investment in health, education, and other services broadly related to human security.

The State has dedicated itself to trade liberalization and to the protection of foreign investment through the signing of various international treaties.[5] The free trade agreement signed with Canada entered in force since August 5, 2011. Domestic laws were created to promote the entry of foreign investment capital into Colombia. Any obstacle to the entry and hiring of foreign personnel[6] has been removed, and sectoral income tax exemptions have been established in order to promote the entry of this type of capital.[7] Colombia has also signed contracts to ensure legal stability for investors[8] and create a regime of free zones.[9]

Attracting foreign investment in the mining and petroleum sectors has been central to this model.[10] Thus, the public policy of hydrocarbons underwent a thorough restructuring process in 2003 to make it more efficient.[11] Importantly, security forces for this sector have been created within the army – the Special Forces – to ensure the protection of infrastructure and personnel associated with the exploitation of these resources.[12] These Special Forces are designated to act against threats such as terrorist attacks, the action of subversive groups, and even actions related to social protests.[13]

The deep commitment of State authorities to this model of development should be aligned with the second axis of action. Colombia, according to its Constitution, is based on the rule of law.[14] This means that the respect and protection of the fundamental rights of all Colombian citizens is its main task and source of legitimacy.[15] Consequently, the ultimate goal of any government action should be aimed at ensuring these rights. It is important to emphasize that rights to decent work and free association among labour groups occupy a crucial place among the guarantees recognized by the Constitution and national laws.[16]

In the case under consideration, the State is in the difficult position of legally respecting foreign investors as well as their host communities in the extractive sector. The national government is the architect and promoter of the oil development policy.[17] It also guarantees legal rights for Canadian investors such as Pacific Rubiales Energy Corp. But at the same time, the national government is responsible for respecting the rights of workers and host communities. At the local level, the mayor of Puerto Gaitán is responsible for protecting the rights of the inhabitants of the town. The mayor also needs to follow the guidelines on economic matters that are directed from Bogotá.

Pacific Rubiales Energy Corp.

PREC is dedicated to the oil business, especially crude oil and natural gas, including processes of exploration, exploitation, production and marketing of derivatives. However, it also holds interests in other related mining and energy sector activities.[18] Currently, it is the largest private company in the country's hydrocarbon sector, and is the second producer of oil in the country after the state-owned Ecopetrol. While it has operations in seven countries,[19] the majority of its projects are in Colombia. It operates in 72 fields[20] – areas that have either been identified with the potential for hydrocarbon exploitation, or which are already in production. Most of its holdings are located in the Orinoquia and Magdalena Medio.

Currently, this company has also established itself as a major political player on the national scene. It is highly present in the mass media[21] and sponsors numerous social causes and sports teams.[22] The only source of uncertainty about the economic outlook and success of the company is the eventual renewal of the concession of Campo Rubiales, a decision that will be taken in 2016 by Ecopetrol. Like the previous actor in this case (the State), the structure of this company is also complex. The company is the result of numerous processes of creation, acquisition, and merger. The current configuration of the company is the result of the fusion in 2008 of two corporative blocks, both of Canadian origin – on one hand, Petro Rubiales Energy Corporation, and on the other, Pacific Stratus Energy Corporation. This merger allowed the company to enter the stock markets of Toronto and Vancouver, endowing it with the financial capacity to compete with large companies.

A second factor that increases the company's complexity is the fact that, probably in an attempt to diversify risk and promote specialization, it has been acting through other companies. In the case of Colombia, these companies include Kappa Energy Holdings Ltd., Petromagdalena Energy Corp., Petrominerales Ltd. and Meta Petroleum Limited. The latter is the direct operator of the oil fields Campo Rubiales, Piriří and Quifa. These companies are all owned by PREC and each one has separate legal entity.

An additional element to consider in this study is that the multinational has contracted several national companies to provide the necessary services for the development of its activities.[23] The main ones that are related to this case study are Intricon S.A., Ismocol S.A., Duflo S.A., and Montajes J.M. S.A. These companies are entirely independent from the TNC. PREC does not own shares in them.

Workers

This is a heterogeneous group, since it is composed of people who face very different situations. Workers can be categorized according to three types of variables. The first concerns the company to which the workers are linked. They can be hired directly by PREC or by one of its contractors. Second, there is the type of contract that binds them to their employer – a fixed or indefinite term. The final factor concerns the worker's attachment or not to a trade union, and if so, to which of the two unions that have relevance in the case.

It is not possible to determine with certainty the exact number of workers directly or indirectly linked to PREC who worked in Campo Rubiales during the period under study here. USO claims that there were 12,000 workers,[24] while PREC refers to 10,000, of which 800 were their direct employees.[25] The lack of clarity is due to the fact that the number of workers at an oil field varies over time.[26] Further, the conditions for workers directly associated with PREC were far better than those of contractors at the beginning of the crisis.

Unions

The role of the unions is a crucial component for the understanding of the problem between PREC and workers. At the heart of the problem is the guarantee of the right to freedom of association for workers vis-à-vis unions. The problem is complicated by the competition between two unions, USO and the Union of Power Industry and Utilities (UTEN), to attract and represent workers.

The Workers' Trade Union of the Petroleum Industry, USO, which represents many of the workers in Colombia's oil industry, is one of the oldest and largest unions in the country. USO has actively promoted a campaign against foreign investment in the extractive sector, and insists that the State company, Ecopetrol, should assume full control of oil exploitation.[27] USO has been the target of violent attacks.[28] In fact, it is the third most victimized of Colombia's array of social organizations, with more than 120 killings of its members in the last twenty years.[29] This persecution has been exacerbated by its stigmatization under the administration of President Uribe (2002–2010), whose speeches linked unions with guerrilla groups.[30]

Recently, the situation seems to be improving for USO. Government discourse under President Santos has taken a radical turn in favor of union activity.[31] The resurgence of the USO has also been linked to a change in its policy strategy. It is not exclusively addressing its discourse to workers. Instead, USO also has directed its messages to host communities of oil projects. This strategy seeks to link the trade union movement with other social movements such as indigenous and environmental groups.[32]

The Union of Power Industry and Utilities (UTEN) provides service to the energy and public utility sectors in Colombia. It was created in 2008 as a division of the industry union SINTRAELECOL, which represents workers from the electrical sector.[33] Initially, the majority of UTEN's members worked in the department of Cauca. However, since 2011, it expanded its geographical base to include workers of the hydrocarbon sector.[34] This decision is closely related to the case under study, a point to which we shall return. UTEN is a unique case regarding unions in Colombia. The official discourse of UTEN defends an "alternative corporate unionism in the XXI century." Consequently, UTEN encourages a constructive dialogue with the business sector. It also understands the dynamics of the economy and recognizes the importance of economic growth.[35]

The union's vision has led it to be identified by other unions as "clientelist," that is, to be an ally of employers. Interestingly, UTEN has been accused of being a business. This observation is supported by the fact that in September 2013 UTEN said that it was prepared to offer to the Government of Honduras about US$300 million to gain control of the National Electricity Company (ENEE), which was mired in a deep financial crisis at the time. Rarely does a union reach such financial power that would permit that kind of investment.[36] The stigma of this union as defending the interests of business has meant that it has become the target of attacks by guerrilla groups, including the Revolutionary Armed Forces of Colombia (FARC).[37]

The Communities of the Municipality of Puerto Gaitán

The final player in this case is the population of the municipality of Puerto Gaitán. Despite its endowment with a wealth of natural resources, the community faces serious gaps regarding respect for human rights and human security. The people of this municipality, which is ethnically diverse, have assumed different forms of organization to present their demands to public institutions and companies operating in their territory. The community associations are the most common, and collectively are represented by the Association of Community Action (ASOJUNTAS). It has played an important role in this case. Other local organizations, such as movements in defense of the environment and of indigenous interests, are also relevant to the case at hand. Finally, a commission of citizens was established in October 2011 to monitor the agreements eventually reached with PREC regarding the hiring of local labour, one of the key demands of the community.[38] This commission has been important to the process of conflict resolution.

Pacific Rubiales' Oil Projects in Puerto Gaitán and Labour Conflict with its Employees and Contractors

Social and Economic Context of the Municipality

Puerto Gaitán is a municipality in the Department of Meta, located in the Orinoco region in east of the country. It is located 190 km southeast of Villavicencio, the departmental capital, and has an area of 19,000 km, making it the fourth largest municipality in the country. The population is around 30,000 people, but a few years ago it was barely 17,000 people.[39] The rise of oil operation is responsible for this increase.

The municipality is located in the heart of the high plain savannas of the Orinoco, an immensely bio-diverse region endowed with numerous water sources. It is also very diverse in human terms. A significant portion of the population is indigenous, with 9,000 people organized into 63 communities belonging to Sikuani, Piapoco and Saliva[40] ethnic groups.[41] Diversity is not the only wealth of this territory; the land is particularly fertile. This soil also has important oil reserves that have begun to be exploited in the past two decades.

Despite the wealth of this town, historically it has been an area with little government presence. This institutional weakness permitted the FARC to control much of this territory in the mid-1980s with little resistance for a decade. In 1995, paramilitary groups such as the Peasant Self-Defense Forces of Meta and Vichada (ACMV) began to appear in Puerto Gaitán, fighting against the guerrillas.[42] Civilians, caught in the crossfire, were the main victims. Both guerrillas and paramilitary groups perpetrated massacres, forced disappearances, forced displacement, and so on.[43]

Oil extraction quickly has become the main economic activity of the region since the turn of the twenty-first century, and the State has increased its power and presence there to protect petroleum production.[44] At the moment, the majority of the population (around 18,000 people) works in the oil industry, and municipal finances depend heavily on this activity.[45] Puerto Gaitán has become one of the municipalities that contribute the most to the national oil production,[46] and was until 2012 the one receiving the greatest amount of royalties.[47] In 2010, this municipality received COL$96 billion pesos for oil.[48] The booming of the oil industry has been accompanied by the emergence and consolidation of agribusiness by national and multinational companies. Thousands of acres are today occupied for the extensive cultivation of soy, corn, palm oil, and timber.

Puerto Gaitán has emerged as a major area for the expansion of the energy and agricultural sectors. In 2014, the national government has declared its intention to convert the high plains region, where the municipality is located, to a developed region. As a result, the government has drawn an ambitious plan involving an investment of COP$9.6 billion (Colombian pesos) for the improvement of infrastructure and public services, and to encourage agricultural and agribusiness development.[49] It has also announced plans for the improvement of roads linking the department with the rest of the country, thereby reducing transportation costs.[50] These decisions, however, have not been accompanied by a program to use the benefits of this growth for the social welfare of the population.

The Index of Unsatisfied Basic Needs in Puerto Gaitán is 65 percent.[51] Poverty is worse in rural areas of the municipality, where the oil and agribusiness projects are located, and where the poverty rate is 83.49 percent.[52] Moreover, the rapid increase in population has led to the exponential rise in land prices and housing, creating a housing shortage that local administration has failed to address.[53]

The safety of the inhabitants of the region has not improved with the economic boom. While the military presence of the State has been increased to guard the oil fields, not much has been done to improve the defense of the population. Residents have become the victims of the Anti-Subversive Revolutionary Army of Colombia (ERPAC), which is a successor of right-wing paramilitary groups after their demobilization in 2006. This criminal gang, as the authorities call it, has been responsible for killings, disappearances, forced recruitment, and displacement. These facts, however, are rarely reported to the authorities due to fear or distrust.[54]

Conflicts over Labour Rights in Campo Rubiales[55]

The presence of PREC dates back to 2008 when, in association with Ecopetrol, it started operating the Rubiales field,[56] which is today one of the most productive oil blocks in the country.[57] It is also active in the blocks of Piriri and Quifa (see Table 2.1).

In early 2011, the production of these blocks, as in the rest of the region, increased considerably. This resulted in an increase demand for workers. Consequently, staff from across the country arrived in the town, but there was no clear plan to manage their arrival. The impact of this wave of people on an impoverished locality with weak local institutions was devastating.[58] This was also recognized by PREC.[59]

The oversupply of cheap labour, combined with the presence of weak institutions, contributed to the abuse of workers' rights. In addition, the oil company delegated contractors to manage the hiring process, without establishing appropriate monitoring and control mechanisms. In this context, PREC's personnel working in three fields at the time had been contracted by outsourcing companies, so workers did not have a direct employment relationship with the multinational. PREC has acknowledged that the surveillance exercised over its contractors to ensure respect for the rights of workers was minimal.[60]

Table 2.1 Oil companies operating in Puerto Gaitán 2008 and 2014

OIL Camp	Cód. ANH	Operator 2008	Operator 2014
Cabiona		Hupecol	New Granada
Caño Sur		Ecopetrol	Ecopetrol
Guarrojo		Hocol	Hocol
Chicuaco		Campetrol	(Área Reservada)
Gabán		Hupecol	(Área reservada
Cocli	135 •	Hocol	Hocol
Sabanero	153	Hocol	Maurel & Prom
Caracara	2,057	Hupecol	Cepcolsa (Cepsa)
Quifa	2,064	Meta Petroleum	Meta Petroleum
Rubiales	2,399 –	Meta Petroleum	Meta Petroleum
Piriri	2,402	Meta Petroleum	Meta Petroleum

Sources: Navas, Op. Cit, (2012) and *Mapa de Tierras* ANH (2014).

Complaints against contractors were numerous, and can be grouped into five categories. First, regarding the conditions of employment, contracts were very short and were managed through intermediaries. This meant minimal job security. Second, wages were less than the TNC paid, and the payment of premiums and mandatory social benefits was decreased. Third, working hours were extended beyond what is permitted by law, without recognition of overtime. Fourth, the accommodations, which must be provided by the companies since the fields are far from the municipal center, were not properly air conditioned. Accommodations for workers were crowded and unsanitary.[61] Finally, foremen were charged on several occasions for treating workers in a degrading manner.[62]

Related complaints were filed by workers of PREC's contractors. These complaints were discussed at various meetings. The result was an agreement signed on March 30, 2011 between the contractors, the TNC and workers which sought to end abuses.[63] This agreement was never fulfilled. Consequently, on July 18, 2011 workers of PREC's several contractors began a work stoppage and blocked the internal roads of Campo Rubiales. The security forces – the army and riot squad police (ESMAD) – intervened and clashed with protesters, numbering nearly 5,000 people. This situation forced the suspension of operations of the field. The scale of the protests, and their impact on the production of one of the major oil fields of the country, immediately aroused the attention of the media.

Negotiations to resolve the labour dispute began the next day. PREC facilitated the dialogue between the parties.[64] While the strike was not conducted by PREC's workers, it was clear that PREC's business was being harmed. From the beginning, USO presented itself as the representative of the workers.[65] The union argued that it was entitled to represent them because about 5,000 workers of the TNC's contractors had membership with USO.[66] The union also stated that the abuse of labour rights was directly attributable to the TNC, therefore, it should act to resolve the labour conflict with workers.[67] Initial meetings among the actors involved in this crisis were unsuccessful and the protests continued. On July 25, 2011 the union first attempted to enter Campo Rubiales' restricted areas – camps, administrative offices and locations under drilling – without the permission of the TNC, which triggered the intervention of the security forces.[68]

USO organized marches that were harshly suppressed by the police, leaving dozens injured and much damage to public infrastructure and property. Despite this, the union was able to obtain the solidarity of the inhabitants of the municipality due to their concerns regarding threats to various facets of human security. Inhabitants of the town had been demanding not only adequate attention to their needs by the State, but also greater social investment by oil companies. Moreover, many residents had objections against the environmental impact of several TNCs, and indigenous communities opposed the displacement that had been imposed on them to allow oil drilling in the lands they had traditionally occupied.[69] The union adopted these demands into its political platform.[70]

The magnitude of the protests, the coverage they received from the media, the cut in oil production, and the threat to the image that the country wanted to portray to foreign investors, led the national government to intervene immediately. The intervention of the State in this case study stands in sharp contrast to the lack of State involvement and tripartite negotiation with regard to other cases treated in this volume. Even before the protests began, on July 15, the Vice President of the Republic of Colombia, Angelino Garzón, declared his interest in the case. He stated that it was a problem caused solely by the contractors of the company, and that all these contracting companies were Colombian.

Thus, on August 3, the Vice President stood as the mediator of a new process of dialogue for the actors involved. Since the protests went beyond labour issues, workers and contractors were not the only ones involved in the dialogue. Indigenous communities and the population of the municipality were also engaged in the conflict resolution process through ASOJUNTAS. PREC was invited in as guarantor for agreements reached in the process. The TNC concurred with the final agreement that was reached. The company argued from the beginning that it was legally bound only to its own employees. However, it claimed that since community complaints over contractors were contrary to Pacific Rubiales' Corporate Social Responsibility policy, it would deal with such issues.[71]

The negotiations led by the Vice President of the Republic involved eight topics of discussion – labour, human rights, environmental concerns, the provision of goods and services, improvement of roads, indigenous affairs, lack of housing, and social investment by the companies (Corporate Social Responsibility). All these fall within the parameter of human security considerations. The discussion group related to labour was made up of the mayor, the Ministry of Labour, contractors, workers, and PREC. Employees submitted a list of 136 petitions on various issues such as wage increases, contractual stability, job placement and hiring of unskilled labour (see Table 2.2).

Due to the extent of the demands, PREC invited other multinational oil companies operating in the town to join the negotiation space, but none did.[72]

USO presented itself within the negotiation process as the leading representative of all workers and the community. PREC never recognized USO's legitimacy, arguing that PREC's workers were not linked to that union.[73] This situation added stress and conditioned the relationship of these two sides throughout the conflict. Importantly, the union lost the support of the community shortly after negotiations began. The violent nature of the protests that continued while the negotiations were carried out led various social organizations, as well as a section of the indigenous communities, to publicly reject USO's methods. This led to questions regarding the legitimacy of the union's presence in the process.[74] All this resulted in the loss of USO's claimed role as the voice of the community. Instead, this position was assumed by ASOJUNTAS and other civil organizations. Later a group of citizens aimed at monitoring compliance with the agreements concerning local recruitment joined this endeavour.[75]

Despite this loss of support, USO persisted with its strategy. This was justified as a means to protest the failure of several promises made by the multinational,[76] as well as the layoffs of more than 4,000 workers linked to the contractors of PREC for the sole reason of having participated in protests. Consequently, the Ministry of Labour opened 40 cases against these employers and eventually imposed some fines to contractors. However, many of the complaints are still pending as of this writing.[77]

Six of the topics within the negotiation process, coordinated by the Vice President, advanced toward agreements. These achievements include commitments on social responsibility from PREC on issues such as transfer of resources to the community and the commencement of studies to construct housing and roads.[78] But negotiations related to human rights and labour issues came to a complete halt. Due to the difficulty in obtaining a negotiated agreement on those themes, USO led new protests and actions. As a result, PREC stopped pumping crude at Campo Rubiales on September 19, 2011. The national government reacted by introducing a new negotiating forum.

This second roundtable,[79] under the coordination of the Ministry of Interior, quickly achieved a cessation of violence, the reopening of oil field activity, and the commitment by PREC to enable USO to visit Campo Rubiales. The speed of this first step contrasted with the difficulty to advance the negotiations on other substantive points.[80] The union insisted that PREC needed to improve the working conditions of both its own employees and its contractors. This demand was completely rejected by the TNC, which asserted its role as simple mediator in the dialogue.

An unexpected event wrecked this additional space for dialogue. On October 6, PREC announced that 850 of its 1,512 direct employees had decided to join UTEN. Although this union had no links with the oil industry, PREC fully supported the entrance of the new union as a means to secure union rights of the workers.[81] This announcement was followed by the signing of an agreement on labour standards between UTEN and PREC. This agreement included three types of clauses. First, it established improvements for workers directly and indirectly employed by the company in terms of wages, working hours and conditions of accommodation. Second, the TNC pledged to increase controls on suppliers and contractors to ensure compliance regarding the rights of the hired staff. Finally, measures for the community of Puerto Gaitán were adopted to ensure that 100 percent of the TNC's contracts and those of its contractors involved the hiring of unskilled local labour. The process of concluding this agreement was accompanied by the Minister of Mines, and was recognized and endorsed by the Vice President's Office, Attorney General's Office, Deputy Prosecutor for Labour Affairs and Social Security, the Assistant Director of the United States Agency for International Development (USAID), and the General Secretary of the General Confederation of Labour-CGT.[82] A few days later, two addenda to the agreement were signed. The first included additional benefits for PREC's workers, and the second, referred to the commitment of the company to acquire, whenever it was possible, goods produced in the town.[83]

This agreement, achieved outside of the official negotiating roundtable, was harshly criticized by USO. It questioned the fairness of the process, and accused the new union of being employer oriented (*patronal*) and completely unaware of the labour problem at Campo Rubiales. It also indicated that the agreement did not recognize the negotiation positions that had been made by USO. Therefore, USO left the negotiating roundtable in Puerto Gaitán when it was still operating, and recommenced protest demonstrations. These protests that USO led culminated in the last days of October 2011, with the capture of Campo Rubiales'

Table. 2.2 Outline of instances of dialogue

Conflict resolution space	Convener	Participants	Agreements reached	Sources
Mesas de concertación local (local agreement working table).	Vice Presidency of the Republic until December 1. In 2013 it is reactivated by the Ministry of Labour. A new timetable was agreed to meet with the other operators of the municipality now that they want to join the table.	Initially it is USO, but then ASOJUNTAS and Veeduría for labour intermediation become the spokespersons of the community.	The working table is installed on August 3 by the Vice Presidency. On September 30 an integral agreement is reached with the community via ASOJUNTAS. On December 1 no labour agreement with PREC was reached (See Table 2.1). Their work table is closed with PREC, but it is reactivated in June 2013 to continue dialogue with the other operators in Puerto Gaitán. This labour agreement was signed with ASOJUNTAS and the Veeduría de Intermediación. USO was not part of this agreement since, as of December 1, the agreement with UTEN still had one month before it had to be signed.	Proceedings of the working table. Excel matrix sent by PREC to the Vice Presidency.

| Mesa de concertación nacional (national working table) | Ministry of Interior and Ministry of Labour. | The USO becomes the chief spokesman. Also advocates for direct employees, which allows inferring that they had at least some affiliated members at this stage of conflict. Ministry of Labour, Ministry of Interior and PREC also participate. | It was raised as a supplementary working table to the local labour working table. USO came with pretensions into six themes:

 1. Salaries and benefits of PREC workers (direct and contractors and subcontractors).
 2. Guarantees for the full exercise of freedom of association by USO.
 3. Real and effective employment of municipality's local labour.
 4. More stable contracts.
 5. Policies for the population living under conditions of manifest weakness.
 6. Reintegration of personnel who had been terminated for contractors since July 19, 2011.

 This table is installed in September 21, 2011. A whole month, until October 21, is given to reach agreements. It was also agreed to restore normal conditions.

 This table is closed the October 21 as the deadline is met and no agreement with PREC. Moreover, it is in October 6 when PREC signs labour normalization deal with UTEN. This agreement with UTEN, as well as the lack of agreement at the national dialogue instance in Bogotá, were the facts motivating a second wave of protests between October 24 and 28, until the repression of the police forced USO to leave Campo Rubiales. | Minutes of September 20, meeting between USO and national government. Minutes of September 21, meeting between USO and PREC. |

Source: self-elaboration.

facilities and the declaration of its closure. The army and the police intervened, leading to violent clashes.[84] The images of the armed forces acting against protesters – disseminated by USO in the mass media – negatively affected the overall image of the company and prompted the solidarity of various sectors of national civil society.[85]

This new wave of protests did not stop the negotiations regarding labour issues in Puerto Gaitán, which eventually reached an agreement that was signed by PREC, ASOJUNTAS and a group of citizens. This new agreement committed the TNC to ensure better conditions for the operations of its contractors, ones that had not been addressed in the agreement reached with UTEN. It covered issues such as job security, the hiring of local labour, labour rights protection, salary increases, and operational stability.[86] An operating committee was created to follow up the agreement.[87]

Subsequent Events to the Signing of Agreements

The signing of the agreements of October and November 2011 did not end labour unrest. USO has insisted that throughout the dialogue process and even after completion, PREC has developed actions to undermine the freedom of association of workers, especially its contractors. USO argued that PREC has prevented the union's access to Campo Rubiales to seek member affiliation.[88] USO also pointed out that PREC has pressured workers to abandon their membership to USO.[89] Moreover, USO referred to the existence of "black lists" containing names of those who did not yield to company pressures. These lists, as argued by USO, have been circulated to oil companies and their contractors to prevent those included on the list to be rehired in the region.[90] This argument is reinforced through criminal complaints filed at the Attorney General's Office by several workers against some of the contractors.[91] The union also notes that, despite promises made by PREC, the company took legal action against some protest leaders and several of them have been prosecuted. USO has also denounced that its leaders in Puerto Gaitán have been threatened by armed groups linked to former paramilitary forces.[92]

All of this stimulated interest by the country's Congress. A senator tried to visit Campo Rubiales in October 2012 to conduct an inspection of the working conditions of employees. He insisted he was not allowed to enter, a claim that was denied by PREC.[93] Likewise, Senator Jorge Robledo led a public debate in the Senate on this issue. Despite several attempts by Robledo's supporters during the following year, this initiative to consider USO's complaints did not continue in Congress. The absence of the Minister of Mines and managers of the TNC prevented the discussion from taking place.

Due to the failure of this debate, and difficulties to judicially force PREC to assume responsibility for the actions of its contractors, in July 2013 several national and international social organizations proposed an Ethical and Political Judgment to the company.[94] PREC was accused of violating human rights, labour rights, indigenous rights and environmental legislation in the context of its projects in Puerto Gaitán. After three days of sessions, an ethical and political tribunal highlighted that the company's actions did not respect workers and communities in the area and demanded its withdrawal from the country.[95] The company was not involved in this process.

Although the agreements reached in October and November 2011 determined the commitments of PREC and its contractors, labour negotiations in the region have not been completed. It is noteworthy that although the protests were directed against the Canadian TNC, the reality is that the abuse of workers' rights has been committed by an assortment of companies. In May 2013, the Labour Board was reactivated, this time under the coordination of the Ministry of Labour. During 2013–2014 this board has held sessions with a number of oil companies in the region with two objectives.[96] First, it has attempted to encourage dialogue regarding the responsiveness of oil companies to resolve concerns from the local population regarding the use of contractors. Second, it has encouraged the development of a conflict resolution mechanism for labour as well as a program to hire workers from the local population.[97]

USO has been integrated into this space and has engaged in discussions with certain oil companies concerning job placement.[98] But USO's position is not comparable to the one it had in the recent past. It has definitely lost the support of the community and an important faction of its former members has separated from the union. Additionally, due to the constant threats, USO has opted in late 2013 to close its office in the municipality.[99]

Actions such as protests and work stoppages have not occurred again. However, according to representatives of ASOJUNTAS, some disagreements persist regarding the implementation of the agreements reached, especially those coordinated and signed by the Vice President of the Republic.[100] PREC has extensively monitored the progress of these agreements, particularly with regard to the commitments made by its contractors and subcontractors. PREC's Sustainability Report 2012 indicates that is has met 95 percent of the commitments it made to workers and the community of Puerto Gaitán.[101] A later report, addressed to the Vice President of the Republic, reports a 100 percent compliance in labour, social, and infrastructure agreements.[102] In the same vein, it has increased the salary of its employees and has indicated to its contractors to act in the same way.

It is clear that working conditions have improved considerably in Campo Rubiales in comparison to the situation at the outbreak of the protests. PREC has implemented improvements for its own employees and strengthened controls over its contractors to ensure better working conditions. For instance, housing conditions have substantially improved: the pictures that were presented in the debate in the Senate in 2012 show crowded *cambuches* where workers used to sleep; now they sleep in accommodations that include more bathrooms, and units that house four workers rather than 20 as was previously the case.

There remains tension between USO and PREC, but the situation of direct conflict has ceased. As noted by a security guard of PREC's oil fields, since 2011 there have not been any protests or disruptions to oil extraction.[103] For those in charge of security in the field, the conflict is perceived as a past event. The atmosphere of normality suggests that many of the workers who initially joined USO became UTEN's affiliates and are generally satisfied with the agreements reached.

Finally, it should be noted that in January 2014 Pacific Rubiales was finally acquitted by the Ministry of Labour in the investigation that had been opened regarding the alleged harassment of members of USO as a result of protests at Campo Rubiales and Quifa. USO had filed complaints with the Ministry in February 2012. Initially, the Ministry acquitted the company, but USO appealed the decision. The Ministry confirmed its decision, which declared that the termination of contracts of USO supporters was not the result of anti-union acts.[104] Criminal complaints against the management of PREC and some of its contractors presented by the USO to the Attorney General are still pending.

Legal Frameworks Governing the Case

The facts that have been exposed reveal a complex situation in which three types of problems are intertwined. The first problem is the alleged violation of the rights of workers by contractors of PREC. The second problem is related to the alleged violation of freedom of association among workers and the persecution of trade unionists. Finally, despite the wealth of the town, the living conditions of the people of Puerto Gaitán require major improvements, and so PREC's Corporate Social Responsibility programs have been called into question. While USO has not fared well during this process, the questions it raised at the beginning of the protests remain highly relevant: What is the legal responsibility of a transnational corporation? Does the TNC need to respond to labour rights violations committed by its contractors? Does the TNC need to take care of the social needs of its host community?

The agreements reached in Puerto Gaitán do not answer these questions because they are designed to address in a timely manner a problem considered to be a local one, when in fact it is an important matter of global concern. To answer these questions, it is necessary to overcome the local approach and situate the dispute within a broader framework of analysis. The law provides such a framework. In the case under study, three different legal systems are pertinent: (1) labour law, which is eminently domestic; (2) regimes for protection of foreign investment, which is mainly international; and (3) the liability regime for TNCs regarding human rights, which combines elements of domestic and global law.

Labour Law

The conflict that occurred in Campo Rubiales began as a labour-oriented issue. It is related to claims of workers supported by a union. Labour law is, therefore, the framework in which to place their demands. Contrary to what might be thought, the aim of the scheme is not the protection of the worker, but to reconcile the interests of the parties involved in a working relationship.[105] Due to profound economic and power differentials between the parties, labour law is concerned with empowering workers through legal benefits and protections. This system has a wide and solid structure. Its basic principles are set by the

Constitution and its main provisions are enshrined in three laws: the Labour Code, Act 100 of 1993 – which refers to the social security system – and the Procedural Code of Labour and Social Security. The treaties signed by the country as part of the International Labour Organisation, as well as the statements and recommendations issued by this agency, are also part of the system.[106]

It is important to emphasize that it is quite irrelevant whether or not the employer is a domestic or a multinational company. The law makes no distinction regarding the obligations to which employers are subject despite their nationality. The legislation also provides a comprehensive set of provisions for the protection of freedom of association, which is conceived as a fundamental right, inherent in the exercise of a labour relationship.[107] Collective bargaining[108] and strikes[109] are placed in the same category. Consequently, these three rights are surrounded by the guarantees necessary for their exercise.

While the employer and employee are the main subjects of these provisions, labour law recognizes and regulates the existence of other actors. This is the case with regard to simple intermediaries,[110] independent contractors,[111] temporary employment agencies,[112] and associated worker cooperatives[113] with workers as dependents.[114] The presence of these actors complicates the employment relationship. However, the rights and obligations of the parties cannot be blurred.

In this particular case, it is necessary to delve into the implications for independent contractors,[115] the category in which PREC's contractors are situated. These contractors are companies[116] that are in charge of work performed or which provide a service to a third party with full autonomy. In more concrete terms, with regard to the conflict raised in Puerto Gaitán, there is no employment relationship between contract workers and PREC.

Exceptional measures, however, can be legally taken to protect these workers. In some cases, the contracting company may be liable, along with the independent contractor, for the payment of salaries, benefits, and allowances.[117] This situation occurs only if the independent contractor performs work that fits into the normal activity of the parent company and, for some reason, is unable to pay its employees. However, this liability does not apply to working conditions, since these are solely the responsibility of the contractor. With regard to the case under study, PREC is responsible when there is a non-payment scenario by the contractor. But this is a relatively small problem in this case, since unpaid wages are just one of the grievances of workers, and these are pertinent only to workers that engage in oil production.[118] Therefore the framework provided by this law provides only a partial answer to the question posed.

Legal Framework for the Protection of Canadian Foreign Investment in Colombia: Multinational Corporations as Subjects of Protection

Since Pacific Rubiales is a foreign investor, the International Investment Law is one of the relevant legal regimes to consider in this case. This legal regime is primarily intended to establish necessary conditions for the massive influx of foreign capital into the country, through the creation of a stable environment and predictable business conditions. The basis of this policy framework is established by rules of the global order that have been voluntarily accepted by the States, such as international public policy and international law agreements. The first are documents issued by international institutions[119] that make recommendations to governments regarding, for example the protection of foreign investment. The second refers to bilateral investment treaties and free trade agreements with foreign investment chapters that establish rules whose purpose is to facilitate the transnational movement of private capital and protective mechanisms for foreign investors.[120] The free trade agreement between Colombia and Canada is located in this category.

International policies and agreements are integrated in the area of domestic law and complemented by a set of national standards such as those in the Constitution.[121] This legal framework – both at the national and international levels – builds on the perception that, due to their lack of citizenship with respect to the country where they were incorporated, investors are in an unfavorable position that has to be balanced. In order to protect foreign investors and avoid any type of discrimination, three basic rules are established. First, the State's obligation to ensure fair and equitable conditions of operation for foreign investors, at least as favorable as those offered to its citizens. Second, the protection of property rights requires authorities to ensure fair compensation for any kind of expropriation. Finally, the principle of resolution of disputes requires that conflicts between investors and the State are resolved expeditiously, with access to international arbitration proceedings. These provisions are central for free investment agreements[122] and free trade agreements. Generally, the protection offered to investors excludes other actors. These agreements do not usually impose obligations on investors to protect people or communities who may be affected, in some way, by the activities of these investors. The responsibility to protect this sector of the population is a duty of the State.

The Free Trade Agreement between Colombia and Canada, which came into force in 2011, deviates slightly from these general features. While it incorporates the three principles of investor protection, it encourages the voluntary adoption of Corporate Social Responsibility programs by foreign investors.[123] It also has three supplementary agreements that address negative impacts of its application in Colombia on issues such as labour,[124] the environment,[125] and respect for human rights.[126] Since PREC is a Canadian company, it is subject to the protection and recommendations inherent in the treaty.

Regulatory Framework of the Responsibility of Multinational Companies in the Field of Human Rights

The final international regime that is related to the case at hand concerns the responsibility of TNCs with regard to human rights. Claims made by PREC's workers, USO, and the community of Puerto Gaitán fall into this framework. These claims are linked to the essential rights of the individual. Unlike the previous two regimes, this one is not fully consolidated. The rules that comprise this regime are recent, and some are still in the process of formation.[127] Moreover, this regime involves two trends that share a controversial relationship – Corporate

Social Responsibility and the regime of non-contractual civil liability. The first focuses on the voluntary nature of companies to make commitments on issues like human rights, environment, and sustainable development.[128] These provisions belong to both international law and domestic law, but they are not legally mandatory. In contrast, the second trend, which is articulated by the State, consists of obligatory provisions that may be claimed in domestic courts. While some authors argue that these two trends are contradictory,[129] it is possible to see them as complementary.[130] Indeed, in the case under study, the two types of provisions are interrelated.

PREC has shown an active interest in Corporate Social Responsibility (CSR). It has its own CSR policy, reformulated in 2012,[131] and has launched several related initiatives, both at the international and domestic levels. Indeed, in January 2011 it signed the Global Compact.[132] This represents a public commitment to 10 principles relating to the respect of human rights, environmental protection, and the fight against corruption.[133] Importantly, respect for workers' rights, including freedom of association, occupies an important place in the Global Compact initiative that has been promoted by the United Nations. In addition, the company has recently been awarded the certification standard EO100 – regarding sustainable development in the oil and gas sector – for Rubiales and Quifa fields.[134]

Locally, PREC is part of Guías Colombia en Derechos Humanos y Derecho Internacional Humanitario since 2012 (translated as Guidelines in Colombia in Human Rights and International Humanitarian Law). It is an initiative that brings together actors from civil society,[135] the national government, as well as domestic and foreign companies[136] operating in Colombia. The full respect for labour rights is part of this commitment, as is the concern for the safety and welfare of host communities.[137] Since 2013 PREC has also been part of a second local initiative, the Energy Mining Committee (CME) that focuses on security and human rights.[138] This is a forum created by the national government in order to formulate recommendations for managing the security of a key sector for the national economy. This committee includes companies of the mining and energy sectors,[139] government agencies,[140] and representatives of the embassies of the United States, United Kingdom, and the Netherlands.

The three initiatives mentioned, along with others such as OECD Guidelines for Multinational Enterprises,[141] are based on the voluntary membership and commitment of companies. Despite their variety, they share several common elements. The first is their *soft law* character, there are no legally binding commitments. However, these commitments can be important to the company's customers and shareholders.[142]

Secondly, these initiatives share common principles.[143] Although the State assumes the main legal responsibility for human rights,[144] companies must refrain from violating human rights and deal with any negative impact on host communities.[145] Related to this principle there are three auxiliary rules that are particularly relevant in this case. First, the principle of due diligence[146] requires that companies anticipate possible negative effects of their activities and take appropriate measures to prevent, mitigate or repair them. In the case under consideration, this requirement implies that the TNC should have predicted the effects of increased oil production, and should have adapted the infrastructure to meet the needs of the growing number of workers. It also implies that the oil industry in a municipality like Puerto Gaitán should have assumed that the company's operations could produce negative consequences for the well-being of the community. Second, the principle of sphere of influence[147] associates the company with the negative consequences of the activity of its partners and other members of the value chain. With regard to the case at hand, this principle implies the responsibility of PREC for possible violations of workers' rights committed by its contractors. Finally, there is the principle of access to reparation mechanisms which requires both States and businesses to take the necessary measures to ensure access to appropriate reparation to those who have seen their human rights violated.[148]

The regime of non-contractual civil liability is also applicable to the case under study. Unlike the regime discussed above, this one has not been designed to link business and human rights. It is part of the foundation of domestic legal systems. In fact, as noted by International Commission of Jurists (ICJ), "[i]n every jurisdiction, despite differences in terminology and approach, an actor can be held liable under the law of civil remedies if through negligent or intentional conduct it causes harm to someone else."[149] This regime allows the civil population to file lawsuits against companies that have violated human rights or been complicit in this. Domestic standards such as the *Alien Tort Claim Act*[150] even recognize the national court's jurisdiction to consider cases from abroad.[151] In Colombia the opportunity to sue a company is an option that so far has only been raised on a theoretical level.[152] In Canada, however, the decision of July 22, 2013 the Superior Court of Justice of Ontario[153] has opened this option. This alternative will be explored in the following section.

Route for Peaceful Conflict Resolution

The analysis of the three interrelated legal frameworks of this case determine that the liability of PREC is not limited to respecting the rights of its own workers. In exceptional cases, the Colombian labour regime imposes upon parent companies obligations regarding the employees of its contractors. The foreign investment law tentatively encourages a commitment to labour. However, a broader commitment is achieved through a complex legal framework that links business with respect for human rights. The principles of due diligence and sphere of influence link the TNC to employees of its contractors and to host communities. Thus, the regime of non-contractual civil liability raises option to take a company to court for the damage a TNC's activities have caused, as well as those produced by its contractors.

The question that arises at this point is whether or not these legal frameworks provide mechanisms through which it is possible to claim the fulfillment of these commitments. As discussed throughout this section, each of the involved legal systems offers alternatives, but none is fully satisfactory. The narrow focus of each of these structures suggests a consideration of their simultaneous use.

Mechanisms of Labour Law

The Colombian labour system offers multiple ways to resolve the conflicts that arise between various parties within an employment relationship. This regime proposes that the company is the place where differences have to be resolved. Therefore, it provides rules for the mechanisms that each employer shall consider to allow workers to present, discuss, and resolve conflicts.[154] Such mechanisms are exclusively structured around the relationship between employer and direct employees, excluding any third party. Despite the usefulness of these mechanisms to address various problems that arise in the labour context, they do not allow PREC to respond to the demands of the employees of its contractors.

A second mechanism is collective bargaining, which can eventually lead to a strike. The latter, rather than a mechanism for conflict resolution, should be understood as a right derived from the freedom of association. The exercise of this right is widely regulated. Thus, a strike can only start when the parties – the employer and its workers – have exhausted a prior stage of direct settlement[155] and if the dispute has not been brought to an arbitration tribunal.[156] Representatives of government, employers, and workers participate in the negotiation process; the latter can be represented by one or more unions. However, it is possible to invite another party as guarantor, if there is consensus between the negotiating parties. This situation was presented in the case under study. PREC acted as a guarantor at the Rubiales field's collective bargaining. PREC accompanied the process, ensuring that it was done according to the rules that govern it. Consequently, while the company made valuable advances regarding the rights of workers hired by its contractors, no assumption of responsibility for eventual labour rights abuses by contractors was made.

Alternative Management of Conflicts Offered by the Colombia – Canada FTA

The Free Trade Agreement between Canada and Colombia has 23 chapters that cover a wide range of issues related to free trade of goods and services and the promotion of mutual foreign investment. Thus, investor protection is extremely relevant. Those individuals or companies who hold this condition, as investor, have certain rights, which are structured around the three main principles that have already been mentioned. However, these rights are not complemented by a catalogue of duties. The treaty establishes the scope of the obligations that are limited to the State members, especially their public authorities.[157] Eventually, particular duties regarding the respect for human rights, labour and environmental issues can be imposed on investors. Nevertheless, this treaty ignores that option and, as noted, promotes the use of non-binding instruments on labour matters. Moreover, it involves three supplementary agreements to resolve conflict generated by the application of the FTA.

Of the various procedures established in these agreements, one could provide an alternative for resolving disputes between Pacific Rubiales, USO, workers and contractors: The process of public communications[158] and annual reports on human rights.[159] This provides a channel for national companies and investors to raise issues relating to the implementation of labour laws in the context of the obligations established by the FTA.[160] Nevertheless, it is not adequate as a mechanism of conflict resolution, and does not entail the adoption of binding decisions. It is difficult to evaluate this mechanism at this point, due to its lack of use and the vagueness of the terms in which it has been created. These points will be developed in Chapter 6, and in the Conclusion.

Options Offered by the Regime of Corporate Responsibility

Before analyzing the system of Corporate Social Responsibility, it is important to note two features of this regime that provide it with a special strength. Although this regime is considered soft law, corporate reputation has an important impact for the TNC. Beyond ethical considerations, companies have a keen economic interest in observing and implementing these commitments.[161] The promotion of human rights and human security has a significant impact on the image of a TNC, which can affect its performance on stock markets, for example. Since PREC has become aware of the value of its reputation, it has endeavored to make public its compliance with various international and regional instruments related to Corporate Social Responsibility.[162] PREC's annual sustainability reports[163] and comprehensive campaigns in the media[164] are demonstrative of this.

This regime provides mechanisms for the resolution of conflicts such as those entailed in this case study. First, Guías Colombia is an initiative that has been designed as a space for the collaborative construction of standards for respectful behaviour towards the IHRL and IHL.[165] Members of this initiative are encouraged to create their own mechanism for receiving complaints and grievances,[166] within a wider context that seeks to achieve conflict resolution. In fact, this general idea embodies a commitment made by the larger project to which authors of this volume belong, a point that will be developed in the conclusion. This mechanism could emerge as a tool for the study and resolution of complaints of those who have been negatively affected by the activity of the company or its contractors, or by the FTA in general. It must provide the confidentiality necessary to ensure the security of the claimant by recognizing and mitigating power asymmetries presented in these situations. Finally, if a violation of human rights is committed by a company or one of its contractors, necessary measures should be implemented to prevent its recurrence and to seek forgiveness.[167] This procedure does not replace State action. It actually requires access to judicial and administrative actions. The State punishes the company or its contractors for any human rights abuse. Thus, this mechanism establishes a forum for dialogue for the parties involved to identify responsibilities, and to plan changes to ensure respect for human rights and the provisions of IHL.

The principles proposed by the OECD seek a similar objective. Failure to comply with the guidelines established by this instrument may be reported to a State entity. In Colombia, this entity is the Ministry of Commerce, Industry and Tourism.[168] Upon receipt of the complaint, a mediation process must be developed aimed at finding a solution. This mechanism has three elements that make it a little more recommendable than *Guías Colombia*. First, it is developed in a neutral environment. Secondly, it culminates with a public report. Finally, the principles of due diligence and sphere of influence are more clearly set out in the OECD principles than in the *Guías Colombia* documents.[169] It should be noted that none of these mechanisms was in effect at the time of the strike.

The Route of Resolution Offered by the Regime of Non-Contractual Civil Liability

This regime provides the opportunity to attend a national court for a judgment. As previously noted, a situation of this nature, involving a TNC with direct or indirect participation in the violation of human rights, has not been presented yet in Colombia. Until recently, this pathway has not been an option in Canada, especially since the refusal by Parliament in 2010 to approve a rule allowing citizens to bring legal proceedings against Canadian extractive companies for events outside the country.[170] However, the decision made in 2013 by the Superior Court of Justice of Ontario in the case of *Choc* v. *Hudbay Minerals Inc.*[171] completely changes this scenario. Through this decision, the court declared admissible a complaint against a Canadian mining company for alleged human rights violations committed by a private security company hired by a subsidiary in Guatemala. While this is a procedural decision, it marks a milestone in the jurisprudence of this country. It recognizes the jurisdiction of Canadian courts for acts committed abroad. It also supports the possibility of linking a TNC to acts committed by its contractor, which goes against the jurisprudential line followed for more than a hundred years in Canada.[172] This step was made possible by the incorporation of soft law instruments of Corporate Social Responsibility – publicly accepted by the Canadian company – which introduced the principles of scope of influence and due diligence.

This decision suggests the possibility of resolving the conflict between PREC, contractors, workers, and unions in the Canadian courts. While the context and type of violations of human rights differ, the core elements of the case are similar. However, this type of alternative has disadvantages that must be evaluated. On the one hand, it transforms the conflict into an essentially legal dispute, which has been identified as a risk by the doctrine. Authors such as McCann, for example, have pointed out that the language of human rights can restrict the social features of the struggle and offer remedies that do not attack the root causes of the problem.[173] Furthermore, a conflict of this kind often lasts for many years. The solution to the conflict, thus, extends over time, while its causes can be deepened.

Lessons Learned

The conflict in 2011 in Campo Rubiales goes beyond a local consideration. Although it took place in a well-defined place, it reflects issues with a global character. It is not an accident that the conflict emerged from the most important oil field in the region, and initial protests turned into an organized movement. Nor is it an accident that claims were directed to Pacific Rubiales, one of the most powerful multinational corporations operating in Colombia. Claims from both the community and the workers, originally channelled through USO, raise questions as to the model of development adopted by the country, characterized by the use of foreign investment, the extractive industry, and multinational corporations as essential elements. Four lessons have been gained with regard to PREC and the broad theme of human security. First, the activity of TNCs takes place in a complex context of social, political, economic, and even cultural tensions. These occur with a distinct historical context, which must be appreciated when a TNC starts and operates a venture. Against this backdrop, demands made by TNCs and FTAs to Colombia – such as the guarantee of a stable, predictable and favorable legal environment – cannot be isolated from the historical and social context.

Paradoxically, society gives meaning to an economic activity. On the one hand, the establishment and operation of TNCs is developed through constant interaction with various social actors. On the other hand, business activity affects the social environment because it is intended to obtain a community's resources for which the community expects to be reimbursed. Beyond a logic of profit maximization and the efficient use of resources, the dynamics of the company cannot be unrelated to the characteristics of the social environment where the operation takes place. On the contrary, it is at this point that the concept of social responsibility makes sense and should be seen as a regulatory element that defines the TNC behaviour.

Second, the commitments made by a company in the context of Corporate Social Responsibility can be particularly effective to achieve human security in the communities in which they operate. The principles of sphere of influence, due diligence, and conflict resolution, which are included in the regime of corporate responsibility, are particularly important, as we have seen. Further, it is crucial for TNCs to establish as a duty the creation of conflict resolution mechanisms.

Although the official position of Pacific Rubiales is that TNCs such as itself have no legal obligations to the workers of its contractors, it agreed to participate in all the forums created for resolving the conflict involving disputes with contract workers. Pacific Rubiales also committed to the provision of additional benefits to employees of its contractors and to the community of Puerto Gaitán. Overall, it has reformulated its own policy of Corporate Social Responsibility, strengthening controls over its contractors and establishing more stable ties with the community. The explanation for this behaviour lies not only on ethical issues, but on the economic value of CSR programs and of corporate reputation in general. This is especially the case for PREC, because the company is traded on the stock market. In this regard, the role of the media in covering the conflict added pressure for PREC to provide a good corporate image.

Nonetheless, it is important to recognize the complex relationship between Corporate Social Responsibility and the protection of human rights. Theories such as shared value, the one inspiring PREC's current policy, have a deep liberal-utilitarian base. It seems difficult to include a real human rights perspective in such a proposal.

Third, investment law is designed to protect investors. Unless there is a change in the structure of this law, attempts to incorporate the protection of people and communities affected by the activity of foreign investors will remain as ineffective annexes. We showed that international investment law is a legal system that was designed with the clear purpose of developing mechanisms for the protection of the transnational mobility of capital. Therefore, this legal system does not regulate the behaviour of TNCs regarding social responsibility.

TNCs enjoy protection from any regulatory action by the State that may affect its ownership or economic expectations. The guarantee of legal stability allows investors to develop an economic activity that is efficient and focuses on maximizing profit. References to regulations on labour and human rights included in international investment agreements are enigmatic. It is unclear whether these regulations are decorative elements of the law, or if they involve a Machiavellian function, that is, they openly legitimize favorable conditions to particular interests of a small social group (foreign investors). In any case, it is difficult to believe that these agreements will change in the short term. Therefore, it is advisable to seek solutions in other mechanisms or normative instances.

Fourth, domestic labour law, despite its high degree of sophistication, is unable to regulate complex relationships generated by the activity of TNCs and their contractors. Colombia has a special regulation for employment in order to deal with disputes between workers and employers. This regulation is governed by principles established internationally. However, the practical capacity of this regulation is limited if labour relations between an employer and a group of workers are not established in a linear manner.

Finally, this case study generates suggestions regarding both corporate and governmental HRIAs as tools to promote critical human security. With regard to corporate Human Rights Impact Assessments, this case demonstrates the significance of various threats to workers rights and to human security that can emerge from corporate use of contractors in the field. These can threaten the public image of the corporation in a manner that can produce negative economic consequences. Thus, if a corporation relies on contractors, a series of human security indicators should be included in a corporate HRIA to determine any negative impacts that may occur regarding workers and the community, so that these may be addressed and remedied. Such indicators might address, for example, the following questions: Does the contractor pay employees a rate similar to the parent corporation? Does the contractor adhere to basic labour laws domestically and internationally? Does the contractor respect unionized employees, and permit free association? Does the contractor have a good record of human rights in the past?

We also observed that, beyond workers, the community played a vital part in both the public protests as well as the conflict resolution process. Hence, community relations are a key aspect of human security and should be included in the HRIA. Indicators should measure the corporation's and the contractor's various social effects on the community, in relation to security, the environment, ethnic rights and so on.

With regard to governmental HRIAs, such as the one involved in the Canada–Colombia FTA, there is much to learn from the case at hand. First, the HRIA needs to be treated as a serious instrument to promote conflict resolution and human security, in contrast to its status through 2014 as being vacant and irrelevant – points that are developed fully in Chapter 6 and in the Conclusion. If the Colombian and especially the Canadian government begin to treat the HRIA as an important tool to promote the interests of both businesses and host communities, this case showcases tripartite negotiation and a strong role of the State as being vital aspects to conflict resolution. Finally, the case also suggests a roster of human rights and human security indicators for a governmental HRIA, ones that are similar to the corporate HRIA noted above.

Notes

1 *Un muerto y diez heridos durante paro en Campo Rubiales*, El Espectador (El Espectador July 19, 2011), www.elespectador.com/noticias/nacional/un-muerto-y-diez-heridos-durante-paro-campo-rubiales-video-285612, (accessed on October 3, 2014).
2 In an interview with an important Colombian radio station the Vice-Minister for Labour Relations of the Ministry of Social Protection, Javier Coca Parga, said that "the problem between the USO and Pacific Rubiales is not responsibility of the government or the company. The problem is between USO and contractors who hire workers affiliated to the union", available at Caracol Radio, www.caracol.com.co/noticias/actualidad/nuevas-dificultades-entre-trabajadores-y-pacific-rubiales/20111024/nota/1567069.aspx (accessed on October 10, 2014).
3 Sebastián, E y Steiner, R *La Revolución Incompleta: las reformas de Gaviria.* (Norma, 2008).
4 Sánchez, B y Urueña, R *Derechos humanos, desplazamiento forzado y desarrollo económico en Colombia: una mirada a partir del impacto del derecho internacional en la política local* en Seminario en Latinoamérica de Teoría Constitucional y política *Derechos Humanos: posibilidades teóricas y desafíos prácticos* (Libraria, 2014).
5 Since August 2014, there are in effect seven FTAs between Colombia Mexico, Chile, El Salvador, Guatemala, Honduras, United States, Canada and the EFTA members (Switzerland and Liechtenstein). There are also in effect four partial tariff preference agreements with Venezuela, Cuba, Nicaragua, and the Caribbean Community (CARICOM), and two agreements with international organizations: the Andean Community of Nations (of which Colombia is a party) and MERCOSUR. Five investment agreements have been signed with Spain, Switzerland, Peru, China, and India. Additionally, there is still pending the ratification of agreements with the European Union, UK, Singapore, Japan, Panama, Costa Rica, and South Korea.
6 In 2010, Law 1429 removed restrictions on the entry of foreign workers and the Decree 834 of 2013 established a particularly simple system for granting visas to investors and their families. See Republic of Colombia, Law 1429 (2010).
7 In 2002, Act 788 exempted from this tax to sectors such as the sale of electricity produced by alternative energy sources, river transport, the use of forest resources and the hospitality industry. See Republic of Colombia, Law 788 (2002).
8 In 2005, Act 963 claims that these contracts ensure that certain standards, central to the development of an industry or service, will not be modified in several years.
9 This is the area within the country where industrial or commercial activities take place under favorable tax and customs regulations which are included by Law 1004 in 2005 See Republic of Colombia, Law 1004 (2005).
10 According to the National Development Plan 2010–2014 "energy-mining sector, where oil exploration is located, is one of the key component of growth in the

country as it generates half of the country's exports and is responsible for attracting two thirds of foreign direct investment." Republic of Colombia, *National Department of Planning, National Development Plan 2010–2014*, pp. 275–276 (2010).

11 Decree 1760 of 2003 created the National Hydrocarbons Agency and assigned it the role of managing and regulating the hydrocarbon resources of the nation. Republic of Colombia, Decree 1760 (2003).

12 The National Army have special battalions, dedicated to the protection of infrastructure power generation including those for hydrocarbon production. Refer also to the strategic map available at www.ejercito.mil.co/?idcategoria=283083 Army (accessed October 15, 2014).

13 Ministerio de Defensa Nacional, *Memorias al Congreso 2012–2013*, 39–40 (2013).

14 Constitución Política de Colombia (1991) Art. 1.

15 This has been pointed out in its extensive jurisprudence in the Constitutional Court. The T-406 of 1992. The paper of Ciro Angarita Baron is the cornerstone of this approach.

16 Constitución Política de Colombia (1991) Arts. 25 and 39.

17 Colombian politics regarding oil are governed by a comprehensive set of standards including constitutional provisions (Constitution of Colombia (1991) Arts. 332 and 360), as well as laws passed by Congress (Laws 141 (1994) and 756 (2002)). The Government, through the National Hydrocarbons Agency, is the main institution that rules this sector.

18 *Profile: Pacific Rubiales Energy Corp* www.reuters.com/finance/stocks/company Profile?symbol=PRE.TO Reuters (accessed January 20, 2014).

19 The company also owns properties in Brazil, Peru, Guatemala and Guyana www. pacificrubiales.com/map-of-properties.html (accessed September 25, 2014).

20 Pacific Rubiales Energy, *Annual and Sustainability Report 2013* (PREC, 2013: 35).

21 Daniel Pardo, *Pacific ES Colombia*, Kienyke (Kienyke October 11, 2012) www. kienyke.com/kien-escribe/pacific-es-colombia/ (accessed January 24, 2014).

22 *Pacific Rubiales fue presentado como Socio Oficial de la Selección Colombia* (Federación Colombiana de Futbol), www.fcf.com.co/index.php?option=com_content&v iew=article&id=3048%3Apacific-rubiales-fue-presentado-como-socio-oficial-de-la-seleccion-colombia&catid=12%3Anoticias-seleccion-colombia&Itemid=31 (accessed January 24, 2014).

23 Correa, G. y Hoyos, Y., *Impactos en los Derechos Humanos de la implementación del Tratado de Libre Comercio entre Colombia y Canadá. Línea base*. Documento 95 Escuela Nacional Sindical (ENS, 2012).

24 Ethical and Political Trial PREC, Bogotá, October 2013, handicraft square. Intervention USO.

25 The company claims that at that time the total number of PREC employees was 1,500. Today that number stands at 3,000. Interview by Sebastian Rubiano with Alejandro Jimenez, manager of Corporate Social Responsibility, Pacific Rubiales Energy. Bogotá, May 27, 2014.

26 Many of Campo Rubiales labour contracts lasted between four and six months, contributing to this fluctuation.

27 USO, *Nuestra USO cumple 91 años en defensa de la soberanía energética y de la clase obrera* (February 14, 2014), Available: www.usofrenteobrero.org/index. php?option=com_content&view=article&id=7823:nuestra-uso-cumple-91-anos-en-defensa-de-la-soberania-energetica-y-de-la-clase-obrera&catid=43:boletin-junta (accessed on October 14, 2014).

28 PNUD, *Reconocer el pasado, reconstruir el futuro. Informe sobre violencia contra sindicalistas y trabajadores sindicalizados 1984–2011* (PNUD, 2012).

29 *Fecode and Educators* appears as the victimized organization, with 921 homicides, followed by Sintrainagro 798; USO 116; Anthoc 58; Sintraelecol 50; Judicial Asonal 47; SUTIMAC 38; and Fensuagro with 37 View: ENS and Colombian Commission of Jurists, *Journal of Human Rights* (ENS, 2012).

30 *Uribe calificó como 'mezcla maldita' apoyos de sindicatos a la guerrilla*, Caracol, (Caracol, July 23, 2007) www.caracol.com.co/noticias/actualidad/uribe-califico-como-mezcla-maldita-apoyos-de-sindicatos-a-la-guerrilla/20070723/nota/456815.aspx.
31 The government of President Santos (2010–2018) has been more favorable to USO and unionism. First, the role of Vice President Angelino Garzón has been key to the position of the union issue on the human rights agenda in Colombia. Second, the Free Trade Agreement with the United States led to the resurrection of the Ministry of Labour – merged in 2003 with the Ministry of Health – and the signing a labour agreement to ban the use of worker cooperatives.
32 Martha Maya, *El vagón sindical se le pega a la locomotora minera*, La Silla Vacía (La Silla Vacía, August 26, 2012), http://lasillavacia.com/historia/el-vagon-sindical-se-le-pega-la-locomotora-minera-35544 (accessed October 15, 2014).
33 SINTRAELELCOL, *Denuncia Pública*, http://sintraelelcol.org/pdf/denunciasindical.pdf (accessed on October 14, 2014).
34 Currently, UTEN is part of Confederación General del Trabajador (CGT), one of the most important associations of Colombian union trades.

35   We are called to be consistent with a new entrepreneurial class in the world that is committed to corporate social responsibility, a concept which of course includes equity as a principle in relations between companies and their employees. We must recognize that our state is increasingly seeking for a balance between these relations. We, the workers of this new century, are certainly very different from what Taylor called the late nineteenth century, cattle men.
       UTEN Hydrocarbons. "Alternative unionism to a new business scheme."
                                                        Newsletter, February 2012

36 Interview with Alejandro Ospina, by Sebastian Rubiano, UTEN union leader. Bogotá, September 15, 2014.
37 In September 25, 2013 in the Village of "Carmelo" Caloto Township, a gang of the sixth front of the FARC attacked two groups of workers affiliated to UTEN. Debate Newspaper (Newspaper Debate September 25, 2013) http://periodicodebate.com/index.php/nacion/seguridad/item/2470-denucnian-atentados-de-farc-contra-trabajadores (accessed October 14, 2014).
38 Citizen oversight is a representative democratic mechanism that allows citizens to exercise vigilance over the management of any public issue. Consequently, they may oversee the work of actors as diverse as public authorities, NGOs, international organizations and even private companies. They are regulated by Law 850 of 2003 View Republic of Colombia, Law 850 (2003).
39 Departamento Administrativo Nacional de Estadística, *Censo Nacional de 2005* (DANE, 2014) www.dane.gov.co. (Accessed on October 15, 2014).
40 The Sikuani ethnic group is found on the list of 34 towns at risk of physical and cultural extermination in Auto 004 of 2009 of the Constitutional Court, representing 92% of the indigenous population of the municipality. See Republic of Colombia, Constitutional Court, Decision 004 (2009).
41 The *resguardos* are collectively owned territories by indigenous communities, these territories are recognized by the state. There are nine *resguardos* in the town: Wacoyo, Awaliba, Victor Pirirí, El Tigre, Unuma Alto, Walliani, Domo Planas, Iwiwi and Corozal.
42 Paramilitary forces have been major actors in the Colombian armed conflict. These are groups formed as private armies and counterinsurgency forces, in the service of landowners and drug traffickers. They have been responsible for massacres and atrocities in the context of armed conflict. In 2005, the government of Alvaro Uribe agreed with the demobilization and disarmament of these groups. Despite this, a part of their local structures has been operating in several regions of the country.
43 Restitution in stormy Puerto Gaitán, Verdad Abierta (Open Truth December 19,

2013), www.verdadabierta.com/restitucion-de-bienes/5071-refund-storm-in-puerto-gaitan. (accessed October 15, 2014). See also UNDP, Op. cit. Note 32, which states that there have been territorial spoils in recent decades in the town of more than 15,000 hectares.

44 According to official information on the website of the National Hydrocarbons Agency, today 98% of the land in the municipality is reserved or allocated for exploration and exploitation of hydrocarbons. View: www.anh.gov.co/Asignacion-de-areas/Documents/2m_tierras_040714.pdf (accessed October 14, 2014).

45 Navas Camacho, L, *Petróleo de Puerto Gaitán: Amazonas a la vista*, (OilWatch Sudamérica, 2012), disponible en web en: www.oilwatchsudamerica.org/doc/ ARTCULO_DEFINITIVO_puerto_gaitan.pdf (Navas, 2012).

46 Currently, production exceeds 250,000 barrels of oil per day (PREC 2013), which accounts for almost a third of the national production.

47 Royalties are economic resources that companies in mining and hydrocarbons sector pay the Colombian government as compensation for the exploitation of non-renewable groundwater resources. Until 2012, mining and hydrocarbons producer municipalities received royalties directly, but Law 1530 changed this situation.

48 This according to official information from the ANH: ANH. *Comportamiento asignaciones directas causadas por la explotación de hidrocarburos según liquidaciones definitivas año 2013.* www.anh.gov.co/Operaciones-Regalias-y-Participaciones/ Regalias/Estadisticas/PublishingImages/Paginas/Regalias-despues-del-SGR/Publicacion%20Comportamiento%20AD%20Causadas%20%20a%C3%B1o%202013%20 -%20Rendimientos%20a%2031032014.pdf (accessed October 14, 2014).

49 República de Colombia, Departamento Nacional de Planeación, *Política para el desarrollo integral de la Orinoquia: Altillanura – FASE I. CONPES 3797 de 2014* (DNP, 2012).

50 *La explosión de Puerto Gaitán.* Semana (Semana 27 de agosto de 2011), www. semana.com/nacion/articulo/la-explosion-puerto-gaitan/245490–3 (Accessed October 14, 2014).

51 PNUD, *El departamento del Meta frente a los Objetivos de Desarrollo de Milenio.* Bogotá (PNUD 2008). Disponible en web en: www.pnud.org.co/img_upload/33323 133323161646164616461646164/odm%20meta.pdf.

52 DANE, Op. cit. *Nota 42.*

53 Semana, Op. cit. *Nota 53.*

54 Semana, Op. cit. *Nota 53*; Verdad Abierta, Op. cit. *Nota 43.*

55 The file of the Colombian Commission of Jurists was fundamental in reconstructing the events until August 2012.

56 Campo Rubiales was discovered during the early eighties by Ecopetrol, but no one realized its potential during the first years. The oil produced by this field is very heavy and its exploitation extremely expensive in that time.

57 The involvement of the Department of Meta in domestic oil production increased from 9% in 2000 to 47% in 2011. Today the production is around 45%. Much of that participation is due to Meta Campo Rubiales crude, which provides 240,000 of the 750,000 barrels (about one third) of the annual national production. View: www. dane.gov.co/files/investigaciones/pib/departamentales/B_2005/Resultados_2011.pdf (accessed October 15, 2014).

58 Velasco, J.D. y Rocha L.A, *Una cadena de conflictos: Errores y aprendizajes de la actividad empresarial en Puerto Gaitán*, (Bogotá: Centro de Recursos para el Análisis de Conflictos – CERAC, 2012).

59 Pacific Rubiales Energy, *Informe de sostenibilidad 2011. Global Compact* (PREC, 2011: 41).

60 Interview wtih Alejandro Jiménez, Manager of Corporate Social Responsibility, Pacific Rubiales Energy, by Sebastian Rubiano. Bogotá, May 27, 2014.

61 Puerto Gaitán is located 190 km to the southeast of Villavicencio, the departmental

capital. El Campo Rubiales, in turn, is 167 km to the southeast of the town of Puerto Gaitán.

62 Ethical and Political Trial to PRE, Bogotá, October 2013, handicraft square. Intervention USO.

63 Ethical and Political Trial to PRE, Bogotá, October 2013, handicraft square. Intervention USO.

64 Sebastián Rubiano. *Interview to Alejandro Jiménez, Manager of Corporate Social Responsibility, Pacific Rubiales Energy.* Bogotá, May 27, 2014.

65 There are conflicting versions that explain how USO got involved with the protests. According to the USO, it was the workers who sought union support during the labour dispute.

66 It has not been possible to determine the exact number of workers affiliated with the union at the start of the protests in July 2011. Despite claims USO of about 2,000 workers, PREC put the number at just over 1,000. Importantly, the multinational always denied the existence of a mass membership of its employees toUSO.

67 According to the union, it is not acceptable that the Canadian company has resorted to third parties to use people who should link directly to the development of their subject. Even less if you consider that the contractors offer their employees a much less favorable environment than those of the multinational. This argument was answered by PREC, which argued that since its purpose is limited, it requires contractors to develop related but necessary services to meet these goals.

68 Throughout the entire conflict USO insisted on entering Campo Rubiales in order to get membership, and to track and monitor working conditions. Related to this point it is important to mention that Campo Rubiales has about 65,000 hectares, so it cannot be totally closed. But the administrative and residential areas, as well the draw-wells zones, have restricted access. During the protests it seems that the control in these areas was even more severe, thus making access for the union difficult.

69 Ethical and Political Trial to PRE, Bogotá, October 2013, handicraft square. Intervention USO. Nonetheless, it is important to clarify that the claims of the indigenous communities were not against PREC. As other social actors, these communities took advantage of the scenario to present a cumulus of demands.

70 As explained in the characterization of the actors, during the last decade USO has improved its ties with grassroots social movements in the areas of influence of the oil fields in which workers operate. Some of its allies are indigenous peoples, community boards and community action organizations, environmental organizations, among others.

71 The position of the company is particularly exposed in the letter that its CEO sent to the International Labour Organisation in October 2011 This document indicated its simple guarantor position in the spaces of negotiation, without any legal responsibility linked to the conflict. Its only intention, therefore, is to "to resolve the controversy between contractors and their employees." USO, in the letter, also insists on respect by the company for freedom of association and other rights workers. Charter Ronald Pantin, CEO of PRE, addressed to the ILO. October 6, 2011.

72 Interview with Alejandro Jiménez, Manager of Corporate Social Responsibility, Pacific Rubiales Energy, by Sebastian Rubiano. Bogotá, May 27, 2014.

73 Interview with Alejandro Jiménez, Manager of Corporate Social Responsibility, Pacific Rubiales Energy, by Sebasitan Rubiano. Bogotá, May 27, 2014.

74 ASOJUNTAS Press, September 14, 2011. Memo of the authorities indigenous reserves of Puerto Gaitán, September 15, 2011.

75 This group of citizens was created on October 25, 2011.

76 Among the commitments made by the multinational was to not retaliate against workers who had participated in the protests and immediately reinstate those who had been separated. Some of these actions depended on contractors and not exclusively PREC.

77 Pacific Rubiales, *Op. Cit, Nota 62.*

78 Agreements on these tables would be achieved 30 September. The agreements are basically commitments between the mayor of Puerto Gaitan, PREC and oversight boards and local action. Agreements on behalf of PREC largely consisted in transferring resources to support investment projects in education, health, roads, infrastructure, recreation, among others.

79 USO, the National Government and PREC, as a guarantor, participated in this second roundtable.

80 USO focussed on six themes: Salaries and benefits for workers PREC (direct and contractors and subcontractors); guarantees for the full exercise of freedom of association by USE; real and effective linking of local labour in the municipality; stability in employment; developing a workplace policy by that takes into account the situation of vulnerable workers; and reimbursement of staff terminated for contractors from the July 19, 2011.

81 However, it seems clear in the same report, that the company reports that "to the date of the event, Pacific had no direct worker affiliation with any union, displacing our need to promote union membership." Pacific Rubiales, Op. cit. Note 62.

82 Act labour standards agreement between representatives of Meta Petroleum and Pacific Stratus and UTEN, October 6, 2011.

83 Addendum No. 1 to the agreement for labour standards in Pacific Rubiales, 19 October 2011 Addendum No. 2 to the agreement for labour standards in Pacific Rubiales, January 18, 2012 In 2014 we have added four more to the labour agreement addendums.

84 The demonstrations were not only protests, although these events were particularly visible not only by the number of demonstrators but also by the magnitude of the response of the security forces. USO also led peaceful actions as the "Caravan of Humanitarian Action" that took place between 10 and 14 October, which was intended to allow the peaceful entry Campo Rubiales and protest against the company and its activities. See in this regard: Tense calm in Rubiales oil field. The Time (The Time July 20, 2011) www.eltiempo.com/archivo/documento/MAM-4694471 (accessed October 15, 2014).

85 Various organizations show support declared a National Oil Strike. This, however, was only observed in the department of Meta. Also the student movement became public support for the USO. See in this regard: National Strike Oil in Meta. USO (USO November 9, 2014) www.usofrenteobrero.org/index.php?option=com_content &view=article&id=2847:paro-nacional-petrolero-en-el-meta&catid=43:boletin-junta (accessed October 10, 2014).

86 Wage board for workers of contractors was made. The minimum wage regardless of the position is now $1.23 million more, and includes a number of additional non-wage benefits. This figure doubled the minimum wage for that year established by law.

87 Labour Act, November 28, 2011.

88 PREC claims that it never banned USO entry to Campo Rubiales and sustains there is a record of the visits the union has made.

89 Ethical and Political Trial to PRE, Bogotá, October 2013, handicraft square. Intervention of USO.

90 Ethical and Political Trial to PRE, Bogotá, October 2013, handicraft square. Intervention of USO.

91 Complaints have been filed against Intricon S.A, Ismocol S.A, Duflo S.A. y Montajes J.M. S.A. Report no. 21036110848812 with the Attorney General's Office, May 30, 2013.

92 Ethical and Political Trial to PRE, Bogotá, October 2013, handicraft square. Intervention of USO. USO has highlighted the prosecution of three workers, who were accused by a prosecutor of instigating terrorism. In mid-2014 the investigations into the three workers were closed for lack of evidence to charge them.

93 In October 2012, left-wing Senator Alexander López tried entering the field with a

workers committee. He assures his entrance was denied. PREC denies this, arguing the Senator did not have any problem accessing the field. The debate between Senator López and the VP of Corporate Affairs and Sustainability, Mr. Federico Restrepo, can be heard here: www.wradio.com.co/escucha/archivo_de_audio/senador-alexander-lopez-y-federico-restrepo-de-pacific-discuten-por-denuncias-en-campo/20121210/oir/1808834.aspx.

94   Among the organizers were USO Funtraenergética, Puerto Gaitán indigenous organizations and international trade union activists – mostly Canadian-of the Public Service Alliance of Canada (PSAC) majority, the Confederation of national trade unions CSN Quebec, the Committee for Human rights in Latin America and parliamentary DHAL quebec Quebec Solidarity Party.

95   The ethical and political courts have become spaces for social movements to denounce what they cannot complain in the courts. Often they loosely emulate the structure of a legal tribunal. This is because there are whistleblowers who file complaints supported in evidence, a prosecutor who leads questioning, and a court that decides on the allegations. But there – no guarantees of impartiality or contradiction right of the accused. Although they are invited, companies rarely attend these forums, believing that these spaces are political, and not suitable for a legal complaint.

96   Labor Act, June 13, 2013; Labor Act, June 19, 2013; Labor Act, 23 July 2013; Labor Act, 31 July 2013; Labor Act, September 25, 2013; Labor Act, 9 October 2013.

97   Aspects such as the revision of wages are no longer part of this table. Parallel to the revival of the labour board, discussion continued on the other seven thematic panels. PREC has participated in all of them since October 2014. The Government reported that it met many of the commitments made to the community there.

98   Labor Act, September 25, 2013 Labor Roundtable with the company Hocol.

99   The closure of this office was verified during the performed visit to the area on June 25–26, 2014.

100 Interview with Stella Novoa, local leader of the Community Action Board of Puerto Gaitán. Puerto Gaitán, September 2014. Interview with Justo Ramirez, local leader of the Community Action Board of Puerto Gaitán. Puerto Gaitán, June 26, 2014, by Sebastian Rubiano.

101 Pacific Rubiales Energy, *Sustainability Report 2012. Global Compact* (PREC, 2012: 13).

102 PREC, Matriz de avance de cumplimiento de acuerdos de la mesa laboral. Documento de la Gerencia de Responsabilidad Social (sin publicar, 2014).

103 Interview with Armando Medina, head of security of Meta Petroleum, in Quifa, Cajúa and Rubiales fields. Puerto Gaitán, June 25, 2014, by Sebastian Rubiano.

104 Colprensa. *Pacific Rubiales fue absuelta por el Ministerio de Trabajo.* La República (La República, October 27, 2013). www.larepublica.co/empresas/pacific-rubiales-fue-absuelta-por-el-ministerio-de-trabajo_75101 (accessed on October 15, 2014).

105 This is the current position with the constitutional principles of 1991, in the sense of ensuring private enterprise and general prosperity (Constitution of Colombia (1991) Art. 2). In particular and in spite of that, there existed an internal work order and in some cases ratification of international instruments.

106 Both treaties such as ILO recommendations are part of the so-called constitutional block. See judgments of the Constitutional Court T-979 2004 MP: Jaime Córdoba Trivedi, C-401 2005 MP: Manuel José Cepeda Espinosa or T-171 2011 MP: Jorge Iván Palacio Palacio.

107 Constitución Política de Colombia (1991) Art. 39 y República de Colombia, Código Sustantivo del Trabajo (1951) Art. 12.

108 Constitución Política de Colombia (1991) Art. 55, initially was limited to public employee unions and subsequently regulated by Decree 1092 of 2012.

109 Article 56 of the Constitution excepted cases of essential public services that so far have not been defined in a single policy (before the 1991 Constitution, Article 430

provided utilities CST more broadly). But they are apparent in the case of Central Banking (1992 Act 31), social security emergency care and pension payments (Act 100 of 1993), public utilities (Act 142 of 1992), justice (Law 270 of 1996) and transport (Act 336 of 1996). See Republic of Colombia, Law 31 (1992); Act 142 (1992); Act 100 (1993); Act 270 (1996); Act 336 (1996).

110 República de Colombia, Código Sustantivo del Trabajo (1951) Art. 35.

111 República de Colombia, Código Sustantivo del Trabajo (1951) Art. 35.

112 República de Colombia, Ley 50 (1990) Art. 71–94.

113 Following the development of activities that exceeded their targets in Colombia there was a major legislative development on the CTA. See:Observatory Labour Market and Social Security, The worker cooperatives in Colombia (Bogotá: Universidad Shown of Colombia, 2007).

114 Associates in the case of CTA.

115 República de Colombia, Código Sustantivo del Trabajo (1951) Art. 34.

116 Colombian law also allows individuals to act as independent contractors and to be responsible for their own employees.

117 República de Colombia, Código Sustantivo del Trabajo (1951) Artículo 34 del CST.

118 This would apply to employees of Ismocol SA, which provides construction and maintenance of pipelines, and support for the operation of fields and oil wells.

119 Examples include the World Bank, the International Monetary Fund or the Inter-American Development Bank.

120 This includes treaties that granted jurisdiction to the international center for the settlement of investment disputes (ICSID) to resolve cases in which Colombia is a party, signed in 1995 and incorporated by Act 267 of 1995. See Republic in Colombia, Law 267 (1995).

121 While the Constitution of Colombia makes no direct reference to the promotion of foreign investment in the country, it is enshrined Article 226, 9 and 227. See Constitution of Colombia (1991).

122 They are treaties between two or more States, through which the rules that govern their domestic investments in the territory of the other partners are established. These treaties are not under the supervision of a particular organ and takes different forms. The most common is the bilateral agreement (BIT for short), which comprehensively addresses the regulation of investment between the parties.

123 Free Trade Agreement between Colombia and Canada. Republic of Colombia, Law 1363 (2009), Art. 816.

124 Parallel Agreement on Labor Cooperation in November 2008. Republic of Colombia, Law 1360 (2009).

125 Parallel Agreement on Environment Cooperation in November 2008. Republic of Colombia, Law 1363 (2009).

126 Agreement on Annual Reports on Human Rights and Free Trade in May 2010. Republic of Colombia, Law 1411 (2011).

127 The first norms in this area were formulated in the early seventies of the twentieth century with the Sullivan Principles and the ILO Tripartite Declaration. However, only 20 years later it is possible to speak of the emergence of a regime of corporate responsibility for human rights.

128 Comisión Europea. *Libro Verde: Fomentar un marco europeo para la responsabilidad social.* (2001) DocCOM (2001) 366 final Disponible en http://eur-lex.europa.eu/legal-content/ES/TXT/PDF/?uri=CELEX:52001DC0366&from=ES (accessed 21 August 2014).

129 Martín-Ortega, O. *Empresas multinacionales y derechos humanos en Derecho Internacional*, 90–92 (Bosch, 2008).

130 SteinhardtFinal del formulario , R, SteinhardtFinal del formulario, R *Corporate responsibility and the International Law of Human rights: The new lexmercatoria* en Alston, P., ed. *Non state actors and Human Rights*, pp. 178–179 (Oxford University Press, 2005).

131 This new policy is based on the concept of "shared value" developed by Michael E. Porter and Mark R. Kramer. Interview with Alejandro Jimenez, Corporate Social Responsibility manager of Pacific Rubiales Bogota, May 27, 2014, by Sebastian Rubiano. Interestingly, this theory criticizes the concept of Corporate Social Responsibility. It is a commitment to rethink the foundations of what has so far been the business management, to conceive the social forces, not just the economic ones, that define the market. See Porter, M & Kramer Mark Creating Shared Value. "How to reinvent capitalism and unleash to the wave of innovation and growth" *Harvard Business Review*, January–February (2011) www.waterhealth.com/sites/default/files/Harvard_Buiness_Review_Shared_Value.pdf (accessed August 24, 2014).

132 Through a statement signed by Francisco Rubiales, president of the company on January 17, 2011, accepted the ten principles and undertook to apply them in the area of influence. www.unglobalcompact.org/system/commitment_letters/13105/original/Pacto_Global_Pacific_Rubiales.pdf?1295390553 (accessed 25 August 2014).

133 This initiative was presented by former UN Secretary General Kofi Anan in the economic forum in Davos in 1999. Press Release SG/SM/6881 of February 1, 1999. Further information is available in www.unglobalcompact.org/ (retrieved 22 August 2014).

134 This standard is promoted by EquitableOrigin and makes up a certification system that companies voluntarily submit. For more information see the website www.equitableorigin.com/ (accessed October 15, 2014).

135 The Foundation Ideas for Peace, which is also the developer, International Alert and CODHES are part of this initiative. The latter, is one of the most important NGOs in the country in terms of forced migration.

136 Companies such as (Anglogold and PR), power generation (Isagen SA), food production (Colombia Nestlé SA) and agribusiness (IndupalmaLtd.a) are integrated into this initiative.

137 Guías Colombia *Documento base* disponible en www.ideaspaz.org/publications/posts/487 (consultado el 22 de agosto de 2014).

138 Pacific Rubiales. *Informe Anual y de Sostenibildad 2013.*

139 In addition to Pacific Rubiales other companies are included: Anglo American, AngloGoldAshanti, Colombian Association of Petroleum, Cerrejón Ecopetrol Equion, Greystar, ISA, ISAGEN, OXY, Rio Tinto, Vetra and Talisman.

140 Presidency, Vice-Presidency, Department of Defense, the Army, the Ministry of Foreign Affairs, the Superintendency of Surveillance and Private Security, the General Command of the Armed Forces and National Police.

141 OECD. *Líneas Directrices de la OCDE para Empresas Multinacionales* (OECD, 2013). http://dx.doi.org/10.1787/9789264202436-es (Accessed on August 22, 2014).

142 SteinhardtFinal del formulario, R, Op. cit. *Nota 131*, pp. 213–215.

143 The Corporate Social Responsibility principles have been identify and systematized by the Special Representatrive of UN Secretary General on the issue of human rights and transnational corporations, John Ruggie on March 2011. Doc. UN. A/HRC/17/31.

144 Naciones Unidas. Doc. UN. A/HRC/17,I.A. 1.

145 Naciones Unidas. Doc. UN. A/HRC/17/31 II.A.11.

146 Naciones Unidas, Doc. UN. A/HRC/17/31 II.A. 17.

147 Naciones Unidas, Doc. UN. A/HRC/17/31 II.A. 13.

148 Naciones Unidas, Doc. UN. A/HRC/17/31 III.A.

149 International Commission of Jurists. *Corporate Complicity & Legal Accountability Report of the International Commission of Jurists. Expert Legal Panel on Corporate Complicity in International Crimes* Vol. 3, 10 (2008).

150 28 U.S.C.§1350.

151 *Doe* v. *Unocal*, 395 F.3d 932 (9th Cir. 2002), *Sarei* v. *Rio Tinto* 550 F.3d 822 (9th Cir. 2008) y *Presbiterian Church of Sudan* v. *Talisman Energy Inc.*, 582 F3d. 244 (C.A.2, 2009), among others.

152 Lina Céspedes y A. Gutierréz. *La responsabilidad civil por actividades peligrosas: Una forma de establecer el nexo entre personas jurídicas privadas y violaciones de derechos humanos en Colombia* 125 *Vniversitas*, 149–186 (2012).

153 *Choc* v. *HUSbay Minerals Inc.*, 2013 ONSC 1414.

154 This is in addition to the regulations regarding rights and obligations of workers and employers.

155 In fact, it is forbidden for the union to promote cessations or stoppages, unless in the case of a legally declared strikes attributable to the employer for failure to pay obligations to workers, according to Article 379 paragraph *Código Sustantivo del Trabajo* amended by Act 584 of 2000.

156 República de Colombia, Código Sustantivo del Trabajo (1951), Art. 452.

157 Free Trade Agreement between Canada and Colombia. Republic of Colombia, Law 1363 (2009), Art. 104.

158 Agreement on Labour Cooperation between Canada and the Republic of Colombia, signed on November 21, 2008, Annex II. Republic of Colombia, Law 1360 (2009).

159 Agreement on Annual Reports on Human Rights between Canada and the Republic of Colombia, signed on May 27, 2010. Republic of Colombia, Law 1411 (2010), Art. 1.

160 Concerns are raised to an instance called "point of contact". This is the body designated by each state to advance all procedures and formalities related to the treaty. In Colombia it is the Foreign Investment Office of the Ministry of Foreign Trade.

161 SteinhardtFinal del formulario, R, op. cit. *Note 131*, pp. 213–215.

162 Interview with Alejandro Jiménez, Corporate Social Responsibility manager of Pacific Rubiales. Bogota, 26 May 2014, by Sebastian Rubiano.

163 These reports are available on www.pacificrubiales.com/sustainability/reports.html (accessed August 25, 2014). These reports are prepared in accordance with the G3 guidelines (2006) of the Global Reporting Initiative (GRI), an application level A+.

164 For example, on August 31, 2012 Kienyke, the influential online magazine published a story on the social commitment of this company. View The Human Factor Pacific Rubiales Kienyke (Kienyke August 31, 2012), www.kienyke.com/historias/el-factor-humano-de-pacific-rubiales/ (accessed August 26, 2014).

165 Beatriz Eugenia Sánchez. Interview with Angela Rivas, coordinator of the thematic area of business, conflict and peacebuilding Foundation Ideas for Peace. Bogota, May 19, 2014.

166 Guías Colombia *Documento base* punto 22.j.

167 Guías Colombia, *Mecanismos de quejas y reclamos atentos a los derechos humanos y el DIH* (2012) available on www.ideaspaz.org/publications/posts/486 (accessed August 26, 2014).

168 Republic of Colombia, Ministry of Commerce, Industry and Tourism, Decree 1400 (2012).

169 OCDE. *Líneas Directrices de la OCDE para Empresas Multinacionales*, pp. 75–78.

170 CANADA. Bill C-300, 2009.

171 *Choc.Hudbay Minerals Inc.*, [2013] ONSC 1414.

172 *Salomon* v *Salomon & Co.* [1897] A.C 22 (HL).

173 McCann, M. *Law and Social Movements. Contemporary Perspectives.* Annu. Rev. Law Soc. Sci.17–38 (2006).

References

1 Norms

Republic of Colombia. Law 50 (1990), Official Journal 39,618.

—— Law 278 (1996), Official Journal, 42,783.

—— Law 790 (2002), Official Journal, 45,046.

—— Act 1151 (2007), Official Journal, 46,700.
—— Act 1359 (2009), Official Journal, 47,545.
—— Act 1411 (2010), Official Journal, 47,867.
—— Act 1444 (2011), Official Journal, 48,059.
—— Act 1610 (2013), Official Journal, 48,661.
—— Decree 205 (2003), Official Journal, 45,086.

2 Court Decisions

Republic of Colombia, Constitutional Court. Judgment C.797, 2000 MP: Antonio Barrera Carbonell.
—— Judgment T-979, 2004 MP: Jaime Córdoba Trivedi.
—— Judgment C-401, 2005 MP: Manuel José Cepeda Espinosa.
—— Judgment T-251, 2010 MP: Nilson Pinilla.
—— Ruling C-608, 2010. Magistrate Humberto Sierra Porto Antonio.
—— Ruling C-609, 2010. Magistrate: María Victoria Calle Correa.
—— Ruling C-915, 2010. Magistrate Humberto Sierra Porto Antonio.
—— Judgment T-171, 2011, MP: Jorge Iván Palacio Palacio.
—— Judgment T-733, 2011, MP: Gabriel Eduardo Mendoza Martelo.
—— Judgment T-965, 2011, MP: Gabriel Eduardo Mendoza Martelo.

3 Books and Book Chapters

Correa, G. y Hoyos, Y. *Impactos en los Derechos Humanos de la implementación del Tratado de Libre Comercio entre Colombia y Canadá. Línea base. Documento 95 Escuela Nacional Sindical.* Medellín: ENS, 2012.

Dueñas Quevedo, Clara Cecilia. *Derecho Administrativo Laboral*, Bogotá: Ibañez, 2011.

Fall, P. y Zaharan, M. *United Nations corporate partnerships: the role and functioning of the Global Compact.* Ginebra: Naciones Unidas, 2010.

Lozano, J., Albareda, L., Ysa, T., Roscher, H. y Marcuccio, M. *Los gobiernos y la responsabilidad social de las empresas: políticas públicas más allá de la regulación y la voluntariedad* Barcelona: Granica, 2005.

López Castaño Hugo, *Trabajadores urbanos independientes. Ciclo de vida laboral y seguridad social en Colombia.* Bogotá: ISS-CIE-Universidad de Antioquia-Ministerio de Trabajo y Seguridad Social, 1990.

Martín-Ortega, O. *Empresas multinacionales y derechos humanos en Derecho Internacional* Barcelona: Bosch, 2008.

Muchlinski, P.T. *Multinational Enterprises and the Law*, Oxford: Blackwell, 1999.

Observatorio del Mercado de Trabajo y la Seguridad Social, *Mitos y realidades de la reforma laboral colombiana. La ley 789 dos años después.* Bogotá: Universidad Externado de Colombia, 2005.

Observatorio del Mercado de Trabajo y la Seguridad Social, *Las cooperativas de trabajo asociado en Colombia.* Bogotá: Universidad Externado de Colombia, 2007.

República de Colombia, Departamento Nacional de Planeación. *Política para el desarrollo integral de la Orinoquia: Altillanura – FASE I. CONPES 3797 de 2014.* Bogotá: DNP, 2014.

Rivas, A, y Miranda C. *Guías Colombia en Derechos Humanos y Derecho Internacional Humanitario: Ejes de trabajo para avanzar en el campo de Empresas y Derechos Humanos en Colombia,* Bogotá: Ideas para la paz, 2013.

SteinhardtFinal del formulario, R. "Corporate responsibility and the International Law of Human rights: The new *lex mercatoria"*. En *Non state actors and Human Rights*, Alston, P. (Ed.) Oxford: Oxford University Press, 2005.

Velasco, J.D. y Rocha L.A. *Una cadena de conflictos: Errores y aprendizajes de la actividad empresarial en Puerto Gaitán.* Bogotá: Centro de Recursos para el Análisis de Conflictos – CERAC, 2012.

4 Articles in Journals

Cespedes, L, y Gutierrez, M.A. "La responsabilidad civil por actividades peligrosas: una forma de establecer el nexo entre personas jurídicas privadas y violaciones de derechos humanos en Colombia." *Vniversitas 125* (2012).

Del Toro, M. "El fenómeno del softlaw y las nuevas perspectivas del Derecho" En *Anuario Mexicano de Derecho Internacional.*Vol. VI. (2006).

Dumberry, P. Corporations as Subjects of International Law: The Question Revisited in Light of Recent Developments in International Investment Law" En 1 *Revue Générale de Droit International Public Vol. 108* (2004).

Mazuelos, A. "Softlaw: ¿Mucho ruido y pocas nueces?, En *Revista electrónica de Estudios Internacionales* Vol. 8 (2004).

Porter, M y Kramer M, *Creating Shared Value. How to reinvent the capitalism and unleash a wave of innovation and growth* Harvard Business Review, January-February (2011).

Ratner, S. "Corporations and Human Rights: a Theory of Legal Responsibility" *3 Yale Law Journal Vo. 111* (2001).

5 Other Documents

Organización de las Naciones Unidas, Informe del Representante Especial del Secretario General para la cuestión de los derechos humanos y las empresas transnacionales y otras empresas, *Principios Rectores sobre las empresas y los derechos humanos:puesta en práctica del marco de las Naciones Unidas para "proteger, respetar y remediar"* Doc. A/HRC/17/31.

Pacific Rubiales Energy. *Informe de sostenibilidad 2011*. Global Compact, 2011.

Pacific Rubiales Energy. *Sustainability Report 2012*. Global Compact, 2012.

Pacific Rubiales Energy. *Sustainability Report 2013*. Global Compact, 2013.

República de Colombia, Comité de Trabajo Interinstitucional para el Seguimiento del Impacto del Acuerdo de Libre Comercio entre la República de Colombia y Canadá. *Primer Informe Anual del "acuerdo en materia de informes anuales sobre derechos humanos y libre comercio entre la república de Colombia y Canadá",* Mayo 15 de 2012. (Proporcionado directamente por el Ministerio de Relaciones Exteriores).

República de Colombia, Comité de Trabajo Interinstitucional para el Seguimiento del Impacto del Acuerdo de Libre Comercio entre la República de Colombia y Canadá. *Segundo Informe Anual del "acuerdo en materia de informes anuales sobre derechos humanos y libre comercio entre la república de Colombia y Canadá",* Mayo 15 de 2013. (proporcionado directamente por el Ministerio de Relaciones Exteriores).

República de Colombia, Comité de Trabajo Interinstitucional para el Seguimiento del Impacto del Acuerdo de Libre Comercio entre la República de Colombia y Canadá. *Tercer Informe Anual del "acuerdo en materia de informes anuales sobre derechos humanos y libre comercio entre la república de Colombia y Canadá",* Mayo 15 de 2014. (proporcionado directamente por el Ministerio de Relaciones Exteriores).

República de Colombia, Vicepresidencia de la República. Cartografía Social Indígena del Departamento del Meta, Bogotá: Vicepresidencia de la República, Programa Presidencial de Derechos Humanos y Derecho Internacional Humanitario – Gobernación del Meta – Secretaría Social y de Participación, 2010.

6 Internet

Reuters. "Profile: Pacific Rubiales Energy Corp.", accessed on September 30, 2014, www.reuters.com/finance/stocks/companyProfile?symbol=PRE.TO.

Kienyke. "Pacific es Colombia", accessed on September 30, 2014, www.kienyke.com/kien-escri"be/pacific-es-colombia/.

Federación Colombiana de Futbol. "Pacific Rubiales fue presentado como Socio Oficial de la Selección Colombia", accessed on September 30, 2014, www.fcf.com.co/index.php?option=com_content&view=article&id=3048%3Apacific-rubiales-fue-presentado-como-socio-oficial-de-la-seleccion-colombia&catid=12%3Anoticias-seleccion-colombia&Itemid=31.

El Espectador. "El país de Pacific Rubiales", accessed on September 30, 2014, www.elespectador.com/opinion/columna-377285-el-pais-de-pacific-rubiales.

Razón Pública. "Pacific Rubiales, herencia de la confianza inversionista", accessed on September 30, 2014, www.razonpublica.com/index.php/econom-y-sociedad-temas-29/3066-pacific-rubiales-herencia-de-la-confianza-inversionista.html.

Newswire. "Pacific Rubiales AgreestoAcquire Kappa Energy Holdings Ltd.", accessed on September 30, 2014, www.newswire.ca/en/story/208749/pacific-rubiales-agrees-to-acquire-kappa-energy-holdings-Ltd.

Newswire. "Acquisition of PetroMagdalenabyPacific Rubiales Energy Corp.", accessed on September 30, 2014, www.newswire.ca/en/story/1013041/acquisition-of-petromagdalena-by-pacific-rubiales-energy-corp-completed-9-0-senior-a-notes-to-be-redeemed.

El Espectador. "Pacific Rubiales compró Petrominerales por $3 billones", accessed on September 30, 2014, www.elespectador.com/noticias/economia/pacific-rubiales-compro-petrominerales-3-billones-articulo-449428.

Foreign Affairs, Trade and Development Canada. "Canada's Foreign Investment Promotion and Protection Agreements (FIPAs)", accessed on September 30, 2014, www.international.gc.ca/trade-agreements-accords-commerciaux/agr-acc/fipa-apie/fipa-apie.aspx.

La Silla Vacía (08–26–2012). "El vagón sindical se le pega a la locomotora minera?" available in: http://lasillavacia.com/historia/el-vagon-sindical-se-le-pega-la-locomotora-minera-35544.

La Silla Vacía (10 de Octubre, 2011). Los indígenas solo existen en época electoral en Puerto Gaitán.

La Silla Vacía (05–05–2011). "En Puerto Gaitán las inscripciones de cédulas aumentan inusitadamente, ¿está Pacific Rubiales detrás?", available in: http://lasillavacia.com/historia/en-puerto-gaitan-las-inscripciones-de-cedulas-aumentan-inusitadamente-esta-pacific-rubiales.

Verdad Abierta (19 de diciembre de 2013). "Restitución tormentosa en Puerto Gaitán". Available in: www.verdadabierta.com/restitucion-de-bienes/5071-restitucion-tormentosa-en-puerto-gaitan.

Guías Colombia (2011) "Mecanismos en quejas y reclamos atentos a los derechos humanos y al DIH", available in http://archive.ideaspaz.org/index.php/guias-colombia/documentos/item/1217-mecanismos-en-quejas-y-reclamos-atentos-a-los-derechos-humanos-y-el-dih.

Marín. D. (2013) *Los principios Ruggie y los informes de Pacto Global dentro de la figura de instrumentos de "softlaw" que vinculan a Empresas dentro del marco de la ONU* en Relatoría globalización, poder y derecho http://relatorestematicos.uniandes. edu.co/index.php/es/globalizacion-poder-y-derecho.html.

Navas Camacho, Luisa María (2012). *Petróleo de Puerto Gaitán: Amazonas a la vista.* OilWatch Sudamérica. Available in: www.oilwatchsudamerica.org/doc/ARTCULO_ DEFINITIVO_puerto_gaitan.pdf.

OCDE (2013), *Líneas Directrices de la OCDE para Empresas Multinacionales*, OECD Publishing, Available in http://dx.doi.org/10.1787/9789264202436-es.

Programa de las Naciones Unidas para el Desarrollo (2012), Reconocer el pasado, construir el futuro. Informe sobre violencia contra sindicalistas y trabajadores sindicalizados 1984–2011, Bogotá: PNUD. Available in: www.pnud.org.co/2012/informe_sindicalismo. pdf.

7 Videos, Interviews, and Meetings

Ethical and Political Judgment to PRE, Bogotá, October 2013, handicraft square. Intervention by the USO.

Statement by Senator Jorge Enrique Robledo at the meeting of the Fifth Committee of the Senate, August 17, 2011, to discuss the situation of oil workers in the area of Puerto Gaitán, Meta. Available in: www.youtube.com/watch?v=WG6M3kdUdMw.

Beatriz Eugenia Sánchez. Interview with Angela Rivas, coordinator of the thematic area of business, conflict and peacebuilding Foundation Ideas for Peace. Bogota, May 19, 2014.

Sebastián Rubiano. Interview with Alejandro Ospina, union leader UTEN. Bogotá, September 15, 2014.

Sebastián Rubiano. Interview with Roger Cardona Communities office of the secretariat of the government of Puerto Gaitán. Campo Rubiales, June 26, 2014.

Sebastián Rubiano. Interview with Giovani Soto, President of ASOJUNTAS. Puerto Gaitán, June 26, 2014.

Sebastián Rubiano. Interview with Armando Medina, head of security of Meta Petroleum, in Quifa, Cajúa and Rubiales fields. Campo Rubiales, June 25, 2014.

Sebastián Rubiano. Interview Marleny Ramírez, local leader of the Community Action Board of Puerto Gaitán. Bogota, June 26, 2014.

Sebastián Rubiano. Interview with Justo Ramírez, local leader of the Community Action Board of Puerto Gaitán. Bogota, June 26, 2014.

Sebastián Rubiano. Interview with Stella Novoa, local leader of the Community Action Board of Puerto Gaitán. Bogota, June 26, 2014.

Sebastián Rubiano. Interview with Alejandro Jimenez, manager of Corporate Social Responsibility of Pacific Rubiales Energy. Bogota, May 27, 2014.

Sebastián Rubiano. Interview with Rodolfo Vecino, president of the USO. Bogota, July 16, 2013.

3 Ethnicity, Episteme, and Gold
The Struggle for Human Security in Marmato

James Rochlin

A clash between two systems of thought is at the root of a contest between Gran Colombia Gold Corporation (GCG) and organized groups from the isolated community of Marmato. One of these entails transnational production, ultra-speed, de-territorialization, and a value system based on monetary worth. The other is rooted in localized ethnic culture that is historically entrenched. It celebrates tradition, a spiritual connection to territory, and a preference for long term, slow-motion sustainability. This problem is indeed surmountable – transnational mining corporations and the community of Marmato can work together for mutual benefit. This can be achieved by State and corporate policies that promote sustainable development, the legalization of traditional miners, and community development as defined by the locals. None of that can be achieved without tri-partite negotiation between the State, the corporation and the community – a strikingly obvious part of the solution that has not yet occurred. What is clearly unworkable is a plan – currently shelved due to relatively low gold prices and community backlash – for an open pit mine and the relocation of a community that predates the Spanish Conquest and today is comprised mostly of Afro-Colombians and Indigenous peoples. The case provides important insights related to ethnic rights, gender rights, sustainable development and other themes that can be helpful for creating human rights indicators for the Human Rights Impact Assessment (HRIA) and its side accords.

In many ways, Marmato epitomizes the sense of magical realism and assorted paradoxes so vividly evoked by the late Gabriel García Márquez. Marmato is isolated, yet hosts an active transnational extractive industry. Its remote, cloud-shrouded and steeply mountainous location is strikingly beautiful, yet sustains environmental damage due to centuries of toxic gold mining and inadequate sewage and waste facilities. Residents bustle along cobblestone streets, along with horse driven vehicles, and with small motorcycles that provide affordable transportation for the locals. Marmato is distinguished by its generally mellow population that is free of the illicit armed groups that populate many sites of extraction in Colombia. The reasons for this vary. Such groups have not established an historical presence in the region, as they have in the case of Segovia and Remedios, which is discussed in the next chapter. Also, the town is difficult to access, and the economy in Marmato may be too unstable to sustain such groups.[1] While the community is proud of its reputation as tranquil and law abiding, traditional miners there are incensed for having been criminalized by the State due to their lack of legal titles for mines – a point to which we shall return.

History and Concepts

Concepts

There are a number of conceptual points that flow together regarding the Marmato case. First is the role of class and production in relation to the contest between a Canadian transnational corporation and a small Colombian town composed primarily of Afro-Colombian and Indigenous peoples. The forces of class and capital have had a clear impact on legal matters, as we shall observe shortly regarding the struggle of traditional miners who abruptly have been declared illegal. Class politics are also reflected in Colombia's State structure, which, in its most recent manifestation, myopically reflects the interests of transnational capital and the extractive sector. Indeed, the country's notorious entrepreneurialism and commitment to capitalism provide the larger framework in which the extractive boom has occurred. Class-based polarization is also at the heart of the urban-rural divide in Colombia, whereby urbanites generally have access to greater wealth and upward mobility than their rural counterparts. Throughout the chapter we shall develop these and other points in the realm of political economy.

Epistemic aspects are particularly relevant here. There is a clash between systems of thought on the part of transnational corporations, on the one hand, and with regard to the community of Marmato, on the other. TNCs, for example, typically conform to the notions of ultra-speed, capital maximization within a zero-sum context, and money as power. Their connection to a particular territory is fleeting. Conceptions of development, within this framework, are linked to profit maximization and quick growth. Often within the system of globalized production, cultural and local knowledge are relegated to the backburner.

The dominant system of thought in Marmato is quite distinct from that approach. This multicultural community is the product of centuries of history as the quintessential capitol of Colombian gold mining. Its customs and forms of knowledge have proven to be resilient. The community moves to a relatively slow rhythm, and its members would like to see its gold extracted in a manner that would last a millennium rather than couple of decades, as it likely would with the establishment of an open pit mine as preferred by TNCs. Its ethnic community has a special relationship to territory, and views this as central to the preservation of its culture. Hence, epistemic themes related to local knowledge, and conceptions of time and space, are central to an understanding of the current struggle in Marmato.

Closely related to this is the politics of circulation – of people, of capital, and of knowledge. As we shall see, there are many dimensions of this apparent in the Marmato case. As we noted, the locals of Marmato prefer a slow-motion circulation of gold from their community, rather than the ultra high speed of open pit mining. The community wishes to benefit from the circulation of global knowledge that can promote sustainability in the region. It has relied on the internet and even a North American motion picture[2] to circulate ideas within a global network of transnational social movements to battle the narrow interests of transnational capital. Due to its location in the mountains of Caldas between the urban, narco-center of Medellin and the coffee country of Manizales and Risaralda, Marmato's gold circulates on local highways along with cocaine (from Medellin), coffee and marijuana (from the Pereira region), and arms for a variety of illicit gangs. The politics of circulation has been the centerpiece of the strategy of organized traditional miners in Colombia, who, along with cohorts in the agricultural sector, have implemented roadblocks to voice their demands to the national government. Halting circulation is a key, peaceful instrument of power. Locals have employed what Paul Virilio has termed "the political control of the highway."[3]

Critical Human Security and the Marmato Case

We noted in Chapter 1 that Critical Human Security (CHS) is particularly relevant to the case studies in this book since its broad concepts provide a coherent approach to the intersection of development, human rights, and security, but can also be molded to the particular context of specific cases. With regard to the specificities of the Marmato case, a number of elements of the CHS approach are especially relevant. First is the broad question of development for whom? The quest by Gran Colombia Gold Corporation for an open pit mine has been energetically opposed by the community of Marmato, as we shall see. Hence, there exits a polarization between two sharply different models of development – one that reflects the interests of a TNC, and another that reflects the interests of an historic ethnic community in Marmato.

With regard to other elements of the approach, CHS emphasizes community values, identity and preservation – this is key in the Marmato case, given that an open pit mine would forcibly relocate the community and perhaps destroy its integrity. Closely related to this is Critical Human Security's emphasis on ethnic rights, which is highly relevant given that almost 70 percent of Marmato's community is either Afro-Colombian or Indigenous. The significance placed by CHS on local knowledge and epistemology is also key in the Marmato situation. Finally, sustainability and the avoidance of ecocide are crucial components of the Critical Human Security perspective, and are highly relevant in the Marmato case given the implications of an open pit mine not only for those residing on the mountain but also due to its potential effects on the Cauca River below. This is Colombia's second largest river. It is the major source of drinking water for the major city of Cali, and also sustains various flora and fauna. The question upon which we shall focus is how to bridge the interests of TNCs with those of the community in Marmato, and hence construct a development model that promotes security and human rights.

Historical Context

The town's name comes from the Indigenous word 'marmaja', a shiny, yellow mineral that closely resembles gold. The Indigenous there had been harvesting gold well before the Spanish arrived. The town of Marmato was claimed by the Spanish in 1537. The Catamas Indigenous were subject to both the Mita system of forced labour for males, and to an encomienda system of agriculture, which entailed a mode of sharecropping that came close to slavery.[4] Subjected by the Spanish to arduous labour and living conditions, and vulnerable to disease, the Indigenous population dwindled hugely by 1625. At that point, the Spanish imported about a quarter million black slaves from the Gulf of Biafra and Central Africa to the province of Popayan to perform work that the almost extinct Indigenous population had been doing (Marmato is currently in the department of Caldas, but Caldas was not created until 1910, and so prior to that time it was located in Popoyan). About 500 of these black slaves appeared in Marmato by 1776. Arriving from the coastal department of Choco, they were viewed by the Spanish as "human beasts."[5] Altogether, this meant the presence of five culturally distinct ethnic groups in Marmato – the Spanish Creoles, the Mestizos, the Indigenous peoples, the Afro-Colombians, and a tiny group of English miners. The Afro-Colombians, in particular, maintained their cultural identity under arduous working conditions, with special yearly festivals where only Afro-Colombians were permitted to attend.[6]

The Popoyan province comprised about half of all Colombia's gold production during the 1700s. The significance of the Marmato gold mines was underscored again in the Wars of Independence from Spain in the 1820s, when Simón Bolívar used Marmato's gold as collateral for British loans to bankroll the war.[7] A handful of multinational gold companies appeared on the scene beginning with the British company "Goldsmith" in 1825, and was followed by a major presence in Marmato by England's West Andes Mining Company in 1869 and Powles-Illingsworth in the late 1920s.[8] Hard times hit the Marmato mines in the 1930s, in the context of the Great Depression and the exit by Great Britain and others from the gold standard. English companies used women and children in the mines at the time to keep salaries low. Many in the town succumbed to illness due to poor sanitation and a lack of adequate medical facilities.[9]

The Marmato mines were administered by the Ministerio de Minas beginning in the 1940s.[10] Importantly, this agency created a legal horizontal division of the Marmato mountain in 1954, with large scale mining confined to the lower zone and with small scale mining in the upper region where the historic center of Marmato is located. It would be in this upper region where an open pit mine later emerged as the center of controversy. Multinational mining corporations increasingly appeared on the scene in the 1970s and 1980s, especially from Canada, the US, and South Africa.

How to Tell the Story

As Gabriel García Márquez has shown through his novel, *One Hundred Years of Solitude*, there are occasions when political history can be best told through literature and art. It is a medium that can convey the emotions and subjective elements entailed in politics that are often overlooked in academic works claiming to be objective. While it lacks the global notoriety that García Márquez's work has earned, a deservedly acclaimed piece of literature in Colombia tells the political tale of Marmato. Gregorio Sánchez Gómez, in *La Bruja de las Minas* (The Witch of the Mines), published a novel in 1938 that examines the social dimensions of an English mine that arrived in Marmato in the early part of the twentieth century, apparently in the 1920s (no specific date is mentioned).[11] Suddenly rumors emerge that a foreign company is about to take over the mines operated by locals. The community's worst fears turn out to be true, when government officials arrive along with a military contingent to announce that the government is working with "interested parties", which turns out to be an English mining company, to take immediate possession of the Marmato mines.[12] The government, the author writes, has arrived with military force "to impose" the interests of foreign capital. When locals converge to protest against the English mine, the military shoots one of them, a woman who strongly voiced her concerns.[13] Subsequently, her soul returns to haunt the foreign owners of Marmato's mine – a witch who represents the interests of local miners and who actively seeks vengeance. The author traces in detail how "many lives were disoriented" by the foreign mining company.[14]

Within a couple of years, however, a "new prosperity" arrived in Marmato, accompanied by the English company's relatively modern mining technology and technical knowledge, and buoyed by the rising global appetite for gold during what is apparently the Roaring Twenties.[15] The primary face of the English company is Mister Stanley, who in many ways foreshadows García Márquez's notorious Mr. Brown. He is unflatteringly portrayed as a womanizing drunk who speaks poor Spanish and who treats the local Indians and Afro-Colombians with racist disdain.[16] The Indians are portrayed as too sick and feeble to work in the mines, and are relegated to positions of domestic servants and the like.[17] The Afro-Colombians endure the mines' tortuous working conditions, and are shown to engage in wild debauches on Saturday nights in an attempt to nullify the pain of their daily exploitation.[18] The novel ends when gold prices plummet, and when the foreign mining company unravels as the boom goes bust. The witch succeeds in her vengeance, placing an economic curse on the mining company. With an 'eye for an eye' mentality, she is also behind the disappearance and death of Mary, the Caucasian daughter of the English company's lead representative.[19]

With the melodrama peeled away, it is striking that so many of the themes present in the novel remain relevant to the broad narrative of Marmato's recent struggle with Canadian transnational corporations. As we shall see, rumors of an open pit mine that spelled the relocation of Marmato's historic community turned out to be true. Tense military standoffs have occurred between government forces representing TNCs and traditional artisanal miners. Racial and cultural factors have been blatantly ignored by TNCs and the government. And the boom and bust cycles associated with extractive commodities have led starry-eyed foreigners to doom.

Actors and Interests

The State

Despite increased American military assistance through Plan Colombia and a much improved security scenario compared to the violent chaos of the 1990s, the Colombian State in the new millennium remains weak in both its regulatory and security capacities. An academic study that examined the success of businesses attempting to navigate the problem of Colombia's weak State found that the most successful cases of business-community relations occurred when large companies pursued policies that elsewhere are typically considered to be the duties of the State. For example, such companies negotiated with guerrilla groups for local peace, they implemented social policies, and in general attempted to fill an institutional void left by a weak and dithering national government.[20]

With respect to State policies regarding the extractive sector in particular, miners recently have been obliged to obtain legal title for their mines through Presidential Decreto 2235, which will be discussed in greater detail later in the chapter. But many of these artisanal miners do not have the time and resources to work with the inefficient State bureaucracy to obtain legal title.[21] More importantly, the State does not seem to have a genuine interest in legalizing them. The State has done little to promote legalization or formalization of traditional miners, a point to which we shall return. The implication is that the Colombian government is not interested in formalizing artisanal miners and prefers instead that these mines fall into the hands of major transnational mining companies. By criminalizing artisanal miners, the mines they claim are worth less than they would be if they were legal, and it creates pressure on them to sell their mines to TNCs. In tandem with Decreto 2235 is Decreto 0934, which prevents municipalities from controlling what is in their community's soil. Hence, this negates Marmato's political control over its territory, and could permit the national State to allow an open pit mine in the community against its wishes. Indeed, ultimate power regarding mining operations in the country is concentrated in the national Ministerio de Minas y Energía.

As noted in Chapter 1, the government of Colombia has a relatively low 'government take' – the total amount the Government receives from the extractive sector through royalties, taxes and so on. This is especially true regarding GCG in Marmato. According to the company's literature, GGC pays royalties of between 0.4 percent and 4 percent to the national government, and a 6 percent special administrative fee for certain of its mining titles payable to local authorities in Marmato. That means a sliding scale of as little as 0.4 percent to as much as 10 percent. A recent study indicates that the country's government take in the precious metal sector averaged only 4.3 percent, when factoring in the considerable concessions and deductions afforded to foreign investors.[22] Colombia's investor friendly policies may come at the expense of development in the country. That is, a higher government take could provide funding for social development projects and poverty eradication.

Certainly the State's weak and poorly developed policy toward legalization has not been sufficient to support the 300,000 traditional miners in their quest to obtain legal title to their mines. This was the central factor behind the miners' strike and roadblocks in the summer of 2013. A policy that criminalizes hundreds of thousands of miners without legal title, while providing hugely insufficient administrative support and technical training for them, has had the effect of supporting TNC ownership and development of the country's non-renewable resources. In terms of social power, then, the national government of Colombia has aligned with Canadian TNCs and against its own traditional miners.

But the State is not a monolith. While the national government appears to have advanced TNC interests and may be a vehicle for TNC power, other levels of the State support traditional miners, such as those in Marmato. In an abrupt about-face, the government of the Department of Caldas, where Marmato is located, declared in 2012 its staunch support for traditional and national miners as key to the Department's economic development, without mentioning TNCs at all in its key economic planning document for 2012–2015.[23] The fever pitch of organized traditional miners became too loud to ignore for politicians seeking re-election in Caldas. The municipal government of Marmato does not favor the open pit mine, and has condemned what it deems to be the criminalization of its traditional miners; the Defensoría del Pueblo, the country's ombudsman agency, has sharply criticized the legalization process as providing insufficient support to national miners – points to which we shall return.

Colombia's Contraloría General de la República (the Government Accountability Office) authored in 2013 the most thorough analysis of the country's mining industry to date. It represented a stinging rebuke of the Federal Government's developmental policy regarding the extractive industry, and based its premises on many of those found in the concept of Critical Human Security. The report noted the dangers of unregulated globalization on developing countries.[24] It pointed out that 40 percent of Colombia's territory lacks legal title for land, and that 86 percent of metals produced in the country are extracted by non-titled miners.[25] There were 9,400 titled miners by the end of 2012, in contrast to the 300,000 members of the Asociación de Mineros Tradicionales who are without title.[26] Lack of regulation, the report emphasized, resulted in environmental destruction, community displacement, and human rights abuses. In fact, the report documented that over 80 percent of the country's human rights violations occur in regions where the extractive sector is located. More particularly, extractive regions of the country hosted 87 percent of the country's forced displacement, 78 percent of attacks against union members, 89 percent of human rights violations of the Indigenous, and 90 percent of human rights violations against Afro-Colombians.[27] All of these concerns raised by the Contraloría are representative of the concept of Critical Human Security – ethnic rights, workers rights, sustainable development, proper state regulation to ensure safety and development, and so on.

Senator Jorge Robledo, a member of the national opposition party Polo Democrático Alternativo, has been an important and vocal critic of the federal government's approach to the extractive sector. He vehemently opposed the Canada Colombia FTA based on what he considers to be the poor record of Canadian corporations in the extractive sector, and in 2010 used the Marmato situation as a case in point regarding questionable human rights policies on the part of Canadian businesses. From his perspective, the national government has been the handmaiden of TNCs in the extractive sector, and has constructed policies to meet their short term financial objectives with no vision of long-term sustainability and stability. In the fall of 2014 he indicated he has witnessed no progress on the part of the Santos Government with regard to formalizing traditional miners, and suggested that the central reason for this is that the national government would prefer to see their mines fall into the ownership of TNCs.[28]

Various government offices, in addition to the Departmental Government of Caldas and the municipal government of Marmato, all support the legalization of the miners. This represents important common ground, and could be the focal point where conflict resolution may lie. Critics argue that support for traditional miners to seek legal title would not only help sustain their livelihoods, their communities and ways of life, but it would promote sustainable development by insisting on methods of extraction that abandon ecocide, such as those that rely on the use of mercury. These groups also oppose the open pit mine in Marmato that various Canadian TNCs have pursued.

Finally, a wider and hugely important question is raised by the Contraloría's document, and that concerns the dangers of extractivism as the primary road to development, which has been the case in Colombia. Many critics have pointed to the boom and bust tendencies associated with a reliance on extraction.[29] We shall return to the issue of the extractivist model of development in the volume's concluding chapter.

Actors and Interests: Gran Colombia Gold

By way of overview, Gran Colombia Gold Corporation by 2011 had consolidated the various corporate mining interests in Marmato that had existed up to that time. We will explore the origins of GCG. We will also trace the aspirations of Canadian corporations since they appeared in 1995 through to their trials and tribulations regarding an elusive open pit mine on the top of the mountain of Marmato, which would necessitate relocating the community. Gran Colombia Resources Inc. appeared in Marmato in the period 1995–1997, and purchased mines in the high zone (where the community of Marmato is located). Conquistador Mines, another Canadian company, also bought various mines in the high zone, and acquired a major concession on the low part of the mountain during the period 1996–2000. The context at the time was the aforementioned vortex of violence occurring in Colombia. Given the backdrop of weakening foreign investment and a severe recession, prices for mine purchases were relatively cheap at the time. Another Canadian corporation, Colombia Goldfields, Ltd., through its affiliate Empresa Minera de Caldas, purchased various mines in Marmato during the 2005–2009 period, when gold became more precious. In a decisive turning point in 2010, Medoro Resources of Canada purchased Colombia Goldfields and consolidated within Medoro all of the previously held mines in Marmato. Finally, in 2011, Medoro fused with Gran Colombia Gold, and produced Gran Colombia Gold Corporation. GCG does not extract gold itself, but relies on its local affiliates to do so. This process facilitates the use of 'contract workers,' and can also obscure exactly how many mines the company ultimately controls, since these are purchased by its affiliates.

Let us turn to a focus on the development of specific plans for an open pit mine and the rationale for moving the historic town of Marmato. With respect to the company's perspective, extremely instructive in this regard is a report from November 2006 by Colombia Goldfields Ltd. (which fused with Medoro in 2011) regarding Marmato. The report essentially provides a justification for relocating Marmato due to what it claimed were the high dangers of landslides and poor standards of development that would be corrected in the new town of El Llano. A sizeable part of that report includes excerpts from a related study earlier in 2006 by Thomas Grail for Mineras de Caldas, SA, which was the local affiliate of Colombia Goldfields. That study emphasized "…the instability of this zone and the extremely high risk of landslides…. In summary, the area is extremely unstable and since the early 1980s numerous studies have indicated the need to relocate the urban center of Marmato."[30] The same study underscored what it viewed as a poor level of development in Marmato. "…There is currently neither a potable water system nor a septic treatment system servicing this entire area…. Roadways designed for limited traffic cannot handle the current traffic patterns and there is no obvious solution to this problem."[31] That report also indicated that past efforts to relocate the community failed.

> The residents in 2002 were relocated due to their homes being subject to a high risk of landslides. Despite this fact, these residents generally (122 out of 154) turned their previous homes over to family members or rented these homes to migrant mine workers.[32]

Importantly, by 2006, it was clear that Colombia Goldfields (through its local affiliate Minera de Caldas) wished to construct an open pit mine and relocate the historic town.

> Minera de Caldas has as one of its primary objectives the relocation of the urban centre of Marmato … Minera de Caldas believes that it can assume a significant portion of the cost of this relocation and will define this level of economic contribution when and if the plans are made available.[33]

The company was fully able to justify its position on the matter: "Ultimately the position of the Company is that the urban centre of Marmato must be moved for humanitarian reasons which fortunately coincide with the needs of the company."[34] What was good for the company would be good for Marmato.

Despite its view that the relocation would be in the best interests of the community of Marmato, it appreciated that the move would involve significant challenges to the community.

> The cessation of current mining activities will have a significant impact on the current population of these residents. The Company has anticipated the requirement to replace current sources of employment during the transition phase between current mining practices and the eventual mining project. The skills required will change significantly, from what is currently available. This transition will further impact the commercial institutions that provide services to the current mining activity.... These opportunities range from employment on an agricultural project to produce citrus products, employment during the exploration phases of this project, and employment in the construction of homes, civic buildings and infrastructure anticipated to complete El Llano (New Marmato).[35]

While the company clearly envisaged a plan for the relocation, it is noteworthy that it did not appreciate the cultural shock to the community that such a move would generate. Nor did it seem to fully appreciate the economic devastation to the community entailed in its surrender of mines and jobs that it had imagined would last at least another eight centuries. We shall return to these points in the ensuing discussion of the community's perspective.

Despite its intention to relocate the community, McGrail's report lamented that "[t]o date, the efforts of the Company have been stymied, as current administrations at both Department and Municipal levels are not publicly in favor of this relocation."[36] Finally, this lengthy Colombia Goldfields Ltd. report by author William Lewis concludes that "Minera de Caldas (its Colombian affiliate) has been purchasing mineral licenses in the Zona Alta portion of the Marmato project since 2005 and now owns more than half of the mines with legal title.... Gran Colombia Gold Ltd. is targeting bulk tonnage, low grade gold and silver deposits at the Marmato and Caramanta projects that are potentially amendable to open pit mining with recovery of precious metals by milling and cyanide leaching or by heap leaching."[37] Here we observe a system of thought that is commonplace among transnational extractive corporations – with its emphasis on mass production/extraction, rapid and sweeping exploitation of resources, and a view of land/space that privileges the realization of economic value over other conceptions of land/space.

Once Medoro had purchased Colombia Goldfields in 2010, rumors swirled anew in Marmato regarding the company's intention to construct an open pit mine and relocate the town to El Llano. The community became particularly alarmed when corporate authorities once again suggested that the town was in danger of a landslide, and that the community should be relocated – echoing the views expressed earlier that moving Marmato was simultaneously good for the community and good for the company's ambition of an open pit mine. When community opposition to an open pit mine and relocation became clear, Medoro contracted an NGO, Ventanas, to win the support of the population to suit corporate objectives.[38] This contest continued when Medoro fused with Gran Colombia Gold in June of 2011.

The company's political connections are noteworthy. The Former Corporate Manager for Medoro Resources is the cousin of President Juan Santos, and its Executive Advisor was Hernán Martinez, former Minister of Mines and Energy for Colombia. Gran Colombia Gold Corporation had been led by María Consuelo Araújo, who was CEO of the organization until February 2014, at which time she became President of GCG.[39] She is the ex-Minister of Foreign Relations and also of Culture under President Uribe. Ms. Araújo quit her position as Foreign Minister in February 2007 in the context of a scandal linking her brother, Senator Álvaro Araújo, to criminal activity committed by paramilitary forces.[40] Her brother, Senator Araújo, was convicted by Colombia's Supreme Court in 2010 of having ties to crimes committed by paramilitary forces.[41]

In a press release by Gran Colombia Gold Corporation on January 9, 2012, the company indicated that the Department of Caldas, where Marmato is located, agreed "to assist Gran Colombia in reaching an agreement with artisanal mines within the Company's concession at the Marmato Project." GCG's tone in the press release was highly positive, and it gave a clear indication regarding how the company would like to see things unfold:

> Under these agreements, the artisanal mines will continue to operate for up to two years, at which time the Company anticipates commencing large scale mining at the Marmato Project. The Company has also implemented an environmental and safety training program for the artisanal miners, which will not only serve to immediately improve environmental and safety conditions at Marmato, but will lay the groundwork for these artisanal miners to be available for employment by the Company at its open-pit mine at Marmato once constructed.[42]

While GCG indicated that it still needed to negotiate successfully with the community of Marmato to proceed with these plans, this press release made clear the intentions and strategies of Gran Colombia Gold Corporation. "In order for the Company to build the open pit operation at Marmato, the existing town of Marmato will need to be moved and the existing residents re-settled to nearby areas including the town of El Llano." This strategy was justified in the name of development and modernization.

> The new town of El Llano will be a planned, modern community with proper streets, sewage, utilities and clean water, which is important in a district where only 53% of the homes have running water and only 56% are connected to the sewage system ... El Llano will not be subject to the periodic landslides that afflict Marmato.[43]

The company also indicated that it hired Social Capital Group, a "company with extensive experience in community resettlement in South America," to provide a plan for the relocation.[44] The vision expressed in 2006 by Mineras de Caldas was set in motion by 2012 by Gran Colombia Gold Corporation. It is important to emphasize that according to an official from the Government of Caldas, despite the statement by GCG in its press release noted above regarding its cooperation with the government, it was never presented with any official documents indicating the company's plan for the open pit mine and has only been informed by GCG's public statements.[45]

Despite high hopes in 2012 when gold prices peaked, Gran Colombia Gold Corporation faced serious hurdles by 2013 in its quest to harvest one of the world's top 20 sites for gold deposits. A company executive indicated in October of that year that the open pit mine project would not move forward given the substantial drop in gold prices from its high in 2012 of about US$1,800 per ounce. He indicated in 2013 that it cost Gran Colombia Gold about US$1,300 an ounce to break even at Marmato. He suggested that the company would focus on underground mining, which produced about 20,000 ounces of gold a year in Marmato.[46] Another executive from Gran Colombia Gold observed at the end of 2013 that the company appeared to have abandoned its goal of an open pit mine due to community resistance.[47] If that is indeed the case, it is highly significant. It means the local community has won in its struggle with a TNC. There are other possible scenarios, including the company's reversal of that view to once again support an open pit mine if gold prices were to rise significantly, or perhaps the company might continue its current process of purchasing privately held mines in Marmato and selling the lot to another buyer in the future. Until early 2015, nothing has been mentioned on the company's website about plans for an open pit mine in Marmato.

Gran Colombia Gold Corporation has implemented significant Corporate Responsibility Programs in Colombia. For example, the company has embarked on an ambitious plan to help traditional miners without title to obtain legal recognition in Segovia – Remedios, Antioquia, the nuances of which are explored in Chapter 4. It sees a five to eight year timeline for that process, and has helped legalize about 2000 miners in Segovia – Remedios in 2014. Further, the company does not use mercury, but instead relies on cyanide – viewed as the less toxic of the two approaches. It also has contributed millions of dollars to major social works projects, such as the construction of a hospital near Marmato.

Actors and Interests: Marmato, the Community Struggle

Marmato's rich history, its ethnic composition, its isolated and beautiful mountainous location, as well as the preservation of its traditional culture and lifestyle, place this community in a class of its own. About 54 percent of its population of about 9,000 is Afro-Colombian and another 15 percent Indigenous.[48] Between 500 to 600 of the community's 3,000 miners belong to the Asociación de Mineros Tradicionales de Marmato (AMTM) – that is, they are traditional miners without title to land.[49] According to the President of the AMTM, there are 551 mines in Marmato by mid 2014, and only 120 have legal title to them (GCG is estimated to have purchased 80 of these). The rest are owned by traditional or artisanal miners without legal title to them, and usually have between two to four people working the mine.[50] About 90 percent of the community is dependent on gold, directly or indirectly. The average traditional miner produced about 4.4 grams of gold a week, worth about US$130, in 2013.[51] According to the leader of the AMTM:

> ...many of [the] traditional miners do not sell their gold to Gran Colombia Gold (or to its local affiliates, such as Mineros Nacionales SAS, acquired through Medoro Resources in February of 2010), due to their lack of credibility with the local population. Instead they take their product to microbusinesses in nearby Medellin which extract more gold and therefore pay better that Gran Colombia Gold would.[52]

The first community effort to organize its opposition to an open pit mine and the relocation of the town became apparent in 2004, with the 'Manifesto of Marmato.' Some rocks fell from high on the mountain down to the historic center in that year, prompting renewed calls by authorities to consider relocating the town to avoid landslides. This was viewed by community members as playing into corporate efforts to relocate the town in order to construct an open pit mine. The Manifesto was in opposition to "...different public entities such as the Banco Agrario, the Registrar, Police and others" to relocate the town to El Llano and thereby acting "...against the integrity, the security, the economy and the work..." of community members. The Manifesto indicated that the landslide was used as a facade "...to facilitate access of the Multinational Mining Corporations" to the riches of Marmato's Gold.[53]

In 2010, Colombia's national ombudsman office, the Defensoría del Pueblo, authored a sweeping review of the country's mining industry and its multiple effects on local miners. Its principal recommendations included a more flexible approach to the process of legalizing traditional miners without title, the provision of legal and administrative assistance to help traditional miners in the process of legalization, and the training of traditional miners to promote environmentally friendly mining.[54] Those recommendations remain vital to support the ongoing struggle of Colombia's traditional miners in Marmato and elsewhere in the country.

In late 2011, the Marmato City Council, along with the Marmato Defense Committee and the Regional Indigenous Council of Caldas (CRIDEC), officially opposed the open pit mining project, and indicated it would attempt to persuade the United Nations Educational, Scientific and Cultural Organization (UNESCO) to declare Marmato a World Heritage Site.[55] CRIDEC also demanded that the government follow the advice of the Defensoría and others, and therefore provide traditional miners in Marmato with assistance in the legalization process. Once again, miners in Marmato enthusiastically seek legalization, but they require administrative assistance and some training to meet legal criteria, and this training is costly.[56] They therefore need economic support from the government to achieve that training. Further, the local office in Marmato of Caldas' Secretariat for Economic Development indicates that Gran Colombia Gold is very welcome in the community of Marmato, as long as it does not pursue an open pit mine.[57]

The struggle intensified in 2013 on three related fronts. The first concerned the protracted battle to prevent an open pit mine and relocation of the community, and the second involved the community's involvement in a nation wide strike by miners and farmers. Despite the fall of gold prices in 2013, and the indication by Gran Colombia Gold that it had given up its immediate intention to construct an open pit mine, community organizers in Marmato continued to believe that GCG remained intent on an open pit mine once gold prices rose. Second, Marmato's traditional miners without legal title to their mines were vital participants in the nation-wide strike. Third, epistemic themes regarding temporal, spatial, and cultural politics represent key fissures between the community and TNCs. Let us proceed to consider those issues.

Local miners in Marmato believe that there is enough gold in the mountain to last them at least 800 years at the current pace of small and medium scale extraction. Here we confront a huge epistemological gulf between extractive TNCs and local community members regarding temporal politics – a clash between slow-motion traditionalism and the hyper-speed of postmodern globalization. In tandem with the epistemic confrontation was a basically material and class-based one that centered around the question of "Gold for Whom'?" – for the community of small miners that has lived off the land's gold for five centuries, or for a Canadian TNC that pays relatively low royalties to the State?

The national strike of traditional miners and of farmers in summer of 2013 was a notable political phenomenon in the country, and highlighted the urban/rural divide that continues to haunt Colombia. Strikers relied on a strategy of roadblocks at key junctures nationally, which had the effect of choking agricultural and others supplies to the country's major urban centers. Here we see the politics of the street and the politics of movement skillfully maneuvered on the part of the rural strikers.

Roadblocks implemented by Marmato's strikers generated particular tension, and became a focus point for community angst against TNCs and the national government. Miners opposed President Santos' highly controversial Decreto 2235 that appeared in 2012, which not only rendered illegal mining without title, but which also provided government armed forces with the power to destroy the mining equipment used by 'illegal' miners. The government has attempted to become the sole vendor of mining equipment and supplies to miners in order to bolster Decreto 2235, though the contraband market for these – as for so many items – is brisk in Colombia.[58]

The President of the Marmato's traditional mining association, indicated that after the strike the government agreed to meet with leaders of the traditional miners, including him. Government officials conducted introductory negotiations with the miners, and the government promised it would consider their concerns seriously. However, by June 2014, the Santos administration made no progress with miners up until the eve of the new presidential elections,[59] and since then appears not to have prioritized this issue.[60] The key demand from traditional miners has remained the legalization or "formalization" as it is called in Colombia.

In order to be formalized, they legally require training with modern equipment, with the proper use of explosives, and with environmental provisions. This requires money the miners typically do not possess, and which the government has not yet been willing to provide.[61] Miners by mid 2014 are feeling the pain of government policies, according to the President of the AMTM, since they must purchase their supplies for inflated prices on the black market. He also indicated that traditional miners want support from the government regarding legal commercialization of the gold they produce, rather than let this fall into the large market of "illegal gold" that fortifies armed illegal groups such as right-wing paramilitaries and leftist insurgents. Finally, traditional miners have also requested from the national government proper social security benefits that are denied to them since they are not part of the formal sector.[62] For Muñoz Gil, the criminalization of artisanal miners is just another example of the practice of political exclusion that predominates in Colombia.[63] As of this writing, the federal government has not yet addressed the demands of miners and appears to be in no rush to do so.

More broadly, a representative of CRIDEC, and a member of a key Indigenous organization in Marmato, indicated that both the attempted encroachment by TNCs of Marmato and the process that criminalizes traditional miners without title amounted to "ethnocide – this is the land of the Indigenous." Adriana Palomino indicated that it is ultimately a cultural clash, and that relocation would destroy the spiritual connection that locals have to the territory.[64] This relation between spirituality, culture, and territory is key. She noted that displacement would have a special effect on gender relations in the community, since Indigenous women are the bearers of spiritual relations for the community. It is worth noting that only 4 percent of Marmato's miners are women.[65] Palomino also expressed horror at the environmental effects of a potential open pit mine. Moving the community, she argued, would break social networks and spiritual foundation that the community has built for five centuries.[66]

Beyond the fever pitch of confrontations over mining in Marmato during 2013, ultimately the struggle will be a long one, according to Yamil Amar, the former mayor of Marmato and the President of the Comité Cívico de Marmato. He suggests that GCG's strategy is to purchase one by one the remaining privately owned mines in the community. In addition, he noted that a strategy of CGC and of the government is to move the key institutions out of Marmato's historic center, and to relocate them to El Llano, as had happened with the respect to the community's hospital in 2006 (for which GCG contributed CAD$2 million).[67]

On the matter of traditional miners, Amar emphasized how unfair he thinks the process has been. He indicated that the Colombian government has been historically very weak and even absent in the Marmato region for much of its existence. It is this weakness and absence of the State that is to blame for the lack of legal title among the community's traditional miners. The "criminalization" of traditional miners, he indicated, was a process led by the national government of Santos at the behest of Canadian extractive TNCs to pressure traditional miners to sell their mines at low prices to the large corporations.[68]

The struggle continues in Marmato as of this writing. Muñoz Gil, the President of the local traditional miners association, said he believed the open pit mine will be stalled until gold prices elevate. It remains impossible by 2015 to determine who is winning or losing, Amar indicated, since the battle is a protracted one. He observed that one of the reasons the community has been able to hold its own against Gran Colombia Gold Corporation and the national government is due to the network of solidarity the group has constructed nationally and globally. These include links the Marmato community has established with Canada's North/South Institute, the Canadian Council for International Cooperation, the Comite Sindical de Quebec, and with Colombia's Escuela Nacional Sindical, among many others.[69]

A lawyer representing Marmato concurred with Amar's analysis. Further, she noted that amnesty and legalization of traditional miners is the obvious solution to the wide problem faced in the country, but that the national government opposes this and prefers to see TNCs dominate mining in the country. We noted that subversive groups and criminal organizations often dominate and extort traditional miners in other locations in Colombia. This factor has been emphasized by the Santos government in its discourse against the "illegality" of traditional miners. However, in so doing, the government has not publicly emphasized the significant distinctions and nuances between miners that it has painted with a single brush as "illegal." According to their lawyer, and to other community members in Marmato, there are no links between artisanal gold miners and criminal organizations in Marmato, which has developed a distinct and peaceful historical trajectory.[70]

In sum, the community of Marmato has faced threats in the realm of Critical Human Security. These include threats to economic survival, cultural heritage, ethical and gendered traditions, environmental assault, displacement and the preservation of localized systems of thought. Class conflict, an epistemic rupture between TNCs and the community, and ethnic issues are among the root factors of the conflict. All this has been facilitated by a weak Colombian State that at the national level appears to act at the behest of transnational capital. Despite its isolation, the community has rallied and has organized itself with astonishing rigour. At least so far, it has succeeded in its goals. Marmato community organizers have been supported by a network of transnational social movements, and this bottom-up global surveillance remains a powerful weapon.

Conflict Resolution: Global Implications

The specificities of the Marmato case are particularly noteworthy. It is the "Gold City" of Colombia, with a historic entrenchment of gold mining in the community that can be traced to predate the Spanish Conquest. This stands in contrast to other regions, where gold mining has come alive only after 2008 with the emergence of the global financial crisis and the renewed role of gold as a safe haven for unstable currencies. The community's ethnic dominance of Afro-Colombians and Indigenous is highly distinct in relation to the largely mestizo population of most other mining communities. Its strong cultural heritage, protected in part by its isolated geographical location atop a remote mountain, also stands in contrasts to the mining boomtowns of late. Yet there are global lessons to be gleaned from the Marmato case on the behalf of the extractive corporations, the State and the community.

Global Corporate Implications

Probably due to a combination of declining gold prices and a fever pitch of community resistance, GCG has abandoned its original intentions of an open pit mine, at least at the time of this writing. Even if gold prices had remained high and GCG wished to proceed with the open pit project, globally networked community resistance remains sufficient to wage a formidable battle with potential victory against the company. A number of ideas flow from this.

Perhaps the most striking implication that is apparent for corporations is the all too common danger of wishful thinking. It is a classic human trait to see what we wish to see, and to turn a blind eye to what is obvious to outsiders with no vested interest. In the Marmato case, Gran Colombia Gold Corporation and its predecessors focused on the great wealth in the upper region of Marmato mountain that could be extracted quickly and profitably through an open pit mine. To the company, the construction of an open pit mine made perfect economic sense, especially against the backdrop of the dizzying escalation of gold prices post-2008 and the apparently powerful political connections wielded by its executives. We noted various documents that demonstrated that the company wanted to believe, as did the predecessor corporations that were amalgamated into Gran Colombia Gold Corporation, that it would be doing the Marmato community a great favor by relocating it to a nearby locale that would be more modern, secure, and better serviced.

At an individual level, when one falls prey to wishful thinking, it can be beneficial to consult a friend or outside observer who is truthful enough to provide a reality check. For corporations, third party consultants can potentially play that role. But this is the case only if these parties are explicitly paid to tell it like it is, as it were, rather than feeling that they are obliged to tell the company what it wants to hear so they can remain on the corporation's payroll. The corporation must then be prepared to accept realities that clash with what it hoped to be the case.[71]

Target communities must be engaged by the corporation, or by its third-party analysts, regarding preferred corporate objectives.[72] Those goals need to be explained honestly and in detail to community members. Businesses and their representatives need to listen carefully to community responses. A fundamental principle of Critical Human Security for corporations to keep in mind is that "Most people derive security from their membership in a group – a family, a community, an organization, a racial or ethnic group that can provide a cultural identity and a reassuring sense of values."[73] Hence, community interests must be fully appreciated by corporations, or there will likely be political clashes that can cost businesses dearly. When company objectives and community interests collide, negotiation and rational persuasion are obvious and important tools. But the company should never place itself in the position of believing that it knows what is best for a community. In the Marmato case, it was clear to any disinterested party that the community did not wish to be relocated, and it did not want an open pit mine. Forced relocation is classic human rights problem in the extractive sector, with an abundance of literature on the topic.[74]

More broadly, a major global implication from this case is that Gran Colombia Gold Corporation would have benefited by performing its own, corporate Human Rights Impact Assessment (HRIA). These are especially useful for projects in the Global South where human rights problems are rife, and where the State is weak. A corporate HRIA would consider the human rights specificities of the particular area of potential investment. It would map out potential human rights problems, and consider mechanisms for dealing effectively with them. Corporate HRIAs consider human security issues such as ethnic and community rights, workers' rights, environmental hazards, security threats from illicit armed groups, and so on. They are ideal tools for the identification, prevention and resolution of human rights problems for corporations. In essence, they protect the corporation from unpleasant surprises that may be antithetical to its financial objectives. These are best designed and performed by third parties who are unhindered by vested economic interests, and who fully engage the community in their analysis. The problems faced by Gran Colombia Gold Corporation would never have occurred had it conducted a proper HRIA.[75]

The historic absence and weakness of the Colombian State, especially in rural areas where extractive industries tend to invest, has been emphasized throughout the chapter. The implication for corporations is that they may have to fend for themselves in target communities. The State failed in its responsibility to provide Gran Colombia Gold with an accurate assessment of the historic cultural and ethnic reality of the community that rendered relocation untenable. In the highly unlikely scenario that the community had accepted Gran Colombia's scheme for relocation, the company would have been responsible for a variety of issues that might have arisen. These include programs for alternative employment, community construction, social welfare provisions, and so on, for which the State would normally assume responsibility. The burden for corporations can be high when the government fails to do its job.

The clearest problem faced by Gran Colombia Gold Corporation in relation to Colombia's anemic State is the fact that the vast majority of miners there are not formalized – they have received no formal training in relation to mining, including environmental and technical training, and fail to receive the social benefits of workers in the formal sector. Gran Colombia Gold has initiated a controversial program of formalization in Segovia and Remedios, which is discussed in the following chapter. The fact that the corporation has assumed this responsibility is extraordinary. Even more extraordinary is the Colombian government's continued failure to develop a plan for the State itself to formalize miners.

Further, while Marmato is unique in the Colombian context due to the general absence of illicit armed groups feeding off the extractive sector, other chapters examined in the volume attest to the vast security problems arising for foreign companies and the community when the State is weak or absent. Overall, then, a major global lesson from the Marmato case is the array of problems corporations may face when the State fails to do its job. As the Ruggie Report emphasizes, the State's primary role is to protect human rights, and the corporations' role is to respect them. Let us consider, then, global lessons for the State emerging from the Marmato case.[76]

Global Implications and the State

Both the Colombian and Canadian governments have contributed to vast problems for communities and corporations vis-à-vis the extractive sector in Colombia. Problems associated with the presence of transnational corporations merit resolutions that are transnational or global. Hence, standards suggested by various United Nations organizations are a good place to start when considering resolutions to a variety of such issues. The Colombian government is not unaware of the profound problems over which it presides. We noted that the Contraloría General de la República has sharply criticized both the Uribe and Santos governments for their policies.

A major lesson here is that the State should formalize miners – this is in the interests of miners, host communities, the corporation, and the State. Marmato's artisanal miners desperately want a government that has the interest and capacity to formalize them and to facilitate better technological knowledge, to provide them with the social welfare benefits afforded to the formal sector, and to provide training and supplies that promote environmentally safe practices. The State should observe a key principle of the International Labour Organization's 1998 Declaration on Fundamental Principles and Rights at Work, which concerns "the respect of employment and occupation."[77]

Complicating the matter further in Colombia's case, the State has created a socially pernicious discourse whereby all informal miners are grouped into the category of illegal miners who fuel the profits of illicit armed groups, and who deny the State proper taxation. All too often, the global media has repeated that discourse uncritically and without investigation.[78] But the Marmato case shows that important variations exist among such miners, and that not all traditional miners are linked to illegal armed groups.

The lack of State formalization of traditional miners perpetuates serious environmental problems. While cyanide rather than mercury is used in the Marmato case, artisanal mining in general is estimated to produce at least 67 tons of mercury each year in Colombia. This a practice abhorred by miners themselves, the communities in which they operate and others who suffer from downstream effects. Further, since 73 percent of all gold winds up in the jewelry trade,[79] and only about 20 of the 66 tons of gold produced in Colombia in 2012 came from formalized producers,[80] jewelry businesses should consider taking an ethical approach to the issue as some of their compatriots have done with regard to so-called blood-diamonds from Africa.

An important global implication here is that not only does the government have to have the intent to formalize workers, it has to have the money to bring the process to fruition. The Colombian State, in a highly ill-conceived manner, has kept the government take on the extractive sector low to promote foreign investment and to achieve macroeconomic growth. But programs such as formalization require vast funding, and the funds accruing to the State are not sufficient to alter significantly its feeble capacity to regulate the sector in the name of human rights and environmental sustainability. Given that over 80 percent of the human rights abuses in the country occur in regions where the extractive sector operates, the government's role in human rights protection has been dreadful in this regard. Further, government funds are inadequate to deliver vastly needed social welfare programs. In other words, the State badly needs to build its capacity to regulate the extractive sector and to better distribute the wealth it receives from it – but a low government take only perpetuates its incapacity.

Regarding the necessity to do more, the Colombian government is not alone. As we noted in the introductory chapter, the Canadian government was instrumental during the 1997–2001 period of formulating a Colombian mining code designed to minimize the government take. While it attempted to serve Canadian corporate interests, it resulted in perpetuating a highly insecure environment for Colombian communities and for Canadian extractive corporations. The Ruggie Report emphasizes that home governments of extractive corporations need to provide crucial support to its corporations investing in the Global South. The Report underscores that "home states have a role in helping businesses respect human rights in foreign territories."[81] But Canada has lagged in this regard. Further, the Harper Government has committed a major error by rendering the Human Rights Impact Assessment and its related side accords to be meaningless and empty.[82] The important global lesson here is that the capacity and tools are there to promote human security for Colombian communities, and better security for Canadian businesses, but a myopic vision to generate quick profits for TNCs has only served to fail all concerned.

Finally, the transition from the current focus on immediate quarterly profits to long-term stability that benefits all concerned can be facilitated in part by tripartite negotiation. But this obvious solution is all too rare in Colombia. The State, the corporation, and the community need to meet in a secure space to voice their interests and concerns transparently, and to proceed to develop a concentric area upon which all can agree. This is an area where the Canadian government can clearly assist. Ottawa should devote resources to help the Colombian State build its capacity for tripartite negotiation in order to achieve conflict resolution.

Global Implications and the Community

The basic lesson to be derived from the struggle of the Marmato community is that organization can be the key to political success. Despite unfavorable odds over the last 500 years, the multi-ethnic community has preserved its culture and its vision for the future. While divisions exist, as they do in any community, we have seen that in the main the community has stood together to oppose the open pit mine and the town's relocation.

A significant implication here concerns the interface between the local and the global. The Marmato case demonstrates the basic notion that a transnational threat requires a transnational response. While the organization of the community itself has been key, it has received crucial support from a variety of global NGOs that have publicized the community's plight. This is an area that can be fortified even further to ensure community interests down the road.

Finally, an important global lesson for community struggles emanating from the Marmato case is to be aware of all legal means available to push forward one's case. The community of Marmato could do better in this realm. The Human Rights Impact Assessment associated with the Canada–Colombia Free Trade Agreement also has important Labour and Environmental Side Accords that could be utilized by the community to press its case. For example, the criminalization of traditional miners whose families have worked the mines for five centuries could represent a significant case in the Labour Side Accord, especially since this has occurred during the period when the Canada–Colombia FTA has been in effect.

These legal tools have received little publicity in Colombia on the part of the Canadian and Colombian governments, and perhaps deliberately so. A major implication from this case, then, is that Human Rights Impact Assessments for corporations, and a revised HRIA and related side accords associated with the Free Trade Agreement, could promote human security and human rights in a manner that is beneficial to communities and corporations alike. We shall develop this point in the concluding chapter. More particularly, this case suggests the development of a variety of human rights indicators that could be incorporated into a helpful HRIA, whether or not it is a corporate or governmental assessment. Specific human security indicators could be developed through a consideration of general problems associated with displacement, informal labour, epistemological clashes, ethnic rights, gender rights and ecocide.

The New Gold Rush in Colombia: Development and Rollercoasters

Table 3.1 clearly indicates the boom and bust cycles associated with gold. In recent history, the end of the Bretton Woods regime combined with doubts about US hegemony and the dollar triggered a rise in the price of gold after 1971. More recently, the rise of the transnational speculative economy witnessed a noticeable uptick in gold prices. The booming economy of China and other BRICS countries post-2006, coupled with the US and European financial crises post-2007, further fueled soaring gold values until its relative collapse beginning in 2013. The historically unstable price of gold has varying implications for the three sets of political actors considered here.

Traditional miners in Marmato are perhaps the least concerned with fluctuating prices of gold. As we have seen, they are in it for the long term, and hope to extract gold in the community for another eight centuries. On the one hand, they prefer higher prices since their income naturally increases. But on the other hand, higher prices could spell more pressure from TNCs to re-initiate attempts at constructing an open pit mine that would mean the end of their 500-year-old community.

Table 3.1 Gold prices for selected years – 1833–2013 average annual prices, US dollars

Year	Price	Year	Price
1833–1871	18.93	1987	447.00
1872–1888	18.94	1988	437.00
1891	18.96	1989	381.00
1900	18.96	1990	383.51
1910	18.92	1991	362.11
1920	20.68	1992	343.82
1929	20.63	1993	359.77
1930	20.65	1994	384.00
1931	17.06	1995	383.79
1935	34.84	1996	387.81
1940	33.85	1997	331.02
1945	34.71	1998	294.24
1950	34.72	1999	278.98
1955	35.03	2000	279.11
1960	35.27	2001	271.04
1967	34.95	2002	309.73
1968	39.31	2003	363.38
1969	41.28	2004	409.72
1970	36.02	2005	444.74
1971	40.62	2006	603.46
1972	58.42	2007	695.39
1973	97.39	2008	871.96
1974	154.00	2009	972.35
1975	160.86	2010	1,224.53
1976	124.74	2011	1,571.52
1977	147.84	2012	1,668.85
1978	193.40	2013	1,530.88
1979	306.00		
1980	615.00		
1981	460.00		
1982	376.00		
1983	424.00		
1984	361.00		
1985	317.00		
1986	368.00		

Source: For 1833–2011, National Mining Association, United States, www.nma.org/pdf/gold/his_
gold_prices.pdf, viewed June 12, 2014; For 2012 and 2013, www.goldprices.com/historical-gold-
prices.htm, viewed June 12, 2014.

The community of Marmato could be shielded from the sometimes pernicious effects of highly speculative and fluctuating gold prices through the diversification of its economy, of which 90 percent is dependent directly or indirectly on the precious metal. The local branch of the Department of Caldas' Secretariat for Economic Development is currently contemplating plans for Marmato's economic diversification, and is considering areas such as agricultural development, the establishment of tourism, and the creation of small industries, some of which might be linked to gold production.[83] But these do not appear on the short-term horizon. A solid niche would need to be established in the realm of agriculture.

Regarding the development of tourism, Marmato's remote location – almost four hours by vehicle from the major cities of Medellin, Pereira and Manizales – would necessitate the investment of considerable resources in hotels, restaurants, and linkages to existing tourist routes. Industrial development would also involve considerable investment in physical plant as well as in constructing a durable business plan. To facilitate any of those possible areas of development, much investment would need to occur in the construction of a safe and sizable road connecting the remote mountain-top community to the highway below. Currently there is only a narrow, dirt and gravel road in place that is sometimes unnavigable in poor weather.

By 2015 Gran Colombia Gold Corporation has been hit hard by the fall of gold prices. Its mega-project of the open pit mine was pinned on gold prices hovering somewhere above US$1,500 an ounce. The company's "break even" price was US$1,322 per ounce in 2013.[84] In the context of collapsing gold prices, it indicated in 2014 that it is aiming for US$950 as its break-even level at existing mines. The corporation's adjusted net loss was US$4.5 million in the first quarter of 2014.[85] Gran Colombia Gold's experience in Marmato has meant painful lessons regarding the power of community antipathy as well as the pitfalls of relying on elevated prices for an historically speculative commodity.

Perhaps the biggest gamble for the actors considered here has been the Colombian State's reliance on the extractive sector as the primary legitimate motor of development. Revenue from gold in Colombia fell 48 percent from April 2013 to April 2014. Oil revenue, which accounts for 55 percent of the country's export revenue, fell 8 percent during the same period despite a 0.5 percent increase in volume. The dangers of relying on commodities and the extractive sector are well known – rollercoaster prices, elevated exchange rates, a tendency for the shrinkage of other key sectors such as manufacturing, and so on. In Colombia's case, this danger is exacerbated by a low government take on precious resources that are non-renewable. Reliance on a bargain basement version of the myth of El Dorado as the primary path to development is another manifestation of global casino capitalism.

Notes

1 Interview by author with Jhon Freddy Muñoz Gil, President, Asociación de Mineros Tradicionales de Marmato, Medellin, June 6, 2014.
2 The movie 'Marmato' was released in 2014, and is directed by Mark Grieco.
3 See Paul Virilio, *Speed and Politics* (New York: Semiotext(e), 1987), p. 27.
4 See A. Gallego Estrada and M. Giraldo Rojos, *Historia de Marmato* (Bogotá: Graficas Caberra, 1997), pp. 10, 18 and 20.
5 See Mary Luz Sandoval, "Habitus productive y mineria: el caso de Marmato, Caldas," *Luna Azul*, #34, Universidad de Caldas, January 2012, p. 150. For a broad history, see also: Carolina Aria Hurtado, "Neo Extractivismo o Desarrollo Local? Conflictos Territoriales y Patrimoniales en el Puelbo Minero de Marmato," MA Thesis, Universidad Mayor de San Simon, Bolivia, 2013. Quote from Gallego Estrada and Giraldo Rojas, op. cit., p. 24.
6 Gallego Estrada and Giraldo Rojas, p. 80.

7 Gran Colombia Gold, "Marmato Overview," October 10, 2012, www.grancolombia-gold.com/operations-and-projects/marmato/overiew/default.aspx. Accessed August 15, 2014.
8 Ministerio de Ambiente, Vivienda y Desarrollo Teritorial, Alcaldia de Marmato, Caldas, *Actualization del Documento Diagnostico* (Manizales: Alcaldia de Marmato, 2007), pp. 9–10.
9 See Gallego Estrada and Giraldo Rojas, op. cit., pp. 217–221.
10 See Hurtado, op. cit., pp. 32–38.
11 Gregorio Sánchez Gómez, *La Bruja de las Minas* (Cali, Caldas: Programma Editorial Universidad del Valle, 2004).
12 Ibid., p. 12.
13 Ibid., pp. 21, 33.
14 Ibid., p. 25.
15 Ibid, p. 36.
16 Ibid., see, for example, p. 37.
17 Ibid., p. 14.
18 Ibid., p. 62.
19 Ibid., see for example, p. 147.
20 See Angelika Rettburg, "Business-Led Peacebuilding in Colombia," Development Studies Institute, Crisis States Programme Working Paper Series, #1, December 2004, pp. 2–8.
21 See Brittany Lambert, Americas Policy Group, "Defending Land and Life in Marmato, Caldas, Colombia: A Call for International Solidarity," Feb 13, 2013, Canadian Council for International Cooperation.
22 Guillermo Rudal Lleras, "Mineria y hidrocarburos en Colombia," in C. Toro, editor, *Mineria, Territorio y Conflicto en Colombia,*" pp. 151–178, figure appears on page 175.
23 Gobierno de Caldas, "Plan Departamental de Desarrollo 2012–2015, Caldas compromise de todos," Manizales, Caldas, 2012.
24 Contraloría General de la República, "Minería en Colombia: Fundamentos para supercar el modelo extractivista," Luis Garay Director of Research, Bogotá, April 2013, p. 11.
25 Ibid., p. 19 and 99.
26 Ibid., p. 24.
27 Ibid., p. 53 and p. 64.
28 Interview by author, Senator Jorge Robledo, Polo Democrático Alternativo, Bogotá, September 15, 2014.
29 See Terry Karl, *Paradox of Plenty* (Los Angeles: University of California, 1997).
30 The quote is from Thomas McGrail, "Scoping Study: Marmato Project, Draft Copy of Report for Minera de Caldas SA," 2006 (no page cited for the report), in William Lewis, "Colombia Goldfields Ltd., NI 43–101 Technical Report on the Marmato and Caramanta Projects, Departments of Caldas and Antioquia, Republic of Colombia, November 14, 2006, p. 105.
31 Ibid.
32 Op. cit., p. 107.
33 Ibid.
34 Ibid.
35 Op. cit., p. 109.
36 Op. cit., p. 107.
37 Op. cit., pp. 111–112.
38 El Ecologo, September 9, 2012, www.elecologo.com, viewed 18 December 2013.
39 Lombardo Paredes Arenas took over as CEO of Gran Colombia Gold Corporation in February 2014.
40 The *New York Times* reported that "…the fallout from the arrest last week of five politicians, including her brother, Senator Álvaro Araújo, on charges of working with

paramilitary squads in a kidnapping case … made her presence in the cabinet untenable." See Simon Romero, "Foreign Minister of Colombia Quits in Scandal," *New York Times*, February 20, 2007.

41 See *Colombia Reports*, "Former Senator Sentence for Paramilitary Ties," March 18, 2010.

42 Gran Colombia Gold Corporation, Press Release, January 9, 2012, Toronto. http://grancolombiagold.com/investors/press-Releases/press-releases-details/2012/Gran-Colombia-progressing-with-Marmato-resettlement1127857/default.aspx, accessed April 12, 2014.

43 Ibid.

44 Ibid.

45 Interview by author with Paula Andrea López Galvez, Profesional Especializado, Jefe Unidad de Minas, Gobernación de Caldas, Septiembre 16, 2014.

46 Telephone interview by author with Roy MacDonald, Vice President Investor Relations, Gran Colombia Gold Corp., Toronto, October 30, 2013.

47 Interview by author, Jose Noguera, Gran Colombia Gold, Vice President Corporate Affairs, Bogota, December 11, 2013.

48 Interview by author, Yamil Amar, Presidente, Comité Cívico de Marmato, and former mayor of Marmato, August 13, 2013.

49 Ibid.

50 Interview by author with Jhon Freddy Muños Gil, June 6, 2014, op. cit.

51 John Giraldo and Rodrigo Grajales, "Marmato's Mining Battle," October 21, 2013, warscapes.com, viewed 30 November 2013.

52 Email correspondence by author with Jhon Freddy Muñoz, President, Asociación de Mineros Tradicionales de Marmato, June 26, 2014.

53 Comunidad de Marmato, "Manifesto Marmateño," 2004 (mimeograph).

54 Gobierno de Colombia, Defensoría del Pueblo, *La Minería de hecho en Colombia* (Bogotá: 2010), pp. 236–237.

55 Mining Watch Canada, "Marmato Municipal Council Prohibits Open-Pit Mining and Resettlement of Historic Center," January 6, 2012, www.miningwatchcanada.com, accessed December 2, 2012.

56 *El Pais*, November 20, 2011.

57 Interview by author with Gloria Stella Moreno, Administradora Pública, Secretaria Desarrollo Económico, Marmato, Caldas, September 5, 2014.

58 Interview by author with Oscar Palacios, Investigador, Departamento de Antropología, Universidad de Caldas, August 12, 2013.

59 Interview by author with Muñoz Gill, op. cit.

60 Interview by author with Paula Andrea López Galvez, Gobernación de Caldas, op. cit.

61 Ibid.

62 Ibid.

63 Ibid.

64 Interview by author with Adriana Palomino, council member of CRIDEC (Marmato Defense Committee and Regional Council of Caldas) and Gobernadora, La Parcialdad Indígena de Cartama, Marmato, August 13, 2013.

65 Mary Luz Sandoval, "Habitus productive mineria: el caso de Marmato, Caldas," *Luna Azul*, #34, Universidad de Caldas, January 2012, pp. 170–194, p. 158.

66 Ibid.

67 Interview by author with Yamil Amar, op. cit.

68 Ibid.

69 Ibid.

70 Interview by author, Gloria Patricia Lopera Mesa, Lawyer representing the community of Marmato, Bogotá, August 19, 2013.

71 This is a common theme in the literature on Corporate Social Responsibility and Human Rights Impact Assessments. See, for example: World Bank Group, International Finance Corporation, "Guide to Human Rights Impact Assessment and

Management," 2011, on line, www.guidetohriam.org, viewed June 25, 2014; Tarek Maasarati, M. Drakos and J. Pajhowska, "Extracting Corporate Responsibility: Towards a Human Rights Impact Assessment," Cornell International Labor Journal, number 135, 2007, pp. 136–170, and especially pages 149–151; Ruggie Report, "Report of the Special Representative of the Secretary General on the Issue of Human Rights and Transnational Corporations and other Business Enterprises, John Ruggie, Guiding Principles on Business and Human Rights: Implementing United Nations 'Protect, Respect and Remedy Framework" New York: United Nations, March 21, 2011, especially pages 13–21.

72 See Danish Institute for Human Rights, Human Rights Compliance Quick Check, op. cit., p. 27.

73 United Nations Development Report, op. cit., p. 31.

74 See, for example, Maasarati, et all, op. cit., p. 139 and Danish Institute for Human Rights, Human Rights Compliance Quick Check, 2006, online, www.hrca2.human-rightsbusiness.org., p. 139.

75 See James Rochlin, "A Golden Opportunity Lost: Canada's Human Rights Impact Assessment and the Free Trade Agreement with Colombia," *International Journal of Human Rights*, vol. 18, #4, 2014.

76 Ruggie Report, op. cit., p. 4.

77 International Labour Organization, "1998 Declaration on Fundamental Principles and Rights at Work," (New York: United Nations, 1998), p. 3.

78 See, for example, Paul Harris, "Illegal Mining Colombia's New Bane," *Globe and Mail*, May 9, 2013.

79 See Mary Footer, "Shining Brightly: Human Rights and Responsible Sourcing of Diamond and Gold Jewelry from High Risk and Conflict-Affected Areas," *Human Rights and International Legal Discourse*, vol. 6, 2012, pp. 160–190, especially page 166.

80 Paul Harris, op. cit.

81 Ruggie Report, "Business and Human Rights in Conflict-Affected Zones: Challenges and Options Toward State Responses," (New York: United Nations, May 27, 2011), p. 3.

82 See James Rochlin, "A Golden Opportunity Lost," op. cit.

83 Interview by author with Gloria Stella Moreno, Secretaria Desarrollo Económico, op. cit.

84 Gran Colombia Gold Corporation, Press Release, March 31, 2014. http://grancolom-biagold.com/investors/press-Releases/press-releases-details/2014/Gran-Colombia-Gold-announces-fourth-quarter-and-full-year-2013-results-meets-2013-all-in-sustaining-costs-targets/default.aspx, accessed July 1, 2014.

85 Gran Colombia Gold Corporation, Press Release, May 14, 2014. http://grancolombia gold.com/investors/press-Releases/press-releases-details/2014/Gran-Colombia-Gold-Announces-First-Quarter-2014-Results-Reports-Fourth-Consecutive-Quarterly-Reduction-in-All-in-Sustaining-Costs/default.aspx, accessed August 12, 2014.

Bibliography

Comunidad de Marmato. "Manifesto Marmateño." 2004 (mimeograph).

Danish Institute for Human Rights. Human Rights Compliance Quick Check. 2006. Accessed December 20, 2013. https://hrca2.humanrightsbusiness.org/.

El Ecologo. September 9, 2012. Accessed December 18, 2013. www.elecologo.com.

Footer, Mary. "Shining Brightly: Human Rights and Responsible Sourcing of Diamond and Gold Jewelry from High Risk and Conflict-Affected Areas." *Human Rights and International Legal Discourse* 6 (2012): 160–190.

Gallego Estrada, A., and M. Giraldo Rojos. *Historia de Marmato*. Graficas Cabrerra: Bogota, 1997.

Garay, Luis. "Minería en Colombia: Fundamentos para supercar el modelo extractivista." Contraloría General de la República: Bogotá, 2013.

Giraldo Herrera, John Harold and Rodrigo Grajales Murillo. "Marmato's Mining Battle." *Warscapes*, October 21, 2013. Accessed November 30, 2013. www.warscapes.com/art/marmatos-mining-battle.

Gobierno de Caldas. "Plan departamental de desarrollo 2012–2015, Caldas compromise de todos." Manizales, Caldas, 2012.

Gobierno de Colombia, Defensoría del Pueblo. *La minería de hecho en Colombia.* Bogotá, 2010.

Gran Colombia Gold Corporation. "Gran Colombia Gold Announces Fourth Quarter And Full Quarter 2013 Results; Meets 2013 All-In Sustaining Costs Targets." March 31, 2014. Accessed May 15, 2014. http://grancolombiagold.com/investors/press-Releases/press-releases-details/2014/Gran-Colombia-Gold-announces-fourth-quarter-and-full-year-2013-results-meets-2013-all-in-sustaining-costs-targets/default.aspx.

Gran Colombia Gold Corporation. "Gran Colombia Progressing With Marmato Resettlement." January 9, 2012. Accessed December 20, 2013. http://grancolombiagold.com/investors/press-Releases/press-releases-details/2012/Gran-Colombia-progressing-with-Marmato-resettlement1127857/default.aspx.

Gran Colombia Gold Corporation. "Marmato Overview." October 10, 2012. Accessed May 15, 2014. http://grancolombiagold.com/operations-and-projects/marmato/over-view/default.aspx.

Grieco, Mark, and Stuart Reid. *Marmato*. Directed by Mark Grieco. Caracas, Venezuela: Calle Films, 2014. Documentary film, 87 minutes.

Hurtado, Carolina Aria. "Neo extractivismo o desarrollo local? Conflictos territoriales y patrimoniales en el pueblo minero de Marmato." MA Thesis, Universidad Mayor de San Simon, Bolivia, 2013.

International Labour Organization. "1998 Declaration on Fundamental Principles and Rights at Work." New York: United Nations, 1998. Accessed December 20, 2013. www.ilo.org/dyn/normlex/en/f?p=1000:62:0::NO:62:P62_LIST_ENTRIE_ID:2453911:NO.

Karl, Terry. *The Paradox of Plenty.* Los Angeles: University of California, 1997.

Lambert, Brittany. "Defending Land and Life in Marmato, Caldas, Colombia: A Call for International Solidarity." *Canadian Council for International Cooperation, Americas Policy Group.* February 13, 2012. Accessed December 20, 2013. www.ccic.ca/blog/defending-land-and-life-in-marmato-colombia-a-call-for-international-solidarity-part-1/.

Maasarati, Tarek, M. Drakos, and J. Pajhowska. "Extracting Corporate Responsibility: Towards a Human Rights Impact Assessment." *Cornell International Labor Journal* 135 (2007): 136–170.

McGrail, Thomas. "Scoping Study: Marmato Project, Draft Copy of Report for Minera de Caldas SA." In William J. Lewis, *Colombia Goldfields Limited, NI 43–101 Technical Report on the Marmato and Caramanta Projects, Departments of Caldas and Antioquia, Republic of Colombia.* Micon International Limited: Toronto, November 14, 2006. www.infomine.com/index/pr/Pa530872.PDF. Accessed April 1, 2014.

Mining Watch Canada. "Marmato Municipal Council Prohibits Open-Pit Mining and Resettlement of Historic Center." January 6, 2012. Accessed December 2, 2012. www.miningwatch.ca/news/colombia-marmato-municipal-council-prohibits-open-pit-mining-and-resettlement-historic-centre.

Ministerio de Ambiente, Vivienda y Desarrollo Teritorial, Alcaldia de Marmato, Caldas. *Actualization del documento diagnostico.* Manizales: Alcaldia de Marmato, 2007.

Rettburg, Angelika. "Business-led Peacebuilding in Colombia: Fad or Future of a Country in Crisis?" *Crisis States Programme Working Paper* (Development Studies Institute) 56 (December 2004): 1–25. www.gsdrc.org/go/display&type=Document&id=1199. Accessed April 6, 2014.

Rochlin, James. "A Golden Opportunity Lost: Canada's Human Rights Impact Assessment and the Free Trade Agreement with Colombia." *International Journal of Human Rights* 18, no. 4 (2014): 545–566.

Romero, Simon. "Foreign Minister of Colombia Quits in Scandal." *NewYorkTimes.com*, February 20, 2007. Accessed December 18, 2013. www.nytimes.com/2007/02/20/world/americas/20colombia.html?_r=0.

Rudal Lleras, Guillermo. "Minería y hidrocarburos en Colombia." In Catalina Toro Pérez et al., editor, *Minería, territorio y conflicto en Colombia*. Bogota: Universidad Nacional de Colombia, 2011: 151–178.

Sánchez Gómez, Gregorio. *La bruja de las minas.* Cali, Caldas: Programa Editorial – Universidad del Valle, 2004.

Sandoval Robayo, Mary Luz. "Habitus productive y mineria: el caso de Marmato, Caldas." *Univ.humanist* 74, (2012). www.scielo.org.co/scielo.php?script=sci_arttext&pid=S0120-48072012000200008&lng=en&tlng=es. Accessed April 10, 2014.

Sumpter, Cameron. "Former Senator Sentenced for Paramilitary Ties." *ColombiaReports.co*, March 18, 2010. Accessed December 18, 2013. http://colombiareports.co/senator-sentenced-for-paramilitary-ties/.

United Nations. *United Nations Human Development Report.* New York: United Nations Development Program, 1994.

United Nations, General Assembly, Human Rights Council. "Guiding Principles on Business and Human Rights: Implementing the United Nations "Protect, Respect and Remedy" Framework." *Report of the Special Representative of the Secretary-General on the Issue of Human Rights and Transnational Corporations and Other Business Enterprises, John Ruggie*, A/HRC/17/31. United Nations, March 21, 2011. Accessed September 4, 2013. www.ohchr.org/documents/issues/business/A.HRC.17.31.pdf.

United Nations, General Assembly, Human Rights Council. "Business and Human Rights in Conflict-Affected Zones: Challenges and Options Toward State Responses." *Report of the Special Representative of the Secretary-General on the Issue of Human Rights and Transnational Corporations and Other Business Enterprises, John Ruggie*, A/HRC//17/32. United Nations, May 27, 2011. Accessed December 20, 2013. www.ohchr.org/Documents/Issues/TransCorporations/A.HRC.17.32.pdf.

Virilio, Paul. *Speed and Politics.* New York: Semiotext(e)/Foreign Agents, 1987.

World Bank Group. International Finance Corporation. "Guide to Human Rights Impact Assessment and Management." 2011. Accessed June 25, 2014. www.ifc.org/wps/wcm/connect/8ecd35004c0cb230884bc9ec6f601fe4/hriam-guide-092011.pdf?MOD=AJPERES.

4 The Gold Trade and Human Security in Segovia and Remedios

Adrián Restrepo Parra,
Wilmar Martínez Márquez, and
Juan José Moncada Carvajal

Since the implementation of the Canada–Colombia FTA, community organizations have charged that Canadian mining corporations have acted in a manner contrary to the promotion of human security. An important historical context is that the State has failed in its role of guaranteeing human rights. In the Segovia–Remedios mining district in Antioquia, Colombia, there has been a multifaceted conflict between traditional miners, Gran Colombia Gold Corporation (GCG), community groups, and a variety of criminal organizations. The two largest threats to human security in the region are a legacy of entrenched social violence and the largest mercury pollution in the world, problems which are not easily resolvable in the short term.

This chapter will begin with an overview of the human security situation in Segovia and Remedios. This will be followed by an analysis of the State's viewpoint as well as the corporation's perspective. A series of recommendations will follow, especially with regard to the development of a new national mining policy and the use of HRIAs. There is a particular set of rights related to human security that is relevant in the case at hand. These include the right to life, the right to work, the right to political participation, and environmental sustainability.[1]

Contextual Aspects of the Case

The nearby communities of Segovia and Remedios are located in the northern portion of the Department of Antioquia. Gold mining has been present in this region since at least 1541 under Spanish colonialism. Similarly to the Marmato case, British mining companies arrived in the area around 1825. The mining industry boomed beginning 1850. As mining companies competed for land and concessions, administrative boundaries became more important. It was in this context that the community of Remedios was established in 1860 and Segovia in 1865. The industry was propelled once again by the arrival of northern technology in the 1880s.

What is especially noteworthy about this case study is the historical entrenchment of violence and the massive environmental destruction caused by the use of mercury during the extraction process. As gold prices rose when the Bretton Woods regime ended in 1971–1973, the population of the Segovia and Remedios region increased by 55.4 percent. This population explosion put extreme strain on already limited government services. As the gold rush hit the region, the country was falling into an increasingly intense stage of warfare between rising leftist insurgencies in the form of the FARC and ELN, rising right-wing paramilitary forces under the Autodefensas Unidas de Colombia (AUC), and a very weak Colombian State. An important context was the burgeoning economy of narcotrafficking that funded warfare and that fueled violence on a number of fronts. Beyond narcotrafficking, other components of the illicit economy were related to warfare, such as extortion, kidnapping for ransom, as well as assorted products linked to contraband trade.

As the gold rush and population explosion arrived in Segovia and Remedios, so too did a variety of illegal armed groups who devoted themselves to feeding off the new and booming economy. Competition between the aforementioned leftist insurgencies and the paramilitaries for gold profits, and warfare between them at the national level that found local expression, prompted huge violence in the region. This was especially the case between 1982 and 1997. A massacre of 43 people in November 1988 by paramilitaries, and another involving 15 people in 1996 were among numerous tragedies that rendered this region to be among the most violent and lawless in the country. This legacy of violence and criminal activity continues to haunt the area. What needs to be emphasized at this point is that Gran Colombia Gold Corporation and other parties were aware when they invested in the region that historically entrenched patterns of violence were in place.

Gold prices fell in the late 1990s, and the economy receded in the area under consideration. As Amnesty International noted in 1996, "approximately 45 percent of the economically active population live in marginal areas in the region and earn a living panning for gold on sites abandoned by TNCs."[2] This kind of mining by artisanal miners is one dimension of the current contest between Gran Colombia Gold Corporation and 196 traditional miners that the country's judicial system says is operating illegally on GCG property.

A new crew of illegal groups, and some traditional ones, continue to operate in the region and perpetrate violence. The FARC has two fronts in the district, numbers three and 34. A smaller leftist group, the ELN, also is present. The strength of three competing right-wing criminal groups was very clear by 2012, the height of the gold boom. These included Los Rastrojos, Águilas Negras, and Los Urabeños. To deal with the problem, the Colombian government implemented the Trojan Plan in October of 2012. This involved the placement of 386 additional police in the communities. As we shall see, community members indicate that this has helped to curb violence.

Critical Human Security in Segovia and Remedios

The case involving the communities of Segovia and Remedios is complex and nuanced. This shall become very apparent when we examine a variety of issues from the differing perspectives of community members, the corporation, and the State. While grave issues prevail, an argument can be made that the situation has been improving. Let us consider the panorama of human security in the region.

Threats to human security have various manifestations. With the strong presence of insurgencies and criminal organizations, and in the context of an historically weak or absent State, violence has prevailed as a principal means to deal with conflict. As we shall see, there have been assassinations and threats against key activists in the community who have protested against the policies of Gran Colombia Gold Corporation. Thus, the politics of fear dominates the region, such that community members are reluctant to criticize the corporation, the illegal groups, and so on. Fear also affects the corporation, which can be the target of extortion, kidnapping, infrastructure damage, and so on. Overall, a major challenge to achieve critical human security in the region is to create an atmosphere of security whereby free speech can flourish. Unless problems can be articulated by the community in a secure manner, they are likely to persist and worsen.

A key aspect of critical human security is effective tripartite negotiation – whereby workers and community members can meet with the corporation and the government to voice problems and to resolve them. But these structures remain absent in the case of the Segovia and Remedios region of Antioquia. This essential communication link is obscured even further when contract workers are employed to fill most positions, since there is no direct contact between workers, the community and the corporation. Instead, workers and the community are left to deal with a corporate affiliate.

As we shall see, another key issue in the case concerns the role of the State in Colombia, and how this affects community-corporate relations. Given the historical absence of the State in the country, we found that in Segovia and Remedios, community members expect the corporation to replace the State in many respects through Corporate Social Responsibility (CSR) programs. The State feeds this problem in Segovia and Remedios by its preference for Gran Colombia Gold Corporation, rather than the government, to lead the process of formalization, or legalization, of traditional miners. That is, the "neoliberal" brand of the Colombian government restricts the growth of an already weak State. Overall, the role of the State is to protect human rights established through a variety of international charters. But Colombia's government is so weak, and so ideologically committed to a limited role in the political economy, that its capacity to fulfill its duty of protecting human rights is severely challenged.

Human Security and Gold in Segovia and Remedios: the Community Perspective

Right to Life

There have been numerous and serious allegations of links between GCG's presence in the region and violence there. It should be clear at the outset that there is no publicly available evidence that the violence in the region has been directly caused by Gran Colombia Gold Corporation. And, as we shall see, GCG indicates that accusations directly linking the company to crime are baseless. Instead, some community members allege that GCG's presence has prompted the arrival of a variety of competing criminal organizations that propagate such violence. What is clear is that there have been assassinations and threats against those who have opposed policies of GCG. Of crucial importance, no charges have been laid, and impunity exists, for the perpetrators of crimes. The lack of State-based conflict resolution mechanisms to deal with the situation remains a huge part of the problem.

The right to life in the mining district has been threatened by the political and armed conflicts in the region, and is centered around the quest for wealth, especially with regard to criminal or insurgent organizations.[3] During the last four decades, much of this violence has been inflicted by illegal armed groups seeking territorial control over resources and activities related to mining. In a region where conflict is often resolved by violence, the result of the situation has been basic threats to human life. One of the strengths of the human security approach is its recognition that threats to security in the South often come from within these countries. In the Segovia-Remedios case, these include outright assassination for political or economic motives, population displacement, as well as a variety of credible threats to instil fear.

Violence has waxed and waned in the region, and since about 2012 the general atmosphere has been calmer. This has been the result, at least in part, of an increase in government security forces in Segovia and Remedios. Part of this relative tranquility was expressed during the recent presidential election process in 2014, where a leftist party won the elections in the town of Segovia. No violence ensued, and this is noteworthy in a community that at the time was witnessing fierce competition between right-wing paramilitary groups – especially the Urabeños and the Rastrojos. This is an encouraging development regarding the prospects for resolving conflicts peacefully in the region.

A major stumbling block that has prevented peaceful conflict resolution is the politics of fear and related limits on free speech. Mine workers, communities and government officials argue that they are entitled to express their dissatisfaction, complaints, and so on with respect to the mining industry that dominates the town. However, some claim they have been the target of illegal armed groups. For example, the representative of the municipality of Remedios said that there exists a strong "culture of fear and nobody wants to complain because something bad could happen."[4] This "culture" is the result of a long history of violence in the region.[5] Apparently, this pervasive fear has resulted in political silence among many.

From the perspective of an official municipal representative from Remedios, the activities of the company, rather than promoting peace and integral security, have indirectly propelled insecurity in the region. This is because the wealth created by Gran Colombia Gold Corporation has attracted major criminal gangs (BACRIM) to the area. This municipal representative suggested that GCG officials:

> ...started giving contracts to operate the mines of the company, and these contracts never existed before, even during the 35–40 years when another company ran the mines before GGC arrived, it was called Frontino.... Here

criminal gangs are strengthened because everyone wants a contract, and whoever wants that contract has to go and talk to the commander of the gang.[6]

Through extortion, backed by threats of violence, these criminal organizations assume control of mining contract ownership and distribution.[7] The representative Remedios indicated

> ...that anyone who dared to publicly denounce the situation became a target. In fact, I did and it was the first threat I ever received. I do not mean by this that it has been the Gran Colombia Gold who has threatened me. But I got a threat by phone, which said do not get involved with multinationals.[8]

A culture of fear, then, limits free speech regarding aspects of the extractive industry. In this case, armed criminal organizations have indirectly exploited the contractual system used by GCG and have used violence to assert their control.

Not only is individual free speech curtailed when the State is weak and criminal organizations are strong, but community development is also stifled. People from communities in the region recount an environment of violence and difficulties in exercising the right to social mobilization and organization. According to the communities, the prospect of miners going out to the streets to protest and express their rights becomes the object of stigmatization, accusations and even killings. A representative from a human rights group, the Cahucopana Organization, states that "two years ago in Segovia there were two miners who went to the radio station to protest against the multinational (GCG), shortly afterwards one of them was murdered."[9] Further, the same NGO observes that "Two union leaders belonging the Agricultural and Mining Association and SINTRAMIN-ERGETICA, Jaminson Adrian Amaya and Nelson Cadavid, were killed on July 27, 2012, after leading a strike in the town of Segovia at the Providence mine (which is owned by GCG)."[10] The Cahucopana Organization also emphasized that, in addition to actual assassinations, threats of assassination are just as powerful in terms of their political effect of creating fear and silence. The NGO underscored the social terror resulting from

> ...the attempted murder and the permanent threat against the life of the miners Jhony Alexander, Juan Felipe and Jesus Mira Arango, and their families. This occurred in the context of a violent territorial dispute waged by Los Rastrojos and Los Urabeños for control of gold mining in the region.[11]

Once again, it is important to emphasize that these assassinations and threats occur in an atmosphere of impunity.

It is significant to note that criticism of the extractive industry comes not only from NGOs, miners, and unions, but also from leading representatives from the local government. From the point of view of the representative of the municipality of Remedios, the presence of foreign companies has not been good for the region, since "all they have done so far is to escalate the conflict ... the only thing that it has brought us has been violence, growth of groups outside the law, and inefficiency."[12] A similar view is expressed by representatives of the Segovia municipality.

An important point of friction in the community has been a protracted labour dispute between Sintramiser (Union of Mineworkers of Segovia and Remedios) and a company linked to GCG, called Strategies and Mines.[13] At issue in that case was the hiring of contract workers through subsidiaries of GCG. Shortly after Gran Colombia Gold assumed mining operations in northeastern Antioquia, it was announced that miners were now to be hired through third party contractors. Among the largest was the company called Strategies and Mines. But the company went bankrupt, and failed to properly pay the workers it had contracted to the GCG mine. This coincided with the local miners' participation in a national strike in the summer of 2013. The Government Secretary for Segovia indicated that "of the five local leaders of the strike, two were murdered when they went to work."[14] Overall, it is the weakness of the State to grapple effectively with illegal armed groups, and the related perpetuation of an atmosphere of impunity, that is a prominent part of the problem.

Right to Work

There are two outstanding issues regarding the right to work and the presence of GCG in the region. One concerns the tension generated by the clampdown on traditional or untitled miners and GCG's ability to exclusively offer legal mining contracts. A second issue concerns difficulties emanating from labour subcontracting. First, it is necessary to acknowledge that informal mining activities traditionally have been dominant in the area. The representative of the municipality of Remedios observed that "before GCG came, when there was Frontino Gold Mine, free contracts were given in concession to several mines of this municipality, so the artisanal miner of Segovia and Remedios could work in peace in mines."[15] This situation changed with the presence of Gran Colombia Gold Corporation, because it claimed with legal backing that some of the mines that were operating informally in the area were actually located on its property, and therefore the company owned them. This conflict between traditional miners and GCG has been difficult for the community to manage, according to the municipal secretary of Segovia.[16]

Instead of a temporary concession in the area, Gran Colombia Gold Corporation has a degree of perpetuity, which is known in Colombian legislation as a Recognition of Private Property (RPP).[17] As such, GCG is the owner of the soil and subsoil. It is important to emphasize that Colombian law does not require it to recognize the informal mining sector. For this reason, Gran Colombia Gold has the legal right to reclaim informal mines located on its property. It has filed 35 administrative injunctions to obtain control of these mines.[18] Local miners say that the company attempts to take mines away from miners who do not agree with their process of formalization, or legalization.

Gran Colombia Gold Corporation has developed a mechanism that allows some informal miners to continue exploiting the mines through the endorsement of operating contracts that formalize, or legalize, the mines and miners. In the area of Segovia and Remedios, there are around 122 informal mining units. Of these, the company has managed to formalize 18 through operation contracts.[19] These contracts that permit formalization are based on two major principles of Colombian law. First, the miner to whom the contract is awarded must accommodate all requirements established by Colombian law regarding labour and the environment. In practice, this means that GCG must ensure that the miner enjoys full workers rights and benefits, and that the company can certify that the miner is familiar with basic safety practices and does not use mercury in the extraction process. Second, all material extracted from the mine must be sold to the company, according to weight or weight processing results set by the company.[20]

It is the second principle above that has drawn the ire of some miners in the region. The representative of the Association of Informal Miners of Segovia and Remedios (Asomina), Hernando Henao, offer the following critique of the process:

> The company orders unilateral contracts, ones that are completely determined by them.... The crux of the problem is that the mine comes up short of my expectations when I deliver them gold. Unfortunately the company usually comes in far below what I know I would get if I took it elsewhere.[21]

Bitterness among local miners against the parameters of this formalization process was clearly expressed in the national mining strike carried out in 2013. To be clear, traditional miners see the stark choice between having their mines legally taken away from them, or submitting to a process of formalization with which they do not agree, to represent a violation of their right to work.

Right to Free Association

After the liquidation of the Frontino Gold Mines in 2010, Gran Colombia Gold legally acquired mines in the area of Segovia and Remedios. Unlike Frontino Gold Mines, GCG has given operation contracts to third parties in order to execute mining activity in the area. One of those third parties that exploited gold in the region was the company Strategies and Mines.

Although the Colombian legal system has taken a different view on the matter, as we shall see, the perception of some miners and many interviewees is that the company Strategies and Mines, rather than being a separate entity from the GCG, has been a direct extension of Gran Colombia Gold Corporation. The president of the Union of Mine Workers of Segovia and Remedios (Sintramiser) had this to say on the matter:

> Gran Colombia has a subsidiary called Zandor Capital. Zandor Capital then hires an outsourcing company called Strategies and Mines that recruits us. We are saying that this process is a shell game and it is illegal – we are actually employees of Gran Colombia Gold.[22]

The dispute emerged when local miners began a discussion group as to whether or not to unionize.

When we were working on the discussion group regarding the union, we met month after month with Dr. María Consuelo Araujo, CEO of Gran Colombia.... Before forming the union, those who were members of the discussion group were called to Medellin. GGC paid for transportation, hotel and food, and they asked us to give them a chance, and not to join the union. Dr. María Consuelo wanted to talk to us.[23]

This type of alleged intervention on the part of GCG in relation to the employees of Strategies and Mines solidified the public perception of the tight link between GCG and Strategies and Mines.

The municipal representative of Remedios concurs with that view.

Gran Colombia has invented a company, it is called Zandor Capital, it was registered in Panama and it was brought to Colombia, it doesn't have any mining experience, the legal representative is Mrs. Maria Consuelo Araujo. GCG did this to legally avoid any responsibility related to the workers or a possible claim for violation of labour rights.[24]

The Government Secretary of Segovia also agrees with that perspective: "people were hired through temporary contracts by a company strongly linked to Gran Colombia Gold. One of the largest was Strategies and Mines which had more than 1,000 workers a year ago (2012), now it has 500 workers (2013)."[25] This relationship between the companies, and the issue of responsibility of GCG towards workers, remain central to a dispute involving the dismissal of workers and the bankruptcy of Strategies and Mines.

In February 2014, after about three years of operation, Strategies and Mines was liquidated. According to some interviewees, this occurred when workers decided to form a union, an event that Gran Colombia Gold Corporation could not tolerate.[26] According to this view, by liquidating the company, they were able to dismiss the newly unionized employees. Beyond that conjecture, it is important to emphasize that there were other crucial factors at play, especially the precipitous decline of gold prices since late 2012. Within that context, a local expert suggests that the company of Strategies and Mines simply was not profitable, and that this explains its liquidation.[27]

At any rate, the liquidation of a large number of miners provoked members of the union to seek a legal injunction forcing Gran Colombia Gold Corporation to rehire them. On February 21, 2014, the Municipal Court of Segovia ordered Strategy and Mines to reinstate those workers dismissed as a result of the company's liquidation. But since it was legally liquidated, it was not in a position to re-hire workers. Importantly, this judicial decision exempted Gran Colombia Gold from liability by considering it a distinct company from Strategies and Mines. As of this writing, an appeal has been waged by the members of the union in order to achieve another verdict whereby Gran Colombia Gold is obliged to acknowledge what the union views at the company's responsibility toward its members.[28] Let us consider this further.

A representative from the Union of Mine Workers of Segovia and Remedios explained that one of the fundamental purposes of the union's creation is to claim the right to be employed directly by GCG.[29] The formation of the union on 24 June 2013 was due to "violation of our rights as workers," especially regarding issues surrounding the dismissal of hundreds of workers since 2012.[30] The official representative of the municipality of Remedios suggested bluntly that "[a]fter they formed a union in Strategies and Mines, Gran Colombia Gold wanted to get rid of the company it order to end the union."[31] This is echoed by the Secretary of Government of Segovia, who observed that "shortly after a workers' union was created, they laid off everybody."[32] These layoffs were twinned with the bankruptcy of the intermediary corporation that hired the newly unionized miners. A representative of Sintramiser mentions that "the union was created in June of 2013. One month later, the mode of voluntary retirement was invented; we realized it was a reaction of Dr. María Consuelo Araujo due to the union formation."[33] Workers and municipal government representatives argue that the right to free association is threatened when newly created unions are decimated by mass dismissals and sudden bankruptcy.

Further, what is important to emphasize is that formalized workers are hired by contractors or intermediary corporations, and not directly by Gran Colombia Gold. Thus, any claim that the worker may have can only be directed toward the intermediary.[34] The model limits worker participation, the union says, because it is designed to prevent the establishment of a direct relationship between the miner and the central company directing the extractive industry, which in this case is GCG.

Another obstacle to corporate-worker negotiations, according to the union, is that the companies do not have expedited communication mechanisms for them to express their concerns. The miners and officials interviewed for this case study emphasized that a poor communication framework has limited dialogue with the company.[35] What is clear is that dialogue is necessary to resolve conflict, and that better structures need to be created to reach that goal.

Right to Environmental Safety

The environmental problems in the mining district of Segovia and Remedios are derived from the processes of mineral extraction, especially regarding the use of mercury and cyanide. The United Nations Organization for Industrial Development in 2010 deemed the region to be the worst in the world for mercury pollution.[36] The use of mercury was reduced sharply with the predecessor of GCG – Frontino Gold.[37] Gran Colombia Gold Corporation has continued with this industrial process that uses cyanide instead of mercury. Cyanide is viewed as the less toxic and dangerous of the two. While cyanide is the dominant approach in the region, there are reports that some miners are still using mercury and then selling their product to GCG.[38] The company is building a treatment plant of minerals to reduce negative environmental impacts.

Water pollution due to dumping of mercury and cyanide are the result of the mining activity developed by formal and informal stakeholders in mining. Currently, both traditional miners and those working for Gran Colombia Gold Corporation are responsible for the pollution. While efforts are being made to improve the situation, the area remains heavily polluted, and this is a clear threat to the human security of the community.

The impacts of mining are apparent throughout the urban environment. The municipal representative of Segovia explained that:

> ...here we have mines in the village and we have many homes that have been affected by mining. You can go to a neighborhood called Briceño and see the cracked houses because of underground mining there. The use of dynamite, and other explosives, makes the earth shake and generates all those cracks.[39]

This problem compromises a variety of urban structures. In March 2014 near-disaster struck at the local hospital in Segovia, when the maternity division, the hospitalization division, and the hospital's sterilization department were evacuated before an imminent crash of the building.[40] The Catholic Church also has cracks in its structure as a result of underground mining. Beyond this, the local air is affected by particulate matter generated by the mines.

Corporate Social Responsibility

In the FTA between Colombia and Canada, Article 816 of the Treaty notes that:

> Each Party shall encourage enterprises operating in their territory or subject to its jurisdiction to voluntarily incorporate internationally recognized standards of Corporate Social Responsibility within their internal policies such as statements of principles that have been approved or which are backed by the parties.[41]

The research we conducted in Segovia and Remedios on the matter of Corporate Social Responsibility of Gran Colombia Gold suggests that many actors have expected GCG to do much more than it has. The official representative of the community Remedios wondered "Where is the investment? Tell me where the Gran Colombia Gold has built a neighborhood, where [it] has made a road for the community in the municipality of Segovia and Remedios?"[42] The Finance Secretary of Segovia claims that:

> The social investment made by the company in the community has turned out to be null. They initially had a private school, and they said that the social investment was related to that school. But now Gran Colombia Gold is turning the school over to ownership by the government of Antioquia.[43]

The situation of the school, as well as complaints regarding the poor condition of roads, have been the aspects most echoed by community members during our visits there.

A much wider issue is at play here, and that concerns the weakness and absence of the Colombian State. We saw above that some community members resent that the school, created and financed first by Frontino and then by Gran Colombia Gold, is being turned over to the government to operate. Those companies indeed made an investment in the land purchase, construction and operation of the school. Education, is in fact, the State's responsibility. However, because the State has not delivered what it should in Colombia, especially in rural areas, community members expect Corporate Social Responsibility Programs to be a substitute for the State. This has been the case with the others case studies in this volume, as well.

The Company

Here we provide the perspective of Gran Colombia Gold regarding issues related to human security. This is based on official company pronouncements, as well as direct company responses to specific questions we posed to it. Let us begin with a general description of the company and its operations in the Segovia and Remedios region.

Gran Colombia Gold Corporation has exploited gold in the Segovia-Remedios mining district since August 2010, when it acquired mining rights in perpetuity that were originally granted in 1852 by the Colombian government to the British company Frontino Gold Mines (FGM).[44] The Segovia-Remedios operations include the mines El Silencio, Providencia, Sandra K, La Carla, La Poma Rosa, as well as La Vertical, where a new mechanized mine will be developed.

Regarding Corporate Social Responsibility and commitment to human rights, the company claims that in order

> ...to succeed, GCG should be an agent of positive change for communities in which it operates. This can only be achieved if communities are transformed properly. GCG's success will lead to positive change in the communities in terms of health, safety, wages, pensions, environment, economic growth, education and stronger communities.[45]

Let us assess how the company views itself in relation to human security.

Right to Life

In response to allegations of GCG's role in violation of various dimensions of human security, the company insists that its presence in the region has actually contributed to the "...reduction of criminal activity. Gold mining is an attractive business for criminal organizations. By organizing mining operations under the management of a public company, GCG fills a gap that otherwise might be occupied by a criminal organization."[46] This point is important. We saw above that community members suggested that GCG has indirectly increased violence in the region since its operations have attracted right-wing criminal organizations that attempt to dominate contract distribution, among other themes. But the company argues that it has actually decreased violence in the region by taking a big portion of the industry out of the hands of such organizations. The company does not recognize that its operation in the region has attracted criminal groups.

Senior figures from Gran Colombia Gold have addressed questions surrounding the relationship of the company to acts of violence against union members. Maria Consuelo Araujo, executive director of the GCG, said that "…we reject all forms of violence."[47] Another executive of GCG, Vice President José Oro, claimed that the allegations of trade unionists that link the corporation to violence have no basis: "Here if you are threatened, is not something that is unusual…. We do not threaten anyone."[48] The company does not dispute that assassinations, threats, and other violations against workers have indeed occurred, but adamantly insists that GCG is not responsible for them.

Right to Work

As opposed to various claims by miners, GCG repeatedly has stated that its presence in the region helps to strengthen the right to work. Gran Colombian Gold emphasizes that in the process of liquidating Frontino Gold Mines, the company met all social benefits owed to miners:

> …we have hosted the majority of the labour force working in the mines of the old company, increasing their basic salaries to almost double of what was previously accrued, we have allocated … an amount that guarantees a pension for 1,600 retirees, and now the challenge is to make the operation 100% sustainable, benefiting even the small mining operations in the municipality.[49]

That response has not muted the complaints of unionized miners of former Frontino mines, since these miners claim that they own the mines over which Gran Colombia has received legal concession.

With regard to complaints surrounding the outsourcing of labour by the company, GCG has argued two points. The first is that it has a model to formalize, or legalize, artisanal miners. According to the company,

> Gran Colombia has created and implemented a business model that offers mining contracts to groups of local artisanal miners. These contracts require the miners to form cooperatives or companies that comply with labour standards, to follow the rules and procedures of GCG, and to operate within the mining plan and deliver gold to the processing plant. The company pays cash to miners according to the US dollar price.[50]

The second point was made by Maria Consuelo Araujo, who said that "from the beginning, the premise of supply and demand established that the contracts would take place through temporary agencies."[51] The company emphasized that boom and bust cycles associated with mining dictate the temporary nature of the work, which necessitates the outsourcing of temporary workers.

The formalization process spearheaded by Gran Colombia Gold is also supported by USAID, Colombia's Ministry of Mines and Energy, the Government of Antioquia, and Corantioquia among other contributors.[52] It is noteworthy that the Government of Canada is not one of the supporters. By October 2014, this process has formalized 2,000 miners and created among them 34 small mining companies. The company indicates that it pays its formalized miners 50 percent of gold's commercial value in the country, and that there are honest standards used to determine how much gold is extracted from the crude material delivered by miners.[53]

Those miners who welcome the initiative of the company through the formalization of labour are exempt from the application of a law that would lead to their expulsion from the territory in which the GCG has the mining rights in perpetuity. Further, the company indicated that mining formalization produces other benefits, for example, it:

> ...provides miners health benefits and pensions, training in health and safety, and [a] safer working environment.... The miners and their families receive regular payments, can open bank accounts and can have access to mortgages and loans. The quality of life increases as miners can support their families and plan their future.[54]

The company estimates that over 6,000 new bank accounts have been opened since it arrived in the region.[55] GCG argues that because it pays significant taxes, this revenue helps social programs throughout the country.[56] According to Gran Colombia Gold Corporation, this kind of business model permits the miner, the State, and the company to win collectively.

Further, the company has emphasized that is has the law on its side. Gran Colombia Gold indicates that according a census conducted by the Government of Antioquia and the National Agency of Mining in 2012, there are 196 illegal mines on the company's site in Segovia. The company said it has given those miners who are operating illegally the option of formalization. It insists that this is good not only for the miners themselves, but also for the community and the country since the standards of mining are applied, the population receives social services, taxes are paid, and so on.[57]

Right to Political Participation

In the case of Segovia and Remedios, the right to political participation is related to the debate regarding the outsourcing of work. We saw that miners claim that when they are outsourced by a company linked to GCG, it prevents them from having direct political relations with the corporation, thus limiting their capacity for meaningful discussion and negotiation. Miners also complained about the firing of 320 people, which they said had been due to their recent unionization. But Jorge Ignacio Noguera, Vice President of Corporate Affairs of Gran Colombia Gold, argued that

...due to reasons out of our reach – such as the fall of the price of gold, the illegal exploitation of titles, the high costs we have to pay for security, the lack of infrastructure – the contract with Strategies and Mines S.A. was terminated.[58]

Further, a legal decision reached by the local court on February 21, 2014 ruled that, on the one hand, Strategies and Mines made a series of violations related to its settlement with workers. But on the other hand, as noted earlier, it upheld that Strategies and Mines and GCG are legally two separate companies.[59]

Communication between the corporation, its workers, and the community represents an important part of conflict resolution mechanisms that can promote human security. As we saw, some miners have criticized its capacity for representation within the company. In response to this, GCG indicates that "it has a mechanism through which workers can file complaints anonymously about methods deemed questionable by them. This procedure is done via Internet on the website of Global Corporate Compliance Inc."[60] It is important to note that the web page is written in English and not Spanish, and includes a level of writing that may exceed the educational level of a miner in the region. However, Gran Colombia Gold indicates that besides the web page, it maintains two permanent offices in Remedios and Segovia that provide service to the workers and community.[61]

Right to Environment

Gran Colombia Gold, since arriving in Segovia and Remedios, has recognized the situation of environmental pollution. María Consuelo Araujo, the former CEO of GCG, said "the company has found a terrible public health situation caused by illegal mining which indiscriminately uses highly hazardous chemicals such as mercury and cyanide."[62] Gran Colombia indicates that it hopes to resolve this problem through training and technology transfer. Carolina Flórez, Chief Executive Officer of Zandor Capital, (the affiliate of Gran Colombia Gold Corporation in the region) said "Gradually we will transfer methods and training to small-scale mining associations, which are within the law, to mine without polluting the natural resources of our country, and to do so without jeopardizing miners' health."[63] Further, the company argues that "there are significant environmental benefits for the community of Segovia because the Gran Colombia Gold processing plant operates in a manner that eliminates mercury exposure."[64] GCG indicates that between 2012 and 2014, its programs of formalization and cyanide use have reduced by 15 tons the use of mercury in the region, and that its work is supported by the Global Mercury Project of the United Nations Organization for Industrial Development.[65] Still, locals are concerned about the mercury already in the ecosystem, and are also very concerned about the effects of cyanide on the population.

Corporate Social Responsibility

Gran Colombia Gold Corporation's perception of its Corporate Social Responsibility contribution in the region is radically distinct from that of other social actors in Segovia and Remedios, who suggest that there is little social investment by the company in their territories. The website of GCG mentions "our social and community programs are designed as catalysts for positive and lasting contributions in the communities where we do business."[66] Carolina Flórez, Chief Executive Officer of Zandor Capital, indicated the company's commitment to CSR through the sponsorship of programs like "*eye care day* that benefit people who have limited access to health services in the mining district."[67] In this same vein, José Oro, Vice President of the GCG, spoke about the school that "we have maintained"[68] and which subsequently has been transferred to the government.

Further, Gran Colombia Gold Corporation indicated that in late 2014 it was developing a plan to prioritize its goals in the realm of Corporate Social Responsibility, and was also developing a plan concerning how best to communicate with host communities. The corporation considers its current project of formalizing traditional miners to be the centerpiece of its CSR programs. It also notes that it is committed to eliminating child labour in the mines.

Part of the reason host communities may undervalue Gran Colombia Gold's CSR contributions is that there is an expectation that the corporation will replace the role of the State in the provision of social services. While this is understandable in context, it is an unreasonable task for the TNC to fulfill. Further, many local miners view the formalization process as an expensive proposition for them, since they suggest that they receive less than half of the income than they would if they operated illegally. This is because formalization involves deductions for taxes, pensions, the provision of social services, etc. These workers, then, see themselves as paying for the formalization process, and do not consider it to be a benefit bestowed on them in the form of CSR from Gran Colombia Gold Corporation.

The State

The Role of the State in the FTA

The State has the responsibility to prevent the violation of human rights and to take the necessary measures to make reparations when violations occur. But the Colombian State is notoriously weak, and violations of human rights, and to human security, often occur within a context of impunity. The Director of Mining Control for the Department of Antioquia indicated that "Segovia is a place where the State has had no credibility among the people, the government historically has been absent in that territory."[69] Similarly, the Secretary of Government of Segovia said "life here has been forgotten by the government ... the government has a very large social debt with Segovia."[70] This absence of the State has facilitated the violation of human security in the region.

Despite its historical absence, and some persistent problems, the situation has begun to improve with increased State security forces that started to arrive in 2010 with the presence of Gran Colombia Gold Corporation. A representative for miners suggested in 2013 that "for at least two or three years the State "is beginning to take care of the region."[71] The Director of Mining Control for Antioquia suggested that that "the State has gained ground ... since GCG arrived."[72] While improvements have been made, no one disputes the huge power of illegal armed groups, and workers have claimed to be victims of a variety of human rights abuses. Once again, what is clear is that the situation is very nuanced.

Right to Life

The launching of the Trojan Plan in 2012 has bolstered the security of the region. This military action has had as its central purpose the eradication of illegal armed groups that are involved in the intimidation and extortion of the community, especially those engaged in mining. Due to this type of State action, the president of the Association of Informal Miners of Segovia and Remedios (Asomina) indicated that "the Trojan Plan has brought very good results, especially by reducing extortion and insecurity. Many small miners and companies who had to leave the region have returned."[73] The representative of Segovia also stated that by increasing the number of armed forces, general security seems to have improved in the area.[74] Similarly, the president of the union Sintramiser said that he has not received any threat to his life. All this creates a scenario that suggests that since the arrival of GCG in the region, the protection of the right to life by the State has been improved significantly,[75] and that the community has benefited from this. But the context is nuanced. While security forces have increased, the booming production of gold continued to attract illegal armed groups and associated deleterious effects.

Right to Work

Let us classify into three groups the sectors of workers that have been affected by the possible violation of the right to work – informal miners, formalized miners, and those dismissed by the company. Informal miners have stated that the arrival of the company has threatened their right to mine. The position of the State at the regional level regarding these events is that:

> ...we must take into consideration the real situation, there is a mining company who is an owner. It is impossible to take the ownership away from the company and give it to the people. That is illegal, and that will never happen.[76]

From this view, GCG's threat to remove illegal mines from its property is consistent with the law, and also requires protection from the State to enforce this law. The problematic issue is the clash between the State's upholding of this law of private property, versus the rights of traditional miners without title who have mined the region long before GCG arrived. In other words, the State is fulfilling its duty to the Canadian transnational corporation, but at the same time has failed traditional miners. It is the historical absence of the State that is the central reason for miners not having legal title to their mines. This represents an important problem that requires political will and the creation of conflict resolution institutions.

The State supports formalization of miners, but appears to be willing to let the corporation, and not the State, take the lead in this process. The Government of Antioquia praises Gran Colombia Gold Corporation for advances GCG has made in formalizing or legalizing traditional miners, since this decreases what the government views as traditional labour lawlessness in the area. In this regard, the Director of Mining Control in the Antioquia Department indicated that the general idea is "to legalize and formalize informal miners to work within the law, and to meet all legal standards; you are giving them operating contracts to demonstrate their legality and to avoid having to remove them by force."[77] From the perspective of the government of Antioquia, formalization is the best and only option.

Further, from the perspective of the regional State or department, the formalization of mining also creates greater security for the miners: "The State has opted to formalize mining units because informality creates risks for the miners … one way or another, and this is the truth, informality can fund armed groups."[78] Formalization appears as a way of protecting miners from criminal mining practices. But again, formalization in this case is "privatized", since it is the corporation that conducts the process.

Second, let us turn to the plight of miners in the process of formalization, and their relation to the State. With formalization comes legal duties that are expensive, such as the provision of social programs, pensions, and so on. The contentious issue arises as to who is to pay for this. This is especially problematic in a region not used to government policies or taxation. The government has argued, quite bluntly, that "legality implies diminishing returns, it implies that people pay social security and invest in having security."[79] Formalized miners receive less money for their gold through GCG because the company is essentially charging them fees for the training involved in the process as well as for the social benefits that result from it. Miners wonder if they are getting proper compensation under this kind of formalization, and wish they had proper input into the creation of such policies.

Formalized miners have also complained that the company violates their right to work because it imposes unilateral contracts. GCG pays the miner for his product at a rate the company determines is correct, but this price is often disputed by miners. The government does not intervene in this dispute because the State cannot be involved in "mediating the employment relationship."[80] In so doing, much power is concentrated in the corporation and it is the miners that are placed in a compromised position.

The third sector of workers considered here are the group of employees who claim they were outsourced by GCG and have been illegally dismissed.

A representative of the Ministry of Labour said: "The mining Code states that the owner of a mine can give all or part of its mine to [a] third party to exploit it."[81] To prove legally that a company outsources or intermediates, it would be necessary to show that they are owned by or work for Gran Colombia Gold Corporation. According to representatives of the State, is not possible to demonstrate this. This relationship requires further legal examination to ensure that policies regulating outsourcing are clearly upheld.

Moreover, GCG's affiliate companies preside over the formalization process. According to the director of Mining Control of the Department, we are "formalizing miners through companies so they are not illegal and so that they produce gold in a regulated manner."[82] From the perspective of the State, rather than breaking the law, the company is developing a fully adequate model of extraction within the departmental and national mining policy. He added that "with 3,000 legalized miners working on a pilot program, it has been discussed how to take this program elsewhere in the country."[83] Once again, the Colombian State wants to see the GCG model of formalization spread elsewhere, thereby ceding to the corporation a function normally performed by the State itself.

Right to Environment

The State is beginning to appreciate the importance of environmental improvement in the region. The representative of mining supervision of the Department of Antioquia indicated that "the protection of the environment is a message that must be demonstrated in Segovia. If you stop using mercury and use clean technology, you will recover your investment and you will gain profit. This is a powerful message."[84] But there is a deeper, underlying problem.

It is important to emphasize that State environmental regulation of mining activity usually strives for damage reduction rather than damage prevention or elimination. A level of continued environmental destruction is permitted to occur along its historic accumulation that, in the case of Segovia and Remedios, has reached the highest in the world in terms of mercury pollution. Human security is surely threatened to the extreme under such circumstances. The major challenge here is to determine how much more, if any, environmental destruction is permissible in the region, and how best to reduce the impact of existing pollution on people and the environment.

Corporate Social Responsibility

Corporate Social Responsibility is not mandatory, it is left to the discretion of the companies. But the State does have a role in promoting CSR on the part of extractive corporations, especially since the State itself is so weak and looks to CSR to fill obvious gaps. The director of the Mining Supervision Department said that "an article of the Mining Code states that companies will need to have a social license to access the territory. But it is not clear what this is."[85] This is an important ambiguity.

This official relates social responsibility to GCG's formalization project.

When Gran Colombia arrived to the territory, it faced a reality: there are people exploiting gold illegally in this area. Therefore it had to take a practical and political decision. It can either displace them, or negotiate with them to achieve formalization.[86]

But the problem is much bigger than the 3,000 member pilot program in the region to legalize artisanal miners. There are estimated to be some 300,000 traditional miners throughout the country.

The Canadian government also has an important role to play here. The Vice President of Gran Colombia Gold indicated that his company very much welcomes the assistance of the Canadian Government with regard to the wider project of formalizing traditional miners in Colombia. "We need the direct support of the Government of Canada to reach this goal."[87] Certainly the Canadian Government can help much more than it has with regard to human security and the extractive sector in Colombia, and we shall return to this point below.

Conclusions and Recommendations

For Colombia, the solution to problems related to human rights and well-being in extractive communities involves the development of a new national mining policy and a program related to the promotion of human security. Such policies would take into account the multitude of issues we have seen in the case of Segovia and Remedios. These include the proper route to formalization, dealing with the challenge of ecocide, eradicating illegal armed groups that feed off the extractive sector, the establishment of strong tripartite negotiation structures, and so on.

Of particular concern is the huge group of miners who the State has recently criminalized – the 300,000 or so traditional or artisanal miners. In the case of Segovia and Remedios, one important dimension concerns those who refuse to be formalized in a manner unilaterally determined by Gran Colombia Gold Corporation. The company launched 35 court injunctions to remove informal miners from its property[88] and out of these four have been enacted as of this writing.[89] It is estimated that informal mining settlements in the area number around 120.[90] A national mining code needs to come to terms with the best way to formalize these miners, and to determine whether the route is through the State or through business. It needs to appreciate the enormous institutional requirements involved to achieve this. This represents a key area for foreign assistance, especially in terms of building State capacity for regulation and conflict resolution.

The human security theme of environmental sustainability is central to the creation of a national mining policy, as the Segovia and Remedios case demonstrates. The absence of the State appears as one of the key factors here. Important questions that require attention are: What level of environmental damage is acceptable? How can the best environmental practices be implemented as soon as possible? What are the best methods to reverse, where possible, accumulated environmental damage? How can human and environmental health be strengthened under such challenging conditions?

A national mining policy might also address the theme of Corporate Social Responsibility. It could seek to delineate exactly what roles are planned for the future development of the State, and which roles should be performed by corporations. Coordination of CSR policies from a variety of corporations though a country-wide mining policy could lead to better overall results by creating a synergy between them.

A national policy also needs to take into account the wide cultural fabric of the country. The clash between the government and 300,000 traditional miners that the government calls "illegal" is also a clash of cultures – between the traditional culture of gold mining in Colombia that has lasted for centuries and the recent corporate culture that is dominated by Canadian TNCs. Thus, a national mining policy needs to appreciate cultural realities, and contend with these in order to resolve conflict.

The national mining agreement would also need to appreciate the social responses to any newfound growth in the State. With Colombia having had such a weak State for so long, there are many implications to consider in this regard. On a legal level, traditional mining has involved oral agreements regarding investments and wages. The shift to written legal contracts requires a State-led outreach or education program. Formalization, and the creation of new legal structures for mining, requires the development of an enormous bureaucracy and the generation of funding to achieve this. Much thought would need to be devoted to how a larger State structure could ensure efficiency and accessibility.

There is also the issue of taxation. The government can help informal workers and the marginalized in highly important areas, including the provision of social security, the prevention of occupational hazards, the provision of stable wages, the enforcement of union rights, the enforcement of working hour regulations, the exclusion of child labour, and so on. But in practical terms, to achieve this would mean the collection of taxes from those in the informal sector that have not previously paid them. We noted claims above that formalized miners with GCG earn less than half of the take-home wages of an informal miner, with the difference apparently made up by social welfare provisions, economic security, and mandatory training. So the establishment of a fair tax system, and a tax culture, requires considerable development. It requires social dialogue with all concerned. This is an area of capacity building in which foreign governments such as Canada can help.

A key factor for resolving conflict is tripartite dialogue between miners, the corporation, and host communities. One milestone toward this was that the national mining strike of 2013 led to the establishment of forums for dialogue between informal miners and the national government. Miners from Northeast Antioquia have engaged in workshops to address their concerns and complaints. While this dialogue is useful, it also needs to involve business. So far, dialogue has stalled, despite the promise of the Santos Government to propel the negotiations and resolve an important pole of rural conflict. Overall, this case study has demonstrated that better dialogue needs to be established between miners, the government, workers, and host communities.

Finally with regard to State development in Colombia, there have been some important advances, but huge gaps remain. There is a clear plan in place to increase the local presence of Corantioquia (the departmental environmental authority) and the National Mining Agency. This additional environmental regulation is highly welcome. It would also be desirable for the Ministry of Labour to draft a special labour regime concerning mining to address the continued controversy over whether or not, in legal terms, companies such as GCG outsource employment in the mining sector.

Regarding the Canadian government, capacity building for Colombia in the areas listed above would help. We noted that Gran Colombia Gold has expressed its strong support for help from Ottawa regarding the strengthening of the process of formalization for Colombia's traditional miners. The Canadian government might also do a more thorough job of monitoring the human security record of Canadian extractive corporations in Colombia. It could assist them to do a better job where possible.

The central recommendation for Gran Colombia Gold is to promote better political inclusion and transparency. The company should consider increasing its dialogue with workers and the community. It would be helpful if this occurred in a tripartite framework that also included the State, so that all major parties are united to resolve conflict. Further, a better and more accessible grievance mechanism for workers and communities needs to be created regarding the activities of Gran Colombia Gold. This needs to provide security for those launching concerns or complaints. There also needs to be a fair and expeditious grievance mechanism established that is consistent with the cultural conditions of the region.

HRIAs and Global Lessons from the Segovia and Remedios Case

HRIAs, in both their corporate and governmental forms, could help improve the prospects for human security in Segovia and Remedios. If the company had implemented a corporate HRIA, it could have anticipated key problem areas and dealt with these. A primary problem is the manner in which Gran Colombia Gold hires workers, that is, through contractors. This is at the heart of many concerns raised by workers and unions. For workers, this can limit their capacity to communicate directly to the corporation, and can provide the corporation with a shield against allegations of unfair labour treatment, human rights abuses, and so on. The problem remains unaddressed, but an early treatment of it through an HRIA would have provided more harmony between the corporation and its workers. This point is relevant to other cases globally where contract workers are dominant in the extractive industry.

A corporate HRIA can also assist GCG with dealing more effectively with the nuances surrounding the historical absence of the Colombian State. This is an important global implication for any TNC in the Global South where the host country is weak. As we have seen, one aspect of this is that the community often expects the corporation to fill the role abandoned by the State. This leads to disappointment and resentment among community members, and frustration for the corporation due to what it views as unfair expectations. The Colombian government has encouraged this through its support of a corporate-led, rather than State-led, process of formalization for traditional miners.

A significant problem that should be addressed in a corporate HRIA for this case is the effect of the presence of GCG on established patterns of violence in the community. The recent bolstering of armed forces has helped reduce the influence of criminal organizations in the area, but they remain powerful. We have observed allegations that the murder of some workers may have been related to their criticism of the company. Death threats have also been hurled, and these can be as powerful as actual murders in silencing a population through fear. In short, an HRIA can provide practical assistance by outlining likely security threats and seeking practical solutions.

An HRIA would also address the huge ecological threat to human security in the region. While cyanide may be less toxic than mercury, extensive pollution by both cyanide and historically from mercury threatens local water supplies and local health. The corporation alone cannot resolve this problem, but an HRIA could point to partners and approaches that address the situation and that attempt to better protect to the health and well-being of community members.

Regarding the governmental HRIA involved in the Canada–Colombia Free Trade Agreement, the case suggests key questions that can generate important indicators to measure threats to human security: How does Canadian investment play into existing webs of violence and security threats, and how will this impact the corporation and the community? What security measures, and social programs, are most effective in reducing such threats? Another set of indicators would pertain to sustainable development. Given the vast extent of contamination already present in the Segovia and Remedios region, what further degree of environmental destruction is tolerable? How can any existing health threats to community members be addressed, and who are the appropriate partners for this?

A governmental HRIA, by both Colombia and Canada, should also address the huge issue of traditional miners in Colombia, and examine the best path towards formalization. The case of Segovia and Remedios demonstrates a corporate path to legalization for miners, but elsewhere this is a vital task of the State. When a corporation unilaterally implements such a process, this concentrates power in the corporation and provides the worker with little power or voice. Rather than empowering the majority, power is concentrated in the corporation. The HRIA needs to analyze this situation in a manner that is fair toward traditional miners, and make a clear and considered determination as to whether the State or the corporation should preside over the legalization of artisanal miners.

A governmental HRIA is best conducted by a third party group of experts from a variety of disciplines. They can provide a balanced view of the overall context of the investment site, and harness the expertise of a variety of fields to formulate helpful suggestions. A third party team to address the case of Segovia and Remedios through an HRIA might involve environmental scientists, water engineers, political scientists, sociologists, legal experts, labour specialists, and anthropologists.

Notes

1 This research involved interviews with various actors involved in the mining conflict in the Segovia-Remedios district. Interviews were conducted with the informed consent of each of the interviewees.
2 Amnesty International, Colombia, "Segovia," November 1996, www.amnestyinternational.org. Accessed February 26, 2014.
3 From 1852 to 2010 mining was performed by the Frontino Gold Mines and since that year by the Gran Colombia Gold.
4 Interview with Hambler Patiño. Representative of Remedios Municipality. December 2, 2013.
5 Grupo de Memoria Historica, 2010.
6 Interview with Hambler Patiño. Representative of Remedios Municipality. December 2, 2013.
7 See: "Guerra de oro en Colombia", (2012). National Geographic. In: www.youtube.com/watch?v=BxaXXo87mQI, accessed January 18, 2014.
8 Interview with Hambler Patiño. Representative of Remedios Municipality. December 2, 2013.
9 Interview with the representative of Cahucopana Organization (Corporation of Humanitarian Action Coexistence and Peace in Northeast Antioquia). Medellín. February 25, 2014. For security reasons the name is omitted.
10 Cahucopana, 2013, 16. Parenthesis were added.
11 Cahucopana, 2012.
12 Interview with Hambler Patiño. Representative of Remedios Municipality. December 2, 2013.
13 Interview with Darío Londoño. President of Sintramiser Union. December 3, 2013.
14 Interview with Carlos Franqui Arango. Government Secretary of Segovia Municipality. December 3, 2013.
15 Interview with Hambler Patiño. Representative of Remedios Municipality. December 2, 2013.
16 Interview with Carlos Franqui Arango. Government Secretary of Segovia Municipality. December 3, 2013.
17 Rama Legislativa Colombiana. Ley 685 de 2001 (Código de Minas). Art. 27. In: www.simco.gov.co/Portals/0/ley685.pdf. Accessed September 1, 2014.
18 Interview with Carlos Franqui Arango. Government Secretary of Segovia Municipality. December 3, 2013.
19 Interview with Hernando Henao. President of the Union of Informal Miners of Segovia and Remedios (Asomina). February 19, 2014.
20 Interview with Carlos Franqui Arango. Government Secretary of Segovia Municipality. December 3, 2013.
21 Interview with Hernando Henao. President of the Union of Informal Miners of Segovia and Remedios (Asomina). February 19, 2014.
22 Interview with Darío Londoño. President of Sintramiser Union. December 3, 2013.
23 Interview with Darío Londoño. President of Sintramiser Union. December 3, 2013.
24 Interview with Hambler Patiño. Representative of Remedios Municipality. December 2, 2013.
25 Interview with Carlos Franqui Arango. Government Secretary of Segovia Municipality. December 3, 2013.
26 Interview with Darío Londoño. President of Sintramiser Union. December 3, 2013.
27 Interview with Marla Uribe. Labour Inspector of the Northeast Area of Antioquia. February 20, 2014.
28 Apparently there is a certain pattern of actions that characterize the births and deaths of firms (companies), especially when a union is formed. Further studies could establish the composition of capital and executive bodies of the companies to refine the accuracy of the financial practice.

29 Interview with Darío Londoño. President of Sintramiser Union. December 3, 2013.
30 Interview with Darío Londoño. President of Sintramiser Union. December 3, 2013.
31 Interview with Hambler Patiño. Representative of Remedios Municipality. December 2, 2013.
32 Interview with Carlos Franqui Arango. Government Secretary of Segovia Municipality. December 3, 2013.
33 Interview with Darío Londoño. President of Sintramiser Union. December 3, 2013.
34 Although Gran Colombia Gold Corporation has its own workers, different from the miners being formalized, it was impossible to access these workers because the company did not address our request for interviews with its staff.
35 Gran Colombia Gold Corporation has a web page and a form to file complaints, but it is in English, which generates constraints for the mining population.
36 Interviews with Darío Londoño. President of Sintramiser Union. December 3, 2013 and with Hernando Henao. President of the Union of Informal Miners of Segovia and Remedios (Asomina). February 19, 2014. See Ministerio de Medio Ambiente, Government of Colombia, www.camara.gov.co/.../gestor.../5335–2013-prop-115-res-min-ambiente, viewed September 9, 2014.
37 Interview with Hambler Patiño. Representative of Remedios Municipality. December 2, 2013.
38 Interview with a miner worker from Segovia. Medellín. November 18, 2013. Due to security reason the name of the miner is omitted.
39 Interview with Luisa Fernanda Rivera. Representative of Segovia City Hall. December 3, 2013.
40 El Colombiano, March 6, 2014.
41 FTA Colombia–Canada, 2010, 60.
42 Interview with Hambler Patiño. Representative of Remedios Municipality. December 2, 2013.
43 Interview with Jairo Arango Londoño. Finance Secretary of Segovia. February 19, 2014.
44 The acquisition of mining rights by Gran Colombia Gold Corporation has been questioned by workers of the Frontino Gold Mines, because, for them, the rightful owners of the mines are the miners themselves. They refer to the so called New York Act of 1979, which they say suggests that Frontino owners should have yielded to their workers the title of the mine as compensation to them for the payment of their debt to the company.
45 Gran Colombia Gold, 2014. En: www.grancolombiagold.com. Accessed September 10, 2014.
46 Gran Colombia Gold, 2014. En: www.grancolombiagold.com. Accessed September 10, 2014.
47 National Geographic, 2012.
48 Roméo Langlois & Pascale Mariani, 2012.
49 Portafolio, November 8, 2010.
50 Gran Colombia Gold, 2014. En: www.grancolombiagold.com.
51 El Colombiano, September 27, 2010.
52 Correspondence by authors with Jose Ignacio Noguera, Vice President, Corporate Responsibility, Gran Colombia Gold Corporation, response in writing to questions posed by authors and dated October 12, 2014.
53 Ibid.
54 Gran Colombia Gold Corporation, 2014. En: www.grancolombiagold.com. Accessed September 10, 2014.
55 Correspondence by authors with Jose Noguera, op. cit.
56 Gran Colombia Gold Corporation, 2014. En: www.grancolombiagold.com. Accessed September 10, 2014.
57 Correspondence with author by Jose Noguera, Vice President, GCG, op. cit.
58 Caracol Radio, January 30, 2014.

59 Segovia, Antioquia, Antioquia Judicial District, Municipal Court, 2014, 26, added brackets.
60 Gran Colombia Gold Corporation, 2014. En: www.grancolombiagold.com. Accessed September 10, 2014.
61 Correspondence with authors from Jose Noguera, Vice President GCG, op. cit.
62 Portafolio, November 8, 2010.
63 Portafolio, November 8, 2010.
64 Gran Colombia Gold Corporation, 2014. En: www.grancolombiagold.com. Accessed September 10, 2014.
65 Correspondence with authors from Jose Noguera, Vice Presidente, GCG, op. cit.
66 Gran Colombia Gold, 2014. En: www.grancolombiagold.com.
67 Portafolio, November 8, 2010.
68 Roméo Langlois & Pascale Mariani, 2012.
69 Interview with Giovani Caro Uribe. Director of Mining Control of the Department of Antioquia. Medellín. December 20, 2013.
70 Interview with Carlos Franqui Arango. Government Secretary of Segovia Municipality. December 3, 2013.
71 Interview with Carlos Franqui Arango. Government Secretary of Segovia Municipality. December 3, 2013.
72 Interview with Giovani Caro Uribe. Director of Mining Control of the Department. Medellín. December 20, 2013.
73 Interview with Hernando Henao. President of the Union of Informal Miners of Segovia and Remedios (Asomina). February 19, 2014.
74 Interview with Luisa Fernanda Rivera. Representative of the City Hall of Segovia. December 3, 2013.
75 As described in the first part of the chapter, Remedios' municipal representative deviates from this diagnosis. For him, the presence of the company has encouraged illegal armed groups to victimize the population. Thus, the State has failed in its role to protect the population.
76 Interview with Giovani Caro Uribe. Director of Mining Control of the Department. Medellín. December 20, 2013.
77 Interview with Giovani Caro Uribe. Director of Mining Control of the Department. Medellín. December 20, 2013.
78 Interview with Giovani Caro Uribe. Director of Mining Control of the Department. Medellín. December 20, 2013.
79 Interview with Giovani Caro Uribe. Director of Mining Control of the Department. Medellín. December 20, 2013.
80 Interview with Giovani Caro Uribe. Director of Mining Control of the Department. Medellín. December 20, 2013.
81 Interview with Marla Uribe. Labour Inspector of the Northeast Zone. February 20, 2014.
82 Interview with Giovani Caro Uribe. Director of Mining Control of the Department. Medellín. December 20, 2013.
83 Interview with Giovani Caro Uribe. Director of Mining Control of the Department. Medellín. December 20, 2013.
84 Interview with Giovani Caro Uribe. Director of Mining Control of the Department. Medellín. December 20, 2013.
85 Interview with Giovani Caro Uribe. Director of Mining Control of the Department. Medellín. December 20, 2013.
86 Interview with Giovani Caro Uribe. Director of Mining Control of the Department. Medellín. December 20, 2013.
87 Correspondence with authors from Jose Noguera, Vice President of GCG, op. cit.
88 Interview with Carlos Franqui Arango. Government Secretary of Segovia Municipality. December 3rd, 2013.

89 Interview with Hernando Henao. President of the Union of Informal Miners of Segovia and Remedios (Asomina). February 19, 2014.
90 Interview with Carlos Franqui Arango. Government Secretary of Segovia Municipality. December 3, 2013.

Bibliography

Amnesty International. *Colombia: Segovia: A Recurring History of Serious Human Rights Violations.* November 1, 1996. Accessed February 26, 2014. www.amnesty.org/en/library/asset/AMR23/061/1996/en/0df7aa30-eace-11dd-b6f5-3be39665bc30/amr230611996en.pdf.

Botero, Laura Victoria. "La Zandor Capital comienza operaciones." *El Colombiano*, September 27, 2010. Accessed February 26, 2014. www.elcolombiano.com/Banco Conocimiento/L/la_zandor_capital_comienza_operaciones/la_zandor_capital_comienza_operaciones.asp.

Cahucopana. "En alto riesgo vida de familia minera en el municipio de Segovia a causa de persecución paramilitar." 2012. Accessed November 20, 2013. http://cahucopana.blogspot.com/2012/10/denuncia-publica-en-alto-riesgo-vida-de.html.

Cancillería de Colombia. *Segundo informe anual del acuerdo en materia de informes anuales sobre derechos humanos y libre comercio entre la república de Colombia y Canadá.* Bogotá: 2013.

Caracol Radio. "Empresa Zandor Capital explica el despido de 320 mineros en Antioquia." January 30, 2014. Accessed February 26, 2014. www.caracol.com.co/noticias/regionales/empresa-zandor-capital-explica-el-despido-de-320-mineros-en-antioquia/20140130/nota/2066220.aspx.

Corporación Acción Humanitaria por la Convivencia y la Paz del Nordeste Antioqueño–Cahucopana. *Informe sobre la situación de los derechos humanos y del derecho internacional humanitario en el nordeste Antioqueño, Año 2012.* Nordeste Antioqueño. Nodo Antioquia: 2013.

Dinero. "Gran Colombia Gold se integra formalmente con Medoro Resources." June 13, 2011. Accessed May 10, 2013. www.dinero.com/negocios/articulo/grancolombiagold-integra-formalmente-medoro-resources/121309.

Gran Colombia Gold. www.grancolombiagold.com. Accessed September 10, 2014.

Grupo de Memoria Histórica. "Silenciar la democracia: Las masacres de remedios y Segovia 1982–1997." Bogotá: Taurus, 2010.

Langlois, Roméo and Pascale Mariani. "Por todo el oro de Colombia." Documentary film. 51:28. 2012. Posted to Vimeo by "alaksandush". Accessed July 17, 2014. http://vimeo.com/43866542.

Matta Colorado, Nelson. "El hospital y un vecindario de Segovia se caen a pedazos." *El Colombiano*, March 6, 2014. Accessed March 6, 2014. www.elcolombiano.com/BancoConocimiento/E/el_hospital_y_un_vecindario_de_segovia_se_caen_a_pedazos/el_hospital_y_un_vecindario_de_segovia_se_caen_a_pedazos.asp.

National Geographic Explorer. "La guerra del oro en Colombia." Documentary film. 44:59. Posted to YouTube by "lanuevageneracion", August 22, 2013. Accessed January 18, 2014. www.youtube.com/watch?v=j0unmbPWMO4.

Periferia Prensa. "¿Qué pasa con la Frontino Gold Mines en Segovia?" March 15, 2011. Accessed May 14, 2013. www.periferiaprensa.org/index.php/ediciones-anteriores/100-ediciones-anteriores/edicion-60-marzo-2011/638-ique-pasa-con-la-frontino-gold-mines-en-segovia.

Portafolio. "Frontino Gold Mines dejó de existir luego de una agonía de 35 años." March 15, 2011. Accessed February 28, 2014. www.portafolio.co/economia/frontino-gold-mines-dejo-existir.

Portafolio. "Gran Colombia Gold emprenderá batalla contra el uso del mercurio en minas." November 8, 2010. Accessed February 26, 2014. www.portafolio.co/economia/gran-colombia-gold-emprendera-batalla-contra-el-uso-del-merc.

Rama Legislativa Colombiana. Ley 685 de 2001 (Código de Minas). Art. 27. Accessed February 26, 2014. www.simco.gov.co/Portals/0/ley685.pdf.

Salazar Vargas, Carlos. *Políticas Públicas y Think Tanks.* Bogotá: Konrad Adenau Stiftung, 2008.

Segovia, Antioquia. Distrito Judicial de Antioquia. Juzgado Promiscuo Municipal. Fallo de tutela N. 00015–2014, February 21, 2014.

TLC Colombia-Canadá. Bogotá: Presidencia de la República de Colombia, 2010.

Vídeos

National Geographic (2012), "Guerra de oro en Colombia". En: www.youtube.com/watch?v=BxaXXo87mQI (Accessed January 18, 2014).

Roméo Langlois & Pascale Mariani (2012), "Por todo el oro de Colombia". En: http://vimeo.com/43866542 (Accessed July 13, 2014).

5 Open Pit Coal Mining in Northern Colombia

Institutional Weakness and the Supremacy of Capital

*Gustavo Rodríguez Albor,
Jairo Agudelo Taborda, and
Ibelis Blanco Rangel*

This chapter examines the case of La Caypa open pit coal mine, which is operated by Pacific Coal Resources Ltd. and located in the department of La Guajira. It analyzes its social effects on the small and isolated communities of Chancleta and Patilla, where the rights of the foreign investor appear to prevail over community interests. The coal mine's operations have produced threats to the human security of community residents. These issues include community displacement, the mine's contamination of the air and water, the loss for many of their traditional economy, labour rights, as well as health problems possibly linked to the mine. The root of this problem is the profound weakness of Colombian political institutions to exercise effective control over foreign investors. What is particularly noteworthy about this case is the tininess of these isolated communities. Hence, this study examines the challenges to achieve human security for a population that lacks the demographic power of the other cases in this volume.

These problems can be addressed successfully, and result in a situation that achieves social benefits for the community as well as a stable and eager workforce for the company. This solution involves strengthening the State's regulatory capacity, increasing the extent and efficacy of Corporate Social Responsibility (CSR) programs by Transnational Corporations (TNCs), and better organization and strategy among community residents to achieve a stronger political influence over community affairs. The case study also discusses important threats to human security that can serve as useful indicators for corporate and governmental Human Rights Impact Assessments (HRIAs).

Context of Coal Mining in Colombia

High commodity prices, the business friendly investment policies of the Canada–Colombia Free Trade Agreement (CCFTA), and support given by the State to the "mining and energy locomotive" of the country,[1] have created incentives that promote coal mining in Colombia. At the moment, the mining sector accounts for about 9 percent of the total Colombian GDP.[2] The El Cerrejón area, where the La Caypa mine is located, contains 90 percent of the coal reserves of the nation.

Mining is historically entrenched in Colombia. It is inherited from the colonial period, when the exploitation of gold was dominant in the country. Oil exploitation gained national prominence in about 1910, within the global context of growing automobile production and the proliferation of industries that relied on petroleum for energy. Also around the turn of the century mining companies in isolated regions of Colombia witnessed technological innovations such as electric lighting, motorized trucks and excavators, and so on. The arrival of the first steam railroads in Colombia in the early twentieth century, and the increasing thirst for coal among burgeoning industries, propelled coal mining in the country.[3] New mines opened in the departments of Cundinamarca, Boyacá, Antioquia, and Valle. With the dawn of globalization and greater demand for coal, in the 1980s the huge coal deposits of El Cerrejón prompted large-scale exploitation through foreign investment.

According to the Mining and Energy Planning Unit (UPME) of the Ministry of Mines and Energy, Colombia is the country with the largest coal reserves in Latin America. In 2015 it has potential resources of 16.992 million tons (Mt) of which 7.063 Mt are measured, 4.571 Mt are indicated, 4.237 Mt are inferred, and 1.119 Mt are hypothetical resources. Furthermore, Colombia is the sixth largest exporter of coal in the world, with a market share of 6.3 percent, equivalent to 50 Mt of coal annually.

The world's largest open pit coal mine, known as Cerrejón, is located in the department of La Guajira. It spans a vein of carbon that is about 60 kilometers in length. It yields high quality product, and is classified as high-volatile bituminous coal. This variety has low contents of moisture, ash, and sulphur, which makes it particularly competitive in the international market. The mining area of the Cerrejón hosts about 50 percent of Colombian coal exports, and 30 percent of the country's traditional exports.[4]

The main economic activities of the department of La Guajira are mining (coal and sea salt), followed by commerce and tourism. At the moment, coal mining accounts for over 50 percent of its Gross Domestic Product (GDP). However, this activity represented only 2 percent in 1975, and so the huge social implications of mass mining are relatively recent for the region. El Cerrejón is divided into three areas: the North Zone, which has measured reserves of 3,000 Mt; the Central Zone, where La Caypa mine operates, with measured reserves of 670 Mt; and the South Zone, with coal reserves of 263 Mt. In these areas coal is exploited by TNCs, and the largest and most important of these is Carbones del Cerrejón Limited (CCL). It is jointly owned by foreign companies including BHP Billiton, Anglo American, and Xstrata Glencore.

La Caypa, then, is an open pit coal mine that comprises 300 hectares, and is located within the El Cerrejón zone. Since 1996 mining operations there have been carried out by the company Carbones Colombianos del Cerrejón S.A. (CCC), under a contract with the owners of the Community of the Cerrejón – a group of private landowners who receive royalties from the corporations.[5] The contract is valid until 2033. On May 6, 2010, Pacific Coal Resources Ltd. purchased S.A., with the mine producing about 1,013 kilotons of thermal coal annually.

Theoretical Considerations

Two elements come together regarding the situation faced by the communities Chancleta and Patilla. The first is the weakness of Colombia's political institutions, especially with regard to the protection of minority rights and isolated populations. The second is the neoliberal style of the State, which further cripples its regulatory capacity. The political institutions of a country are crucial to ensure political inclusion and equity.[6] In the case of Colombia, the development of strong political institutions has been constrained by patronage, corporatism, authoritarianism, inefficiency, and by a concentration of power among elites.[7]

Further, the neoliberal model – business-friendly policies combined with low social welfare expenditures – is associated with what some have called "predator growth."[8] It is economic growth without real development, since profits are repatriated to other countries and the standard of living for the majority of the host country remains stagnant.[9] With regard to the mining sector in particular, economic growth generates relatively few jobs since this sector is capital rather than labour intensive. In Colombia, the extractive sector counts for a very small part of the workforce, only 1.2 percent of those formally employed.[10] In the coal industry, employee remuneration is lower in comparison to other sectors. For example, the coal sector pays employees between COL$15,000 and COL$38,000 pesos per COL$100,000 pesos of gross operating surplus, compared with COL$600,000 and COL$900,000 pesos generated by agriculture.[11] In the regional area of La Guajira, where much of the coal mining sector is concentrated, 62 percent of the population lives in poverty.[12]

The challenges faced by the community of La Caypa are subsumed within the concept of human security. The threats to human security in the region come in the form of displacement, disease, political repression, as well as abrupt ruptures of order at home, at work, and in the community. Indeed, the critical human security approach emphasizes the basic needs of economic survival, health, social development, and environmental sustainability. It emphasizes political inclusion and empowerment of the marginalized to improve their situation. The chapter will focus on these themes.

Human security is a global concept accepted by the international community.[13] It must be guaranteed by all three levels of the State – national, regional, and local. To achieve human security support is required from actors such as multilateral organizations, civil society organizations (CSOs), and TNCs through corporate responsibility programs.[14]

Historical Context

The small communities of Chancleta and Patilla are located in the large municipality of Barrancas. About 45 percent of the town's subsoil is devoted to the open pit mine. These two districts are characterized as among the "rural" zones of the larger municipality.[15] The town was founded in 1664 when Spaniards used this territory as a resting area and for shipping freight from Valledupar to Riohacha. In 1672, Barrancas parish was established, and in 1892 it became a municipality in the department of Magdalena Grande. In 1965 it became part of the department of La Guajira.[16]

The settlement of Chancleta was formed in the early twentieth century, with the arrival of eight families that were the basis of the population until the 1980s. The Patilla community was formed around the same time. The residents of both communities are Mestizos who traditionally have worked in agriculture. Chancleta is located about 400 meters from the La Caypa mine, while Patilla is located about 800 meters from the operating area. Mining exploitation here started in 1993, when the Chilean company Caypa S.A. was established.

The extraction of coal throughout the area of El Cerrejón has been controversial. While transnational corporations and the government emphasize the benefits of coal extraction in La Guajira, social discontent prevails in the region. Coal mining in the area directly involves 15 districts – Espinal, Palmarito, Cabeza de Perro, Sojori, Tabaco, Chancleta, Roche, Patilla, Zarahita, Manantial, Caracolí, Oreganal, Las Casitas, and Barrancón and El Descanso. Some of these communities include Indigenous populations, such as the Wayuu, as well as Afro Colombians.

The arrival of the mining industry was accompanied by a discourse of progress and development. But mining activities have disrupted the economic and cultural traditions of the community, whose livelihood had previously relied on hunting, fishing, and agriculture. With regard to the establishment of open pit mining in the Cerrejón region, the indigenous group Wayuu has insisted that the dispossession of community territory to establish coal mines occurred without the mandatory consultation ensured by the Colombian Constitution as well as international treaties.[17] In addition to the claims of dispossession of the land by indigenous communities, large-scale coal mining has created air, water, and land pollution. Widespread coal dust has apparently resulted in respiratory ailments affecting residents and workers, a point to which we shall return. Community residents have also complained of hearing problems due to the noise produced by machinery and explosive blasting.[18]

Recognizing the widespread threats posed by coal mining to the human security of the communities of Patilla and Chancleta,[19] in 2006 the company CCL initiated a process of resettlement for the residents of these two villages, geographically relocating them to New Chancleta and New Patilla. However, as we shall see, this project has been met with mixed success.

History Through Art

The works of writers such as Gabriel García Márquez and José Eustasio Rivera unveil social tensions experienced by rural residents that host TNCs in the commodity sector. Chancleta y Patilla seem to reproduce the magic realism embodied in the story of *One Hundred Years of Solitude* by Gabriel García Márquez, where a bucolic setting is the backdrop for vibrant transnational activity. In the case of García Márquez's fictional Macondo, foreign capital is introduced with the arrival of 'Mr. Brown', an American who represents the sudden appearance of multinational banana plantations in the country. He was a dazzling and strange figure, and was noticed when he brought the first automobile to the region. The banana monoculture became the sole source of wealth and employment for the community, producing huge social effects for the residents. The inhabitants left behind their original occupations and became the banana plantation's employees. A stark social division was the result.

A camp of wooden houses with zinc roofs[20] ... coexists with the American people ... a people apart ... with palm-lined streets, houses with netting windows, white tables on the terraces and fan blades hanging from the ceiling, and extensive blue lawn dandies and quails.[21]

The problem in the relationship between the banana company and its employees lay in the multiple devices through which the multinational corporation sought to maximize profits at the expense of the well-being of workers. In García Márquez's narrative, the slaughter of banana workers occurred against the backdrop of their allegations that the United Fruit Company attempted to evade its social responsibility to the workers, who were hired by a contractor and not by the company directly. Therefore, the responsibility for decent pay, medical services and working conditions was not directly assumed by the company. In the case of Chancleta and Patilla, the same problem – the outsourcing of miners and associated questions regarding corporate responsibility – was a factor in labour strikes and other social strife.

In *La Vorágine*, by José Eustasio Rivera,[22] the politics of rubber extraction in the Amazon is addressed. This Colombian author realistically portrays themes of social injustice as they occur in a remote area where the government is all but absent. Rubber was produced in the jungle area of Putumayo by Indigenous Colombians, who suffered a variety of human rights abuses under conditions approaching debt peonage. Eustasio Rivera's piece examines the controversies related to the influx of foreign capital as a means to achieve development. Both of these themes are relevant to the case at hand.

Both novels explore the social effects on isolated communities of Colombia's weak State and TNC engagement in the commodity sector. In the case of Macondo, isolation is understood as the subjugation of the State first by colonization and then by multinational companies. Eustasio Rivera's work suggests the isolation of the jungle as a metaphor for the entrance to the unknown, and as a location that is ripe for foreign entities to assert their control in the absence of the Colombian State. Social tension and community resentment of foreign corporations are the common results.

Actors and Interests

The State

The Colombian State is not adequately prepared to regulate the mining industry, nor is it prepared to promote social justice in local communities. The National Mining Code of 2001 sought to promote the modernization of the extractive industry. However, a legal case was made against it in Colombia's Constitutional Court because the Code did not entail an adequate process of consultation with Indigenous peoples – such as those who reside in the department of La Guajira where Pantilla and Chancleta are located. The new mining code was implemented in 2010, but in 2011 was declared unconstitutional with regard to the issue of indigenous rights.[23] When the two-year deadline expired on May 11, 2013, the government indicated that it would reform the Mining Code of 2001 rather than write an entirely new policy, and promised that the process would entail proper consultation with ethnic groups. A new code was promised for 2015.

According to the World Bank's *Doing Business 2014*,[24] Colombia ranks sixth in protecting investors among the 189 economies evaluated. This business-friendly environment has encouraged Canadian TNCs in the extractive sector to operate in Colombia. With a mining boom dominating Colombia's economy at the dawn of the twenty-first century, the government slowly began to create various institutions to cope with the influx of foreign investment in the sector. This includes the creation of the Mining and Energy Planning Unit in 2013,[25] as well as the National Mining Agency and the National Environmental Licensing Authority in 2011.[26] Some progress is occurring with respect to State capacity building vis-à-vis the extractive sector, but it remains at a nascent stage and is too early to gauge the results.

It was noted earlier that a controversial relocation program was launched for the residents of Chancleta and Patilla in 2006. Some residents relocated to the new communities and were unhappy about the results, while others remained in the original towns. While we shall develop this theme in a later discussion of the community's perspective to human security, for now the point is that a large part of the social failure of this relocation is due to the absence of the State in the process. The national government needs to work with the local government of Barrancas and TNCs in the region to coordinate an appropriate response to community concerns. A tripartite negotiation between the State, the corporation, and the community is necessary to enable a successful negotiation that benefits both the community and the TNC.

The national and departmental governments have not yet been sufficiently responsive to the reality of abuses of human security in the region, with some key agencies claiming that they are unaware of any problems in the communities considered here. In fact, the Presidential Office on Human Rights indicated it had no knowledge of any human rights or human security problems in the area. A representative from that agency said no formal complaint or inquiry has been made regarding difficulties associated with the relocation or any other problem, but that the agency would investigate any issues formally raised.[27] Residents apparently are unaware of mechanisms to raise human rights complaints nationally. This suggests that the government should promote a greater awareness of national programs available to communities, and to make these accessible to residents.

In the case of the departmental government for La Guajira, a key agency is Corporación Autótonoma Regional de La Guajira (Corpoguajira), which is in charge of the administration and protection of natural resources. It also is mandated to represent the voice of communities on these matters. A representative from Corpoguajira indicated that it had received specific complaints regarding environmental problems from the large CCL mining operation (that produces more than 90 percent of the coal in the region), but no complaints had been received regarding pollution from Pacific Coal Resources' La Caypa mine.[28] Once again, the community requires better information regarding the availability of governmental channels to address their problems, and needs to organize itself to utilize such channels.

Beyond the lack of tripartite negotiation, another problem concerns the centralization of power in Bogotá, and the isolation and apparent powerlessness of the local government. There are indeed information channels between the central government and foreign investors. But typically there is muted dialogue between transnational corporations and local governments where the operations are performed, because the municipal authorities often are not seen to possess any real power. Against this backdrop, some residents do not view the State, national or local, to be of much practical use in their daily lives: "The police come here when they chase smugglers of fuel.... The army comes when they think there might be guerrillas here. The mayor only comes whenever he needs a political vote."[29] That kind of perception of the State has some important consequences.

One of these consequences is that local communities unfairly expect the corporation to fill gaps left by the State. A local resident complained that "The transportation system here is a mess, it doesn't work,"[30] and that the coal company should address this. Others complain that the school for the original communities of Chancleta and Patilla was removed after residents were relocated to the new sites, but that there is no adequate transportation available for their children to attend other, distant schools.[31] As a result, "the students have to drop out of school because they do not have transportation."[32] Schools and roads are the responsibility of the State. But Colombia's government is so weak, so absent in many places, that communities do not expect much from the State, and look to corporations to fill their needs. There is no question that corporations should indeed make reparations to communities in which they cause harm, and should also promote Corporate Social Responsibility Programs. But the corporation should not be in the position to perform basic duties for which the State is responsible.

When the corporation does perform duties normally performed by government, such as the financing of medical visits by residents, the appearance of a conflict of interest can occur. One resident shared a story regarding her daughter's apparent pulmonary illness, which she attributed to pervasive coal dust in the air.

> She had a check-up at the doctor's office, and it was paid by (the company) CCC. I think there might be a conspiracy between the company and the doctor, because he says the tests do not show that my daughter has anything wrong with her. But all the time she feels that there is something wrong with her lungs.[33]

Hence, political complications can arise when the corporation plays a role that should be done by the government.

The Colombian State needs to be strengthened not only to provide basic services such as education and transportation, but to fulfill the State's duty to protect and respect human rights. This duty is beyond dispute, and Colombia has ratified: the Universal Declaration of Human Rights; the International Covenant on Civil and Political Rights; the International Covenant on Economic, Social and Cultural Rights; the American Convention of Human Rights; the Pact of San José; the Additional Protocol to the American Convention on Human Rights in the Area of Economic, Social and Cultural Rights; and the Protocol of San Salvador, among others. Further, the National System of Human Rights and the International Humanitarian Law was created in 2011 in Colombia, months after the signing of the Free Trade Agreement between Colombia and Canada. All the necessary legislation is in place regarding what the State *should* do. But the Colombian government does not yet have the capacity to meet its responsibilities in this regard.

Let us turn to the local level of government and focus on the broad municipality of Barrancas in which the communities of Chancleta and Patilla are situated. Barrancas' development plan, "The Progress Continues 2012–2015," borrows a term from the national government when it deems mining to be the "the locomotive of development."[34] The 'plan' anticipated that production of coal would increase about 88 percent between 2007 and 2015.[35] But that projection appears to be far too optimistic, since coal prices have fallen over 60 percent between 2011 and the beginning of 2015. Rather than growth, the industry has confronted a sharp decline in production, and the municipality apparently did not anticipate this. The concluding chapter will develop ideas related to the possible crash of the Colombian commodity sector.

Despite overly optimistic economic projections, what is striking about Barrancas' official plan is the detail and sophistication of this 249 page document. It vividly outlines many of the problems in the community. For example, it emphasizes that the poverty rate there is 71.18 percent, or about double the national figure.[36] It ranks near the bottom of the list, at 944 nationally, regarding the availability of social and recreational programs for youth.[37] The percentage of students achieving satisfactory or better achievement rates for Grade 9 students was 4 percent for math, 10 percent for science and 15 percent for reading comprehension.[38] The level of low birth weight babies grew from 6.5 percent in 2005 to 7.6 percent in 2009.[39] The report documents too little public space for community enjoyment, with much of the existing public space poorly maintained.[40]

The municipal development plan lists high among its many problems the "low participation rate among its citizens on public matters."[41] This is crucial. Not only is there insufficient contact between the community and the national government, but the residents of Barrancas apparently do not view the municipal government to be sufficiently efficacious to participate in local politics.

The two small and remote districts of Patilla and Chancleta receive very little mention in the municipal plan, which was written when the relocation process for these communities was envisaged but not yet fully enacted. It observes, for example, that "The exploitation of coal ... gravely affects the environment of ... Patilla and Chancleta," and that the deterioration of the environment of those communities necessitated their relocation.[42] However, no problems or controversies surrounding the relocation are mentioned in the plan.

While the development plan is very careful to avoid any direct criticism of the coal mining industry, it points to a number of problems associated with it. For example, it indicates that air pollution from carbon particulate is an obvious problem for the town, but no precise measurement of this is noted. Similarly, it acknowledges high levels of noise from the mine that disturbs the community. It also emphasizes the frequent problem of coal dust settling into drinking water, as well as other contamination from the mine at the town's water sources.[43] While these problems are also obvious to visitors to the region, better data regarding pollution measurements could strengthen the community's case to convince government authorities to address the problem. Overall, the municipal plan does an especially good job for a remote and poor community of assessing problems and setting goals. It represents a solid starting point to map out existing threats to human security. In this sense, it is an important source of information if Pacific Coal Resources were to initiate a corporate HRIA, or if the governmental HRIA associated with the CCFTA wished to include clear human rights indicators regarding Canadian investment in the extractive sector.

The Corporation: Pacific Coal Resources Ltd.

Pacific Coal Resources Ltd. (PCR) is a mining company based in Canada.[44] It has the distinction of being the only company in Latin America exclusively devoted to coal mining.[45] It has a presence in La Guajira, and has other operations in the departments of Atlántico, Boyacá, Santander, and Cesar. Its purpose is the extraction and production of coal, asphalt, and coke asphalt. The company is the result of a series of acquisitions of several companies that began in the 1990s. Primo Gold Ltd. was established in 1990, and underwent a name change three times. In 1994 it switched its name to Primo Resources Ltd., in 1999 to Primo Resources International Inc. and in 2003 to Vega Gold Ltd., which later changed its name to Vega Resources Inc.[46] In 2010, it began a process to merge with another company, Pacific Coal S.A. (PCSA). With the merger complete, on March 11, 2011, the company changed its name to Pacific Coal Resources Ltd.[47]

PCR and its executives are well connected in the realms of Colombian politics and energy corporations. The current CEO of the company, Hernán Martínez Torres, served as Minister of Mines and Energy in Colombia between 2006 and 2010 and has also been a member of the Board of Directors for Medoro Resources, which eventually merged into what is now known as Gran Colombia Gold Corporation. In terms of other corporate ties, it is worth emphasizing that PCR's operations are related to the interests of Pacific Rubiales Energy Corp. (PREC) in Colombia, which has 14.35 percent of PCR's shares. Among other entitlements, Pacific Rubiales has the right to nominate one member to the board of directors of PCR during regularly scheduled elections.[48] Six of the 13 members of the board of directors of Pacific Coal Resources are associated with

Pacific Rubiales at the time of this writing.[49] In addition, Blue Pacific Assets,[50] another extractive corporation in Colombia, has a 20.85 percent stake in PCR. Executives of PREC are also associated with Blue Pacific Assets.[51]

In practical terms, PCR has delegated the operation of the La Caypa mine to its CCC subsidiary, which was acquired through its predecessor, Vega Resources Inc., in May 2010. Carbones Colombianos de Cerrejón, in turn, recruits mine workers for three associated cooperatives to carry out the exploration, extraction, and transportation of coal and related products. Also, the procedures related to the Environmental Management Plan have been given to CCC.[52]

Pacific Coal Resource's strategy has focused on the increase of mining production, reduction of costs, and the consolidation of debt. In terms of its cost reduction strategy, the company's direct personnel was reduced from 41 to 35 workers between 2013 and 2014. The company struggles with profitability as of this writing. In April 2014, a press release from Pacific Coal Resources Ltd. indicated that it made a profit of CAD$2.4 million in 2013 after losing $30.7 million in 2012.[53] However, it announced in August 2014 that it would miss annual production forecasts due to adverse geological conditions that included "naturally occurring burning of the coal mantles in addition to the mantles being affected by the presence of a geological fault."[54] These problems, combined with cascading coal prices, will no doubt have an impact on an already weak Corporate Social Responsibility portfolio, a point to which we shall return.

Overall, the mining reforms implemented by the Colombian government since 2001, and bilateral agreements such as the Free Trade Agreement signed with Canada in 2011, have favored foreign investors such as Pacific Coal Resources Ltd. Given the context of a country with a weak institutional framework and a strong neoliberal view that limits the further development of State capacity, the result has been the creation of incentives for foreign investors that do not necessarily coincide with the welfare of society.

The Community: Chancleta and Patilla

For almost 100 years the communities of Chancleta and Patilla have survived despite the near absence of the State regarding the provision of public goods and the protection of human rights. In 2006 a relocation process commenced that has fractured the community, and has threatened the economic and cultural survival of the residents. Those who live in both the original and relocated communities need to travel on unpaved roads for about 40 minutes to get to their adobe houses from the commercial center of Barrancas. For the residents who have not been relocated, there are no streetlights, or any other public service. The only school that existed was demolished following the construction of New Chancleta and New Patilla. There is no police presence in the area, instead security is carried out by the private security personnel of the companies CCL and CCC. Further, for those who did not relocate to the new communities, there is no boundary between the mine and the homes of residents – these communities essentially live in a mine. Let us further explore the implications of the relocation program.

The result of the relocation process was that 75 families were relocated from the two communities to the two new ones, with 25 families or about 100 people remaining at the original sites. Some chose not to relocate, and others returned to their original properties shortly after the initial move. There are a variety of reasons for this. Although infrastructure is better in the new communities, people there do not have an area to develop their traditional activities such as hunting, herding, or fishing. This is very significant, since it means they no longer can perform their traditional livelihood. Their cultural ties to the land, and to their traditions, have been severed. There are also complaints regarding the quality of water in the new communities, especially regarding its saltiness. In addition to questionable quality, the availability of water is also a problem. Further, the amount paid to the owners for their original property did not exceed US$1,000, which some viewed as too low of a price to justify a move to the new community. Also, the move to the new community was staged in different phases, which left time among those who had not moved to generate doubts about the new community and ultimately choose not to move. In general, there has been discontent among the population regarding the process.

Some of the residents of Chancleta and Patilla who agreed to be transferred have openly expressed their dissatisfaction with the new location. One resident said, for example,

> Go to New Patilla, you will realize that the people there are suffering. Yes there is energy and light, but water from the aqueduct is salty. We can use it to bathe and to wash dishes and pots, but not to drink. Obtaining drinking water here is a serious problem.[55]

One resident observed that "once these people who are relocated try to pay utilities, they will need to sell the house because they do not have the money to pay for services."[56] Thus, community expectations have not been realized with the relocation.

Those who did not relocate also expressed criticism of the situation.

> Certain people were prioritized for the relocation, there are some that are indigenous, and others who had lived here for years. So they were on the top of the list, and I understand that. But they relocated others before me who had lived here for a very short period of time, who had not lived here as long as I have.[57]

Thus, there were perceptions that the process was not handled fairly, and that some were favoured. Further, the loss of their traditional means of survival, subsistence agriculture, means that both the old and new communities suffer from severe economic and social problems. There is no agricultural land available in the new communities, and because the old communities are situated alongside the bustling mine with high quantities of coal dust, subsistence agriculture has all but disappeared. This has created economic hardship for many.

Finally, it is important to reiterate that neither Pacific Coal Resources Ltd. nor its subsidiary CCC conducted the relocation process – the relocation began in

2006 prior to Pacific Coal Resources Ltd.'s purchase of the CCC in 2010–2011. The community relocation was conducted by the large, non-Canadian company, Carbones de Cerrejón Ltd. (CCL). It is that company which oversees most Corporate Social Responsibility programs in the broader region due to its size. That is, because CCL is the largest of the coal producers in the region, it causes most of the coal-related problems there and has assumed responsibility for broad CSR programs in the greater area – a point to which we shall return. CCL also had the support of the World Bank and the Municipality of Barrancas during the move. Despite CCL's role as organizing the relocation, residents look to the current owner of the mine and its subsidiary, Pacific Coal Resources Ltd. and CCC respectively, for responsibility of the social effects caused by the relocation.

In essence, the communities of Chancleta and Patilla have been destroyed. The geographical fracture of the new and old communities has weakened the social bonds between residents. In just three decades the mining companies present in the area have used the strategy of dispossession and displacement to dominate the land for their interests.[58] Chancleta and Patilla, despite having a century of existence, have been dismembered and destroyed to serve the interests of a mining company. This has occurred in the context of the country's dedication to the "economic locomotive" of mining.

There are a number of important issues here related to human security. The first concerns various controversies surrounding community displacement and fracture. Another theme is the absence of needed tripartite negotiation. Community residents we interviewed felt that the company had most of the power during the negotiation process regarding relocation, since the community had no other party to serve as their advocate, or to help mediate the negotiations.

Environmental aspects of human security are important here. Atmospheric emissions of coal particulate occur daily. The coal dust negatively affects the quality of the air for inhabitants of Chancleta and Patilla. During busy periods at the mine, it is easy to see the coal dust on the leaves of trees, on top of the soil, all over household goods, and even floating on water. As a result, many residents complain about health problems manifested by a dry cough, bronchitis, ocular dryness, dizziness, and abdominal pain. According to statistics from Our Lady of Pilar Hospital in Barrancas, 15 percent of the total hospital consultations in 2013 were with residents who complained of these types of problems.[59] It must be remembered that many of those affected only go to the hospital when they cannot tolerate the disease, and so many cases presumably go unrecorded.

PCR has attempted to deal with the negative impact of coal in the air by implementing a plan of spraying key areas with water.[60] The strategy uses water tankers to spray over three kilometers of dirt roads leading to the mine throughout the day. This prevents coal dust that has settled on the roads to become airborne due to the almost constant tractor traffic to and from the mine. However, this solution brings other problems, especially those related to water conservation. Every hour of irrigation requires 10,000 liters of water that are taken through pumps from the Rancheria River. Due to a recent drought in the region, and a history of weak access to drinking water for residents, this problem is particularly important.

The Community – Disputes and Contractors

About 240 miners at La Caypa have been contracted by two outsourcing companies, Strategic People and Caribbean People. Both companies are subcontracted by the company Mining Project Operations, which was hired by Pacific Coal Resources' subsidiary, CCL.[61] For the miners, these kind of layers obscure issues related to corporate responsibility toward their workers and the host community. For example, when doubts arise as to the safety of a particular job, it is unclear to miners which company is ultimately responsible for the situation.[62] Similarly, when workers at the mine are sometimes expected by the contractor to purchase tools necessary for their job, miners wonder if the core company, Pacific Coal Resources, is aware of the problem.[63]

The issue of corporate responsibility toward workers was also related to a major strike that began on January 22, 2012. It was led by 200 workers from the contracting company Strategic People and 40 from the company Caribbean People. According to Ever Causado, leader of the Union Sintramienergética, on October 1, 2011 a list of demands was presented by the union to the companies. The key request was a pay raise at the La Caypa Mine that is in line with the average pay of the coal sector in the region. At other companies such as Drummond, for example, workers such as shovel operators are paid more than those performing the same work for PCR, according to the union.[64] Further, the union claimed that overtime pay is not properly calculated by the company. Finally, the miners' union requested better programs for industrial safety and for nutrition, as well as transportation to work, and a permanent ambulance on site.[65] Negotiations stopped on January 7, 2012, when the contractors indicated that they were not empowered to negotiate the economic issues of the union's petition. At the end of 2012, in the context of the company losing almost US$31 million for that year, the contractors dismissed over 200 workers.[66] Those who were not terminated continued to experience the same working conditions.

Corporate Social Responsibility and the Community

Pacific Coal Resources Ltd. has CSR programs that are focused on community management and education. These include: (1) information and communication programs regarding mine activities; (2) the provision of work, when possible, for citizens of Chancleta and Patilla; (3) environmental education programs that include recreational activities and environmental clean-up nights; (4) the study of impacts from the mine throughout the larger region; and (5) an environmental education program in schools.[67] Some community members view this as insufficient. One resident commented that "Well, PCR has given us very little compared to the harm it is causing. They give us a small amount of water, but there are no available jobs at the mine for residents."[68]

Besides being workers, many miners are also parents, whose great concern is that their children will have access to some kind of public technical training. One resident told us, "Miners and the people who live here do not have money to send our children to school to study a for a career.... Mining is a dead end."[69]

Some parents worry as they watch their teenagers and children who are young adults sit idle.[70] Miners expect financial assistance from TNCs for the training of their children, because such support has not been provided by the government. Once again, when the State fails in its duties, the community looks to the foreign corporations to fill the gap.

There are two reasons why Pacific Coal Resources, through its subsidiary CCC, does not implement a fuller Corporate Social Responsibility plan. A first argument put forward by the company is that the dominant mine in the region is run by Carbones del Cerrejón Limited (CCL), which exploits more than 20 million tons per year while Pacific Coal Resources, at its La Caypa mine, barely reaches one million tons per year. Therefore, PCR argues that the great majority of negative effects from coal mining emanate from CCL and not from Pacific Coal Resources, and that this is recognized and accepted by the corporations and the community.[71] The second reason is that CSR programs are completely voluntary. There is no legal requirement for PCR or its subsidiary to do more than they are already doing. The limits of CSR programs in the community have led residents to criticize the company for not doing more. But the corporation is frustrated that the community expects the company to provide services that should be offered by the State – in terms of housing, welfare policies, roads, security services, and so on.

Corporate Responsibility vs State Responsibility on Human Rights

Both the corporation and the State should do more with regard to human security in the regions under consideration in this study. The Ruggie Report, which is discussed in the introductory chapter, notes that Corporate Social Responsibility is not a legal duty, but companies must work with the State to respect human rights.[72] Further, it is important to note that the Ruggie Report indicates that TNCs should "deal with the negative consequences on human rights due to its participation in the area."[73] We have observed that the State, for its part, is barely present in Patilla and Chancleta. This absence of the State means the lack of basic services in the region. It has also created a scenario whereby community members expect the corporation to fill the huge gap left by the State. The Santos Government has promised a greater respect for human rights and for the general human security themes apparent in this case. For example, the Presidential Program on Human Rights and International Humanitarian Law has promised a 20-year program to build the State and to improve economic, cultural, social, and environmental rights.[74] But those promises have not yet reached fruition.

Basic public services – such as the provision of water, electricity, education, health care, etc. – are an important part of the human security framework. The State should take the lead in the provision of these, but corporations, through CSR programs, can help. There is much to be done in La Guajira, according to government statistics regarding the satisfaction of basic needs in the regions of extraction in 2012. The departments of La Guajira and Cesar, the major coal producing areas of Colombia, have a 76 percent dissatisfaction rate with basic public needs, in contrast to the national average of 54 percent. In terms of the infant mortality rate, the region of La Guajira reported 32 deaths per thousand of live births, while the national average is 18 deaths. We also saw that access to education is a problem for the residents – not only for grade school children but also for teenagers and young adults who require training to get work outside of their communities where little opportunity exists.

Both the corporation and the communities indicate that they want to improve the situation. PCR is currently developing a plan to implement best practices for the benefit of the communities of Chancleta and Patilla, and wants to ensure that these practices are framed within the economic realities of the company. Meanwhile, the leaders of these communities have indicated their eagerness to engage in dialogue with both the corporation and the State to improve living conditions and human rights. This would necessitate the construction of inclusive political institutions and the implementation of tripartite negotiation, but these have not existed here since the founding of Colombia in 1821.

Small Communities and Social Power

Compared to other case studies in the volume, the communities of Patilla and Chancleta are at a clear disadvantage regarding the political strength required to secure the achievement of human security. This is because the communities are so small. They do not have the demographic strength to pressure government, and their isolated location also serves to keep them out of the national spotlight.

In this sort of case, what may be required is for the community to form an organization that can attract NGOs, both national and global, to their cause. So far, the situation faced by Chancleta and Patilla has attracted the fleeting interest of national and global NGOs. But no concrete or lasting assistance has been provided. One resident, for example, indicated that "Here we have been visited by some NGOs, but we have not received any help. A representative from one NGO comes almost every year, interviews us about the conditions, but overall, not much is done."[75] More community organization is required to attract the enduring attention of NGOs with a clear capacity to help. Community organization is key to exert pressure on various levels of government and to obtain attention from the media. We shall return to these points in the section below.

Recommendations and Global Lessons

Based on this case study, we pose some suggestions to improve human security in the region. Since the themes we treat here are common to other operations throughout the Global South, there are global implications that can be drawn from them. There are a number of general threats to human security that emerge from the case at hand. These include the social effects of relocating a community to promote mining activity. The highly complex issue of displacement deserves special attention. Other prominent human security themes derived from this case include the localized social effects of a weak State, the loss of traditional livelihoods due to mining activity, and basic weaknesses in labour relations due to the use of contract workers in a manner that may obscure corporate responsibility. We also observed threats to human security in the form of illness and environmental hazards. So the focus becomes how the State, the company, and the community can address these problems.

Let us start with recommendations for the corporation. Given that, by its own admission, the Corporate Social Responsibility program for Pacific Coal Resources Ltd. is in a nascent stage, the company needs to ensure that it is familiar with the literature regarding CSR, human security, and key documents such as the Ruggie Reports. Since it has already been operating in the area for almost four years as of this writing, the development of its CSR program should be accelerated. Pacific Coal Resources requires a state-of-the-art panorama of the human security landscape in order to prepare the Best Practices program to which it is committed. This would entail the careful consideration of human security themes such as workers' rights, relocation and displacement, cultural rights, health and environmental rights, as well as the provision of the basic social services that are lacking in the area. Most importantly, the corporation needs to improve the communication circuit between the community and the corporation when community needs are assessed and CSR programs are developed.

There is the question of what the corporation could do by itself, what it could do in cooperation with other businesses, and what it could do alongside the State. The corporation has emphasized that it is small compared to the other coal mining companies in the area, and that it needs to have a CSR program commensurate with its fiscal capacity. The company has also struggled for profitability in the context of falling coal prices. It may find that its limited funds are better spent in coordination with other businesses and the State. A broader, coordinated effort can mean better results in the provision of basic services to the community, for example. Thus, one recommendation is for the corporation itself to push for tripartite negotiation between the State, other businesses, and the community to develop an efficient and coordinated plan to provide basic public services and to achieve the objectives of human security noted above.

Pacific Coal Resources Ltd. would benefit from studying the successes and failures of the CSR programs of other corporations. Certainly PCR's connection with Pacific Rubiales Energy Corp., which is a much larger company with a sophisticated CSR agenda, can facilitate helpful assistance and advice in this realm. It can also work through established business groups in the extractive sector to press for a common stance among corporations regarding the absence of the State and the subsequent implications for companies. As will be discussed in the concluding chapter of this volume, corporations in Colombia often work within a culture of individualism and avoid cooperative efforts to confront the government on common themes. With corporations competing against one another and not finding common ground as a group, they lose the strong collective power they would have vis-à-vis the government.

Finally, Pacific Coal Resources Ltd. could benefit greatly from initiating a corporate Human Rights Impact Assessment. This would be especially beneficial as a primary step to coordinate the development of the company's CSR program.

This is a well-established tool that can identify the broad threats to human security faced by the community and the corporation. In this case, most of the human rights indicators are already clear. The municipality of Barrancas has produced a document outlining many of the weaknesses of the community's social services, as we observed. The displacement theme should be prominent in an HRIA for this corporation, with a particular focus on how existing problems can be addressed almost a decade after the relocation process commenced. Broader human security themes such as community health, environmental threats, labour relations, and so on, are also clearly apparent in this case. The establishment and conduct of an HRIA should involve a highly inclusive approach with the community. Once these are clearly mapped out, a coherent plan can be developed to measure the progress toward achieving these goals. For the company, the HRIA can help promote better relations with the community and with labour. This can mean the diminishment of costly labour problems such as strikes, the development of a more enthusiastic work force, and a more secure environment in which to operate.

The Colombian State

In essence, the Colombian State does not have the institutional presence in Patilla and Chancleta to perform adequately its duty as a guarantor of human rights and human security. The question is where to start. Certainly the provision of basic services is essential – clean drinking water, electricity, policing services, access to education, and so on, all areas that require immediate attention in this case. A tripartite consultation between the government, business, and the community could further hone the prioritization of specific needs for the community.

Here is where a governmental HRIA could assist Colombia. The problems apparent in this case study are not peculiar to Chancleta and Patilla. Environmental degradation, displacement, health threats, inadequate respect for culture and ethnicity, and abuses of workers' rights are common themes in Colombia's extractive sector. These represent important indicators for Colombia's annual HRIA, so that problems can be identified and then measured to promote success in human security. Important nuances in these general themes can be discerned through case studies

One reason why some communities that host the extractive sector do not attract enough State presence is that it is more politically expedient for the national government to prioritize urban residents of the country, since this is where the vast majority of votes are. This problem is exacerbated by the relatively tiny size of the communities of Patilla and Chancleta. A mechanism needs to be established that balances the interests and rights between urban and rural populations of the country. A governmental HRIA could help in this regard by mapping out areas in the country where human security threats related to the extractive sector are likely to occur, so that specific programs can be developed that target remote and virtually forgotten areas like Chancleta and Patilla. Otherwise, these communities are likely to face the same fate of isolation and solitude as depicted in García Márquez's tale of Macondo.

We have stressed the importance of tripartite negotiation throughout the chapter, but it is also crucial to fortify communication links between the local community and the national government. Community residents require a program that informs them of their human rights and workers' rights, and that provides them with a safe and proper means of launching a grievance or concern. The government's presence in the region could be enhanced through internet communication. But for this to be successful, the community would require greater access to online computers. Community members would also need assistance navigating websites, and with writing and reading related messages.

The Community

The small size of the community is the biggest challenge to its political power. So the focus turns to how the community can maximize its power to promote human security. Capacity building programs for community organization could be helpful. The development of a national network of NGOs and academic institutions working in the extractive sector is being developed by the authors of this volume, and this may assist small and isolated communities to obtain the information they require to advance their interests to the national government and other authorities.

Beyond reducing the influence of geographical isolation and lack of information, cyber connectivity within a network of NGOs can compensate for the lack of political clout in small communities by making them part of a larger and more politically powerful entity. This is probably the most viable and economical vehicle for the community to begin the process of empowering itself. But there are obvious challenges. Tiny communities need to be educated as to how internet connectivity can empower them, and they must have access to this service on a regular basis. As we saw, literacy is a major challenge in the communities involved in this case study, so non-written forms of internet communication such as Skype may be particularly important in such cases. Further, community members require information as to what resources are available online, and which national and global NGOs are relevant to their struggle. Overall, the community would likely require some initial outside assistance from an NGO or other group that could help it build support nationally and globally to counter the isolating effects of its remote location and small population.

Notes

1 "Plan Nacional de Desarrollo, 2010–2014 Prosperidad para Todos. Capítulo III," DNP, https://colaboracion.dnp.gov.co/CDT/PND/4C.%20Cap%C3%ADtulo%20III.pdf, accessed September 9, 2014.
2 "Exportaciones," DANE, accessed August 16, 2014, www.dane.gov.co/index.php/comercio-exterior/exportaciones, accessed August 16, 2014.
3 Gabriel Poveda Ramos, Historia Económica de Colombia en el siglo XX (Medellín: Universidad Pontificia Bolivariana, 2005), p. 163.
4 Allison Benson, "La Guajira y El Cerrejón: Una historia de contrastes", *Revista Económica Supuestos*, Febrero 1, 2011, http://revistasupuestos.uniandes.edu.co/?p=1517#cita-1, accessed 10 September 2014.

5 This group is credited with the ownership of some lands in the Central Zone of El Cerrejón.

6 Daron Acemoglu and James A. Robinson, *Por qué Fracasan los Países. Los orígenes del poder, la prosperidad y la pobreza*, (Barcelona: Deuto, 2012), p. 60.

7 See Gustavo Rodríguez Albor, "Calidad de las instituciones y su relación con el desempeño económico: un análisis de la región Caribe Colombiana," *Revista de Economía del Caribe*, No. 5, 2014. Viewed February 14, 2014, http://rcientificas.uninorte.edu.co/index.php/economia/article/view/1251/794.

8 Amit Bhaduri, "Predatory Growth," *Sanhati*, 9 April 2008, http://sanhati.com/articles/739/, accessed August 19, 2014.

9 Amit Bhaduri, "Predatory Growth."

10 Sergio Silva Numa, "La minería en Colombia: la maldición de los recursos naturales," *El Tiempo*. 16 Enero, 2014, consultado agosto 19, 2014, www.eltiempo.com/archivo/documento/CMS-13366835.

11 Ibíd.

12 Kevin Howlett, Colombia´s poverty rates shock as millions on 1.5 US a day," *Colombia Politics*, Julio 11, 2013., www.colombia-politics.com/poverty, accessed 19 August 2014.

13 Jairo Agudelo Taborda, Ed. *Variables Sociopolíticas de la Cooperación Internacional para el Desarrollo en América Latina y El Caribe*. (Cartagena: Universidad de San Buenaventura, Escuela Latinoamericana de Cooperación y Desarrollo, 2011).

14 Ibelis Blanco Rangel, *Alianzas para el Desarrollo*, (Cartagena: Universidad de San Buenaventura, Escuela Latinoamericana de Cooperación y Desarrollo, 2011).

15 See Municipio de Barrancas, *Plan de Desarrollo 2012–2015, El Progresso Continua*, Departamento de La Guajira, 2011, p. 80. http://barrancas-laguajira.gov.co/Nuestros_planes.shtml?apc=gbxx-1-&x=3112134, viewed August 12, 2014.

16 Barrancas-laguaria, "Nuestro Municipio," Viewed August 15, 2014. www.barrancaslaguajira.gov.co/informacion_general.shtml#historia.

17 Observatorio de Conflictos Mineros en America Latina, "Pronunciamiento de los pueblos y comunidades afectadas por megaproyectos mineros en La Guajira," November 11, 2011, Conflictosmineros, www.conflictosmineros.net/contenidos/10-colombia/9018-pronunciamiento-de-pueblos-y-comunidades-afectadas-por-los-megaproyectos-mineros-en-la-guajira, accessed August 19, 2014.

18 Ibíd.

19 For this case study, we only emphizise the small communities of Chanclleta and Patilla. But the CCl has conducted this process of resettlement in other communities of the Barrancas Municipalities.

20 Gabriel García Márquez, *Cien años de soledad*, (Madrid: Real Academia Española. 2007), p. 210.

21 Ibíd., p. 261.

22 José Eustasio Rivera, *La Vorágine*, (Bogotá: ABC, 1945).

23 Sebastián Rubiano Galvis, "Bueros," informal academic paper, http://library.fes.de/pdf-files/bueros/kolumbien/09382.pdf, accessed August 25, 2014.

24 See "Doing Business," Grupo del Banco Mundial, 11 Septiembre, 2014, http://espanol.doingbusiness.org/rankings, accessed September 11, 2014.

25 See, "Quienes somos", UPME, www1.upme.gov.co/quienes-somos, accessed September 11, 2014.

26 See, "Funciones de la ANLA", ANLA, www.anla.gov.co/contenido/contenido.aspx?catID=1298&conID=8033, accessed September 11, 2014.

27 Jhon Riaño, representative of the Programa Presidencial de Derechos Humanos, by Ibelis Rangel, October 24, 2014.

28 Fanny Mejía, public representative, Corporación Autónoma Regional de La Guajira, Interviewed by Ibelis Rangel, June 4, 2014.

29 Remedios Palmesanos, Resident of Patilla, interviewed by Gustavo Rodríguez Albor, May 17, 2014.

148   *G. Rodríguez Albor* et al.

30 Jaider Fontalvo, Worker at la Mina Subterránea de Caypa, interviewed by Elimar Pontón, May 17, 2014.
31 Jaider Fontalvo, Worker at la Mina Subterránea de Caypa, interviewed by Elimar Pontón, May 17, 2014.
32 Remedios Palmesanos, interviewed by Gustavo Rodríguez Albor, May 17, 2014.
33 Ibíd.
34 Municipio de Barrancas, *Plan de Desarrollo 2012–2015*, op. cit. p. 190.
35 Ibid., p. 162.
36 This poverty rate is from 2011. Ibid., p. 45.
37 Ibid., p. 47.
38 Ibid., pp. 93–98.
39 Ibid., p. 50.
40 Ibid., p., 131.
41 Ibid., p. 217.
42 Ibid., p. 191.
43 Ibid., page 161.
44 "Pacific Coal," Pacific coal Resources Ltd., www.pacificcoal.ca/files/PAK%20-%20Q2%202011%20MDA.pdf, accessed August 24, 2014.
45 "Impactos en los Derechos Humanos de la implementación del Tratado de Libre Comercio entre Colombia y Canadá," PASC, www.pasc.ca/sites/pasc.ca/files/u6/Colombian-Base-TLC-final1.pdf, accessed September 21, 2014.
46 "Pacific Coal Resources Ltd.," Gurufocus, www.gurufocus.com/stock/VGGGF, accessed August 26, 2014.
47 "Pacific Coal Completes CDN$201,825,000 Private Placement and Reverse Takeover of Vega Resources Inc," Prnewswire, www.prnewswire.com/news-releases/pacific-coal-completes-cdn201825000-private-placement-and-reverse-takeover-of-vega-resources-inc-117792093.html, accessed August 26, 2013.
48 Ibíd.
49 Serafino Lacono, Miguel de la Campa, Ronald Pantin, José Francisco Arata, Miguel Rodriguez y Hernan Martinez, "Pacific Coal," Pacific Coal Ltd., www.pacificcoal.ca/Corporate-Information/Board-of-Directors/default.aspx y "Pacific Rubiales," Pacific Rubiales Energy Corporation, www.pacificrubiales.com/corporate/board-of-directors.html, accessed August 26, 2014.
50 "Impactos en los Derechos Humanos de la implementación del Tratado de Libre Comercio entre Colombia y Canadá," op. cit.
51 See "Alianza en negocio maderero de socios de Pacific Rubiales con firma canadiense," *Portafolio*, Marzo 11, 2011, www.portafolio.co/detalle_archivo/DR-11154, accessed 26 August 2014.
52 Autoridad Nacional de Licencias Ambientales- ANLA- Resolucion 0175, ANLA, accessed October 31, 2014. www.anla.gov.co/documentos/11499_res_0175_260214.pdf.
53 Pacific Coal Resources Ltd., "Pacific Coal Resources Ltd. announces 2013 year-end financial results," April 29, 2014, p. 1. www.pacificcoal.ca/newsroom, accessed February 10, 2014.
54 Pacific Coal Resources, Ltd., "Pacific Coal Resources Ltd. Announced 2014 Second Quarter Financial Results and Operational Update," August 29, 2014, p. 3. www.pacificcoal.ca/newsroom. Viewed October 27, 2014.
55 Jesús Perez, Worker at la Mina la Caypa and resident of Patilla Nuevo), Interviewed by Gustavo Rodríguez Albor, May 16, 2014.
56 Remedios Palmesanos, Interview by Gustavo Rodríguez Albor, 17 May 2014.
57 Jaider Fontalvo, Interview by Elimar Pontón, May 17, 2014.
58 Gueorgi Kossinets, and Duncan J Watts, "Origins of Homophily in an Evolving Social Network," *American Journal of Sociology*, #115, 2009, pp. 405–450.
59 Interview by Elimar Pontón, Doctor Margarita Solano, Sub Director of Scientific Information, Hospital Nuestra Senora del Pilar de Barranca, July 12, 2014.

60 Jaime Álvarez, Manager of Security, Environment and Community, La Caypa Mine, Pacific Coal Resources Ltd., Interview by Elimar Pontón, July 14, 2014.
61 "Otra Huelga de obreros contratistas del sector carbonífero, esta vez en la mina Caypa, Guajira," Escuela Nacional Sindical, Septiembre 17, 2014, www.pasc.ca/fr/node/3749, accessed 17 September 2014.
62 Jaider Fontalvo, Interviewed by Elimar Pontón, May 17, 2014.
63 Jesús Pérez, Interview by Gustavo Rodríguez Albor, May 16, 2014.
64 "Otra Huelga de obreros contratistas del sector carbonífero, esta vez en la mina Caypa, Guajira," op. cit.
65 Ibid.
66 Indepaz, "Minería – Territorios y transformaciones – Proyectos, permisos y protagonistas en la Sierra Nevada de Santa Marta-Cesar, La Guajira y Magdalena," INDEPAZ, www.indepaz.org.co/wp-content/uploads/2012/10/PERFILES-PROYECTOS-SNSM-NOVIEMBRE-DE-2012.pdf., accessed September 17, 2014.
67 Jennifer Manjarrez, Coordinator for Social Programs of Pacific Coal Resources Limited, Intervied by Elimar Pontón, May 17, 2014.
68 Jaider Fontalvo, Interviewed by Elimar Pontón, May 17, 2014.
69 Jaider Fontalvo, Interviewed by Elimar Pontón, May 17, 2014.
70 Manuel Maestre, Worker at La Caypa mine, Interview by Elimar Pontón, May 16, 2014.
71 Jaime Álvarez, Interviewed by Elimar Pontón, July 14, 2014.
72 Humberto Fernando Cantú Rivera, "Empresas y derechos humanos: ¿hacia una regulación jurídica efectiva, o el mantenimiento del status quo?," *Anuario mexicano de derecho internacional,* vol. December 13, 2013.
73 Ruggie Report, see "Global Business Initiative," Naciones Unidas, www.global-business-initiative.org/wp-content/uploads/2012/07/GPs-Spanish.pdf, accessed September 4, 2013.
74 See Programa Presidencial de Derechos Humanos y Derecho Internacional Humanitario, "De la violencia a la sociedad de los Derechos, propuesta política de Derechos Humanos en Colombia (2014–2034)," www.derechoshumanos.gov.co/Observatorio/Publicaciones/Documents/140801web-Libro-1-propuesta-politica-publica.pdf, accessed September 5, 2014.
75 Wilmer Palmesano, Eneida Vanega y Wilmer Palmesa, community leaders in Patilla, Interviewed by Gustavo Rodríguez Albor, November 13 and 14, 2013.

Bibliography

ANLA. "Funciones de la ANLA." Accessed September 11, 2014. www.anla.gov.co/contenido/contenido.aspx?catID=1298&conID=8033.
Acemoglu, Daron, and James A. Robinson. *Por qué fracasan los países: Los orígenes del poder, la prosperidad y la pobreza.* Barcelona: Deuto, 2012.
Agudelo Taborda, Jairo, ed. *Variables sociopolíticas de la cooperación internacional para el cesarrollo en América Latina y El Caribe.* Cartagena: Universidad de San Buenaventura, Escuela Latinoamericana de Cooperación y Desarrollo, 2011.
Benson, Allison. "La guajira y el cerrejón: Una historia de contrastes." *Revista Económica Supuestos,* February 1, 2011. Accessed September 10, 2014. http://revistasupuestos.uniandes.edu.co/?p=1517#cita-1.
Bhaduri, Amit. "Predatory Growth." *Sanhati,* April 9, 2008. Accessed August 19, 2014. http://sanhati.com/articles/739/.
Blanco Rangel, Ibelis. *Alianzas para el desarrollo.* Cartagena: Universidad de San Buenaventura, Escuela Latinoamericana de Cooperación y Desarrollo, 2011.
Cantú Rivera, Humberto Fernando. "Empresas y derechos humanos: ¿Hacia una regulación jurídica efectiva, o el mantenimiento del *status quo*?" *Anuario Mexicano de Derecho Internacional* 13 (2013): 313–354.

DANE. "Exportaciones." Accessed August 16, 2014. www.dane.gov.co/index.php/comercio-exterior/exportaciones.

DNP. *Plan nacional de desarrollo, 2010–2014 prosperidad para todos.* "Capítulo III: Crecimiento sostenible y competitividad." Accessed September 9, 2014. https://colaboracion.dnp.gov.co/CDT/PND/4C.%20Cap%C3%ADtulo%20III.pdf.

Escuela Nacional Sindical. "Otra huelga de obreros contratistas del sector carbonífero, esta vez en la mina Caypa, Guajira." *Agencia de Información Laboral,* January 25, 2012. Accessed September 17, 2014. www.ens.org.co/index.shtml?apc=Na-;17;-;-;&x=20166833#.

Eustasio Rivera, José. *La vorágine.* Bogotá: ABC, 1945.

García Márquez, Gabriel. *Cien años de soledad.* Madrid: Real Academia Española, 2007.

Grupo del Banco Mundial. "Doing Business." September 11, 2014. Accessed September 11, 2014. http://espanol.doingbusiness.org/rankings.

Gurufocus. "Pacific Coal Resources Ltd." Accessed August 26, 2014. www.gurufocus.com/stock/VGGGF.

Howlett, Kevin. "Colombia's Poverty Rates Shock as Millions on 1.5 US a Day." *Colombia Politics,* July 11, 2013. Accessed August 19, 2014. www.colombia-politics.com/poverty.

INDEPAZ. "Minería – Territorios y transformaciones – Proyectos, permisos y protagonistas en la sierra Nevada de Santa Marta – Cesar, La Guajira y Magdalena." Accessed September 17, 2014. www.indepaz.org.co/wp-content/uploads/2012/10/PERFILES-PROYECTOS-SNSM-NOVIEMBRE-DE-2012.pdf.

Kossinets, Gueorgi, and Duncan J. Watts. "Origins of Homophily in an Evolving Social Network." *American Journal of Sociology,* 115 (2009): 405–450.

Lacono, Serafino, Miguel de la Campa, Ronald Pantin, José Francisco Arata, Miguel Rodriguez and Hernan Martinez. "Pacific Coal." *Pacific Coal Ltd.* Accessed August 26, 2014. www.pacificcoal.ca/Corporate-Information/Board-of-Directors/default.aspx.

Municipio de Barrancas. *Plan de desarrollo "El progresso continua 2012–2015".* Departamento de La Guajira, 2011. Accessed August 12, 2014. http://barrancas-laguajira.gov.co/Nuestros_planes.shtml?apc=gbxx-1-&x=3112134.

Observatorio de Conflictos Mineros en America Latina. "Pronunciamiento de los pueblos y comunidades afectadas por megaproyectos mineros en La Guajira." Conflictosmineros.net, November 11, 2011. Accessed August 19, 2014. www.conflictosmineros.net/contenidos/10-colombia/9018-pronunciamiento-de-pueblos-y-comunidades-afectadas-por-los-megaproyectos-mineros-en-la-guajira.

Pacific Coal Resources Ltd. *Management's Discussion and Analysis.* August 29, 2011. Accessed August 24, 2014. www.pacificcoal.ca/files/PAK%20-%20Q2%202011%20MDA.pdf.

Pacific Coal Resources Ltd. "Pacific Coal Completes CDN$201,825,000 Private Placement and Reverse Takeover of Vega Resources Inc." *PRNewswire.com.* Accessed August 26, 2013. www.prnewswire.com/news-releases/pacific-coal-completes-cdn201825000-private-placement-and-reverse-takeover-of-vega-resources-inc-117792093.html.

Pacific Coal Resources Ltd. "Pacific Coal Resources Ltd. Announces 2013 Year-End Financial Results." April 29, 2014. Accessed February 10, 2014. www.pacificcoal.ca/Newsroom/News-Releases/News-Releases-Page/News-Release-Details/2014/Pacific-Coal-Resources-Ltd.-announces-2013-year-end-financial-results/default.aspx.

Pacific Coal Resources, Ltd. "Pacific Coal Resources Ltd. Announces 2014 Second Quarter Financial Results and Operational Update." August 29, 2014. Accessed October 27, 2014. www.pacificcoal.ca/Newsroom/News-Releases/News-Releases-Page/News-Release-Details/2014/Pacific-Coal-Resources-Ltd.-Announces-2014-Second-Quarter-Financial-Results-and-Operational-Update/default.aspx.

Pacific Rubiales Energy Corporation. "Pacific Rubiales." Accessed August 26, 2014. www.pacificrubiales.com/corporate/board-of-directors.html.

PASC. *Impactos en los derechos humanos de la implementación del tratado de libre comercio entre Colombia y Canadá.* Accessed September 21, 2014. www.pasc.ca/sites/pasc.ca/files/u6/Colombian-Base-TLC-final1.pdf.

Portafolio. "Alianza en negocio maderero de socios de Pacific Rubiales con firma canadiense." March 10, 2011. Accessed August 26, 2014. www.portafolio.co/detalle_archivo/DR-11154.

Programa Presidencial de Derechos Humanos y Derecho Internacional Humanitario. *De la violencia a la sociedad de los derechos: Propuesta para la política de derechos humanos en Colombia (2014–2034).* Accessed September 5, 2014. www.derechoshumanos.gov.co/Observatorio/Publicaciones/Documents/140801web-Libro-1-propuesta-politica-publica.pdf.

Rubiano Galvis, Sebastián. "La regulación ambiental y social de la minería en Colombia: Comentarios al proyecto de ley de reforma al código de minas." *Friedrich Ebert Stiftung—FESCOL, Foro Nacional Ambiental.* Accessed August 25, 2014. http://library.fes.de/pdf-files/bueros/kolumbien/09382.pdf.

UPME. "Quienes somos." Accessed September 11, 2014. www1.upme.gov.co/quienessomos.

United Nations, General Assembly, Human Rights Council. "Guiding Principles on Business and Human Rights: Implementing the United Nations "Protect, Respect and Remedy" Framework." *Report of the Special Representative of the Secretary-General on the Issue of Human Rights and Transnational Corporations and Other Business Enterprises, John Ruggie*, A/HRC/17/31. United Nations, March 21, 2011. Accessed September 4, 2011. www.ohchr.org/documents/issues/business/A.HRC.17.31.pdf.

6 The Canada–Colombia Free Trade Agreement

Imbalances in the Legal Rights and Responsibilities of Canadian Investors in Colombia

Gus Van Harten

Introduction

Other chapters of this volume outline case studies that involve conflict between Canadian investors, especially in the resource sector, and other actors in Colombia. The case studies raise questions about the conduct of Canadian investors in matters of environmental protection, labour and community relations, and human rights protection. Not all Canadian investors should be tarred with the same brush, yet it appears that some have behaved poorly in Colombia.

The main question examined in this chapter is the extent to which misconduct of Canadian investors could be facilitated or sheltered by the Canada–Colombia Free Trade Agreement (CCFTA).[1] The chapter focuses on the CCFTA's provisions for powerful protections for Canadian investors with respect to their treatment and regulation by government authorities in Colombia. Central to these protections is the broad right of Canadian investors to initiate claims against Colombia in international investor-State arbitration and the corresponding power and broad discretion of the arbitrators to review and discipline Colombian sovereign activity and to order payment of public funds, without any monetary limit, to Canadian investors. While it is too early in the experience of the CCFTA to draw firm conclusions, the legal framework clearly establishes new pressures on Colombian governments to modify their behaviour in order to avoid financial and reputational risks associated with foreign investor claims.

The chapter also examines provisions in the CCFTA's side agreements on labour and the environment[2] and the associated Canada–Colombia Human Rights Agreement.[3] The aim is to assess whether these other mechanisms provide a complementary framework of responsibilities for Canadian investors in order to ensure they respect robust standards of environmental, labour, and human rights protection. They clearly do not. Canadian investors are not subject to any binding and actionable responsibilities to respect environmental, labour, or human rights standards. Further, the limited obligations placed on Canada and Colombia to ensure that basic standards are protected are accompanied by a weak enforcement mechanism which, among other things, would depend on foreign investors' home country to initiate a review of the host State's alleged failure to uphold basic standards. Finally, in its reports to Canada's Parliament on human rights implications of the CCFTA – which are mandated by the Canada–Colombia Human Rights Agreement – the Canadian government has adopted a methodology that permits it to ignore entirely the conduct of Canadian investors.

As a result of the imbalance between the rights and responsibilities of Canadian investors in Colombia, as stipulated by the CCFTA and associated agreements, the CCFTA clearly elevates the bargaining position of Canadian investors relative to domestic constituencies in Colombia and to those bodies of the Colombian State that may seek to limit poor conduct by Canadian investors. This does not mean that Colombian governments have no options to regulate Canadian investors or encourage good behaviour but, in the face of an imbalanced legal framework, the CCFTA legal framework clearly may hamper the ability of Colombian officials to counter misbehaviour of Canadian investors in matters of environmental protection, labour relations, and human rights. As such, opportunities provided by the CCFTA for Canada and Colombia to check Canadian investors' poor behaviour and encourage their responsible behaviour were not acted on in the conclusion or in the implementation of the CCFTA itself, its labour and environmental side agreements, or the Canada–Colombia Human Rights Agreement.

Canadian Investor Rights in the CCFTA

The CCFTA's investment chapter provides extensive rights and protections for Canadian investors in Colombia.[4] Most importantly, the chapter incorporates an investor-State arbitration mechanism that allows Canadian investors to bring claims for compensation against Colombia where any exercise of sovereign authority – whether by a Colombian legislature, government, or court – is alleged to have violated the investor's substantive protections under the CCFTA.[5]

The protections in question include an entitlement to no less favourable treatment than treatment received by Colombian investors or other foreign investors in Colombia, an entitlement to compensation in the event of a direct or indirect expropriation of assets, and insulation from so-called performance requirements (in essence, conditions imposed historically on foreign investors in various countries to increase their contribution to the domestic economy).[6] Perhaps most importantly – due to the broad power it gives to the arbitrators who resolve foreign investor claims – the CCFTA entitles foreign investors to "fair and equitable treatment" and "full protection and security".[7] These concepts may sound benign and are purportedly limited in the treaty to a minimum standard of treatment in customary international law.[8] However, in numerous cases, they have been given an expansive meaning by arbitrators to include ambiguous notions of "proportionality" in the treatment of foreign investors, protection of "legitimate expectations" of investors, and entitlement to a stable legal and regulatory framework, all of which give very broad discretion to arbitrators to require retrospective compensation of foreign investors by the State.[9]

These rights and protections for Canadian investors in the CCFTA are broadly similar to other trade and investment treaties concluded by Canada, Colombia, and many other countries, mostly during the 1990s and 2000s. Since the late 1990s, an increasing number of claims have been brought by foreign investors under such treaties, leading to decisions by investor-State arbitration tribunals in hundreds of cases.[10] Colombia came to conclude treaties that provide for investor-State arbitration at a relatively late stage.[11] Colombia's acceptance of the powers of investor-State arbitration is marked especially by the entry into force of the Colombia–Spain bilateral investment treaty (BIT) in 2007, followed by the entry into force of other treaties which provide for investor-State arbitration in Colombia's relations with significant capital-exporters including BITs with Switzerland (2009), China (2012), and India (2012) and FTAs with Canada (2011) and the US (2012).[12] As such, Colombia is one of few countries that consented to investor-State arbitration – while in the capital-importing position – after it was clear that foreign investors were using the treaties creatively to seek very large amounts of compensation from States for their exercise of their regulatory powers. In turn, it may be said that Colombia has assumed uncertain but potentially major financial liabilities associated with investor-State arbitration at a time when the risks were, or should have been, well-known.

In Colombia's case, no known investor claims have yet been filed under a treaty that provides for investor-State arbitration. This is perhaps surprising given the willingness of US and Canadian investors to resort to investor-State arbitration in the event of a conflict with a host State.[13] It might be explained by a relatively investor-friendly or US-friendly position on the part of governments in Colombia. Alternatively, it might be explained by a general perception of specific investors that business opportunities in Colombia outweigh the benefits of arbitration claims. In any event, Colombia is at an early stage of its exposure to investor-State arbitration, making it difficult to evaluate its experience to date and to predict if and how Colombia may be subject to future claims.

The experience of other countries in investor-State arbitration suggests that Colombia will face claims in time. First, Latin American and Caribbean countries have been subject to a relatively high number of claims compared to other regions.[14] Second, while Colombia has arguably in recent years taken a more investor and US-friendly position than countries such as Bolivia, Ecuador, and Venezuela – which might reduce the prospect of investor claims – countries with a similar political outlook, such as Mexico and Peru, have faced numerous claims and have been ordered to pay significant amounts of compensation.[15] Third, resource companies appear to have resorted to investor-State arbitration more often than companies in other industries and the arbitrations in this area have tended to generate relatively high awards.[16] For these reasons, it is reasonable to conclude that Colombia has assumed potentially serious liabilities arising from investor-State arbitration in its BITs and FTAs and that those liabilities may affect government decision-making in Colombia.

To illustrate, there are various investor-State arbitrations that involved conflicts broadly similar to those described in the case studies in this book. In *Mobil & Murphy Oil* v. *Canada*, a tribunal ordered open-ended compensation to an investor after adopting a narrow interpretation of an exception in the North American Free Trade Agreement for provincial requirements that foreign and domestic companies meet minimum research and development expenditure levels as a condition of approval of their offshore oil production activities.[17] In *Oxy* v. *Ecuador No 1* and *Oxy* v. *Ecuador No 2*, Ecuador was ordered to pay well over $2 billion in compensation to the US oil giant Oxy after an extensive conflict over the company's operations and contractual relationship with Ecuadorian State agencies.[18] In *Metalclad* v. *Mexico*, the tribunal adopted a very expansive approach to concepts of indirect expropriation and fair and equitable treatment and awarded compensation to a US investor after permits were refused and relevant lands converted to a park.[19] These actions followed longstanding local opposition to the investor's proposed hazardous waste facility.[20]

None of these cases are based on precisely the same facts as potential conflicts between Canadian investors and governments or other constituencies in Colombia. Yet they reveal how resource conflicts have led to arbitration claims and, in some cases, shockingly large awards of compensation against States.[21] In earlier analyses of trade agreements and globalization, the case against investor-State arbitration was based on researchers' anticipatory assessments of how the treaty rights and protections for foreign investors would be interpreted by tribunals.[22] Now the required speculation is much diminished by the evidence that claims have been brought, tribunals have interpreted investors' rights and protections expansively in numerous cases, and very large amounts of compensation have been awarded.[23] Presumably, the public record of claims and awards against States has been assessed by Colombian officials and will play some role in Colombia government decision-making that affects Canadian or foreign investors with access to investor-State arbitration. In turn, it is fair to assume that the bargaining position of foreign investors in their regulatory relations with the Colombia State will be elevated relative to the position of other constituencies in Colombia who do not have access to any, let alone a similarly powerful, international enforcement mechanism for their rights or interests.

Beyond the known record of investor-State arbitrations, there is a prospect that Canadian and other foreign investors have behind closed doors threatened to bring claims against Colombia. It is possible that such actions may influence Colombian governments in their dealings with Canadian investors involved in conflicts with other constituencies. The prospect of behind-the-scenes pressure by Canadian investors is associated with wider debates about the prospect of regulatory chill arising from investment treaties.[24] Yet it is very difficult for outside observers or the public to track the outcome of threatened claims or associated pressure which is often not a matter of public record and does not lend itself to comprehensive tracking without extensive interviews with serving or past officials who may not be willing to disclose their experiences in government.

Even so, one situation in which investors have used investor-State arbitration to pressure governments, off the public record, came to the attention of the present author in a visit to Colombia in 2013.[25] In particular, it was reported by sources with insider knowledge that a Spanish investor in the private health care sector threatened to bring an investor-State claim against Colombia due to decisions of Colombian courts to require private health providers to provide lifesaving medicines to patients who could not otherwise afford them. Reportedly, the threatened claim did not materialize following an apparent settlement by Colombian authorities. Also, while the threatened claim was discussed openly within government for a period of time, at a certain point officials stopped discussing it internally and neither the claim nor any resolution was reported publicly.

On this basis, it appears that a Spanish investor employed investor-State arbitration in order to pressure the Colombian government to change court decisions attributable to the State, without public knowledge. Also, considering that the present author learned of this information through non-exhaustive research, it is reasonable to expect that other threats of claims have been made and that the Colombian government is aware of its potential liabilities and may change its behaviour accordingly in some cases. The key for present purposes is that there is a realistic prospect for Canadian investors to exercise greater leverage over Colombian officials due to the availability of investor-State arbitration in the CCFTA, the broad rights and protections for Canadian investors, and the prospect of massive financial liability associated with arbitrator power under the CCFTA and similar treaties.

Moreover, the CCFTA and other treaties that provide for investor-State arbitration have prompted the Colombian government to alter its institutional structure to minimize its risks of liability. In 2013, the Colombia government adopted reforms by which to evaluate and reduce risks of investor-State arbitration and to educate officials across the government about Colombia's newly-assumed treaty obligations to protect foreign investors.[26] Among other things, a special commission – the Comisión Intersectorial para la Atención de Controversias Internacionales de Inversión – was established to manage high-level political decision-making in the event of a conflict with a foreign investor and to define the role of Colombian State entities that respond to such conflicts.[27] One ministry, the Ministry of Commerce, Industry and Tourism (MCIT), was given the lead role to deal with investor-State disputes and resolve disagreements within the Colombia government at meetings involving the President's administrative office, the other affected State entity, and MCIT.[28] MCIT was also given custody of all relevant documents and authority to keep documents confidential, presumably facilitating confidential settlements of threatened or actual claims by foreign investors.[29] MCIT has also initiated a training course for Colombia State officials concerning Colombia's commitments to protect foreign investors under trade and investment treaties and how to observe those commitments.[30]

These reforms reveal how institutional structures and bureaucratic resources have been altered and redirected – and the role of one Ministry elevated – to give greater attention to the rights and protections of Canadian investors as a result of Colombia's acceptance of investor-State arbitration. Colombian government decision-making has been affected in significant ways by the CCFTA and other treaties, to the benefit of foreign investors relative to other constituencies with conflicting rights or interests. The nature and extent of these effects is difficult for outside observers to identify beyond the conclusion that they elevate the position of foreign investors' rights and interests in government decision-making at high levels.

The consequent advantages for foreign investors relative to other actors stem from the breadth and rigour of language in the CCFTA on foreign investor protection and the CCFTA's provision for a powerful and binding mechanism of enforcement that is available directly to foreign investors. Investor-State arbitration is extraordinarily powerful when compared to other forms of international adjudication because of the power it gives to foreign investors and for-profit arbitrators to review and discipline States acting in their sovereign capacity.[31] The power of investor-state arbitration in the CCFTA is highlighted by its requirements that Canada or Colombia (1) submit to international arbitration at the demand of any foreign investor, (2) answer for their conduct with reference to wide-ranging and binding obligations to protect investor rights, and (3) submit to the power of arbitrators to direct public compensation, without any monetary limit, to a foreign investor in awards that are highly-enforceable.[32] These elements are the essence of a system calibrated with care to put effective constraints on sovereign behaviour, where that behaviour is judged unlawful by a tribunal whose members are chosen partly by the foreign investor in the process to which no other affected party has access. In the next section of this chapter, this mechanism for protecting foreign investors is compared to other mechanisms contained in the CCFTA, its side agreements, or the Canada–Colombia Human Rights Agreement that might ensure respect for foreign investor responsibilities alongside their rights and protections in the CCFTA's investment chapter.

Canadian Investor Responsibilities in the CCFTA

The elaborate investor rights and protections in the CCFTA's investment chapter presumably reflect the CCFTA's purposes – as described in its preamble – to '[e]nsure a predictable commercial framework for business planning and investment" and perhaps to "enhance the competitiveness of their firms in global markets".[33] Yet there are other purposes of the CCFTA that relate to the responsibilities of foreign investors in relation to labour rights, environmental protection, and human rights. These include the treaty's purposes:

- to undertake investor protection "in a manner that is consistent with environmental protection and conservation"
- to "enhance and enforce environmental law and regulations"
- to "protect, enhance and enforce basic workers' rights"
- to "promote sustainable development"
- to "encourage enterprises operating within their territory or subject to their jurisdiction, to respect internationally recognized corporate social responsibility standards and principles and to pursue best practices."[34]

By itself, these other statements of purpose in the CCFTA's preamble have little concrete meaning – other than as an interpretive guide – unless they are accompanied by clear rights and enforcement mechanisms to achieve the purpose. The question in this section is whether and how the CCFTA, its side agreements, and the Canada–Colombia Human Rights Agreement advance these other purposes in a meaningful way, compared especially to the CCFTA's provision for broad and rigourous foreign investor rights backed by the power of investor-State arbitration.

Three aspects of the CCFTA are examined in this respect. Each offers a potential means to ensure respect for investor responsibilities alongside their elaborate rights. First, the CCFTA's investment chapter includes exceptions and reservations that recognize an ongoing role for Colombian State entities to regulate Canadian investors. Second, the CCFTA includes side agreements on labour and the environment that purport to ensure respect for investor responsibilities and related standards of labour or environmental protection. Third, the Canada–Colombia Human Rights Agreement, which was concluded in conjunction with the CCFTA, was said to offer protections against human rights violations in Colombia alongside the other mechanisms in the CCFTA. In particular, this Human Rights Agreement was concluded in response to criticism in Canada that it should not conclude a trade agreement with Colombia due to the country's poor human rights record.[35] Each of these aspects is reviewed to assess its rigour in ensuring respect for investor responsibilities relative to the CCFTA's rights and protections for investors.

A Clauses in the CCFTA Investment Chapter

The CCFTA's investment chapter has various exceptions and reservations to preserve regulatory space for Colombia in its relations with investors. These include (1) moderating language on the concepts of fair and equitable treatment and full protection and security for foreign investors which limits the meaning of these concepts to the meaning to the customary minimum standard of treatment,[36] (2) moderating language on indirect expropriation which outlines a range of factors for tribunals to consider when characterizing indirect expropriation and which states that "good faith, non-discriminatory measures ... designed and applied to protect legitimate public welfare objectives, for example health, safety and the protection of the environment, do not constitute indirect expropriate",[37] (3) exemptions of existing discriminatory measures or performance requirements from relevant CCFTA obligations not to adopt such measures or requirements,[38] and (4) an exception for performance requirements that concern the protection of human, animal or plant life or health and concerning the conservation of natural resources.[39] These clauses provide space for Colombia to continue to apply domestic regulatory requirements to Canadian investors. They make clear that there is room for the government to take steps to ensure that foreign investors respect domestic regulatory requirements for lawful investor behaviour, emphasizing health and environmental considerations (not, for example, labour relations or human rights protection).

However, the clauses have important limitations.[40] First, they are established as exceptions to the general rule in the treaty of wide-ranging and robust investor rights and privileges. As such, they do not establish Colombia's right to regulate, and any corresponding investor responsibilities, as an equal partner in the

CCFTA legal structure.[41] Second, the extent of regulatory space that is preserved by these exceptions is unclear and open to interpretation by the arbitrators. In various cases to date, similar investment treaty clauses on the national security of States faced with an economic crisis have been interpreted narrowly by tribunals in favour of broader rights for foreign investors and, in turn, greater State liability.[42] Third, many exceptions apply only some of the treaty's investor rights. For example, the clauses noted in items (3) and (4) in the previous paragraph of this chapter are limited to the CCFTA's prohibitions on performance requirements; they do not extend the CCFTA's general exception for health and conservation measures to other State obligations in the CCFTA's investment chapter. Overall, the exceptions emphasize that the Colombian government retains space to regulate but also leave in place a prospect, in all cases, that Colombia will be found to have violated the CCFTA where the exceptions do not apply or where arbitrators interpret them narrowly.

There is also a provision in the CCFTA's investment chapter that states that Canada and Colombia "should not waive or otherwise derogate from, or offer to waive or otherwise derogate from, [domestic health, safety or environmental] measures as an encouragement for" foreign investment.[43] This clause is expressed in hortatory (non-binding) language due to its use of the term "should" instead of the "shall" language in the CCFTA's provisions for investor rights and protections.[44] Also, the clause cannot be enforced through international arbitration – whether initiated by a private party or by the State – including investor-State arbitration under the CCFTA.[45] Instead, it relies on one State party to the treaty to raise concerns about the other State party's alleged violation of the obligation by making a request for consultations, in which case the other State merely "shall make every attempt through consultations and exchange of information to address the matter".[46] In comparison to the extensive and highly-enforceable powers of investors and arbitrators in investor-State arbitration, this mechanism for ensuring that Canada and Colombia do not downgrade health, safety, or environmental controls in favour of foreign investors' rights and interests is extraordinarily weak. It provides no recourse to any person or constituency who has been mistreated by a foreign investor, with or without complicity of the State, other than to push Canada or Colombia to request consultations and hope that the consultations lead to changed behaviour.

Similarly, the CCFTA contains a clause on Corporate Social Responsibility. This clause states that Canada and Colombia should encourage investors to engage voluntarily in good conduct. In particular:[47]

> Each Party should encourage enterprises operating within its territory or subject to its jurisdiction to voluntarily incorporate internationally recognized standards of corporate social responsibility in their internal policies, such as statements of principle that have been endorsed or are supported by the Parties. These principles address issues such as labour, the environment, human rights, community relations and anti-corruption. The Parties remind those enterprises of the importance of incorporating such corporate social responsibility standards in their internal policies.

This clause obviously gives the responsibilities of the Canadian investor an inferior status in comparison to their rights in the CCFTA. First, it is again hortatory. Canada and Colombia "should encourage" good corporate conduct rather than take steps to ensure it. Even if such steps are taken, the CCFTA provides that investors are expected only to "voluntarily incorporate" unspecified standards of Corporate Social Responsibility in their operations. In effect, Canada and Colombia have merely agreed to encourage each other to encourage investors voluntarily to avoid poor behaviour. The clause is not completely worthless. Yet it falls very far short of any meaningful implementation of investor responsibilities. Other than the consultation mechanism discussed above, it gives no recourse to private parties or State entities where a foreign investor has misbehaved. It is not subject to international arbitration or any other form of enforcement and adjudication. It contrasts starkly with the power of investor-State arbitration as a mechanism to protect foreign investors.

B   The CCFTA's Labour and Environmental Side Agreements

A second aspect of the CCFTA that could implement investor responsibilities is its side agreements on labour and the environment.[48] The question here is whether these side agreements – in comparison to the CCFTA's provisions on investor rights and investor-State arbitration – would allow other constituencies or the Colombian government to initiate a binding adjudication that could lead to a meaningful remedy in a dispute with a foreign investor or, alternatively, with a State that failed to ensure that a foreign investor met rigourous labour or environmental standards. Neither side agreement comes remotely close to doing so, as I discuss below. In turn, the side agreements maintain the gross imbalance between investor rights and investor responsibilities in the CCFTA.

The CCFTA's side agreements lay out general obligations of Canada and Colombia to protect labour rights and the environment, respectively. They are framed using binding language ("shall") and are more detailed than the vague provisions on health, safety, and on Corporate Social Responsibility in the CCFTA's investment chapter. Thus, according to the labour side agreement:[49]

> Each Party shall ensure that its statutes and regulations, and practices thereunder, embody and provide protection for the following internationally recognized labour principles and rights:
>
> a.   freedom of association and the right to collective bargaining…;
> b.   the elimination of all forms of forced or compulsory labour;
> c.   the effective abolition of child labour…;
> d.   the elimination of discrimination in respect of employment and occupation;
> e.   acceptable conditions of work with respect to minimum wages, hours or work and occupational health and safety; and
> f.   providing migrant workers with the same legal protections as the Party's nationals in respect of working conditions.

This obligation is supplemented by further duties of each State not to derogate from its domestic labour laws so as to encourage trade or investment,[50] to ensure private access to domestic proceedings to enforce labour rights,[51] and to promote compliance with its labour laws.[52] Similarly, the environmental side agreement contains this general obligation:[53]

> Recognizing the sovereign right of each Party to establish its own levels of national environmental protection and environmental development policies and priorities, and to adopt or modify accordingly its environmental laws and policies, each Party shall ensure that its environmental laws and policies provide for high levels of environmental protection and shall strive to continue to develop and improve those laws and policies.

Besides this, Colombia and Canada are obligated to "effectively enforce, through government action, its environmental laws", not to "encourage trade or investment by weakening or reducing the levels of protection afforded in its environmental laws", and to:

> ensure that [the Party] maintains appropriate procedures for assessing the environmental impacts in accordance with national law and policy of proposed plans and projects, which may cause adverse effects on the environment, with a view to avoiding or minimizing such adverse effects.[54]

On the face of it, these appear to be significant obligations for States in the protection of labour rights and the environment. Yet they emerge as very weak obligations when compared to the States' commitments to protect investors in the CCFTA investment chapter. First, they are limited to domestic laws and regulations that may create investor responsibilities and do not provide for any new treaty standards of investor responsibility or related State responsibility in the manner of the CCFTA investment chapter's elaborate investor rights. Second, they establish either a weak process, or virtually none at all, to enforce the obligations.

On the first point, the obligations in the side agreements would be equivalent to the CCFTA's investor rights and protections only if the treaty's investment chapter limited its protections for foreign investors to provisions in each country's domestic laws. Yet the CCFTA investment chapter obviously goes well beyond committing Canada and Colombia not to derogate from domestic protections for foreign investors. Rather, the CCFTA imposes an extensive range of relatively sweeping obligations to protect investors.[55] Thus, while investor rights and protections are identified and defined in detail in the CCFTA, its side agreements limit the protection of labour rights and the environment – and corresponding investor responsibilities – to a State's domestic laws. There is no attempt to regulate foreign investors directly or to provide for any investor responsibilities in the treaty alongside investor's rights under the CCFTA's investment chapter.

Further, in the environmental side agreement, there are very broad limitations on the State's obligation to ensure protection of the environment in their domestic laws. For example, there is no obligation for Canada or Colombia to strengthen domestic environmental protections or otherwise satisfy international standards. Instead, there is a non-binding obligation to "strive to continue to develop and improve" domestic environmental laws and policies. This obviously contrasts with the elaborate treaty-based rights of foreign investors under the CCFTA that are independent of domestic law and establish minimum standards from which a State cannot derogate.

Also, the environmental side agreement has a broad affirmation of the right of Canada and Colombia to regulate (and, by implication, de-regulate) freely in environmental matters. In broad language, the side agreement affirms "the sovereign right of each Party to establish its own levels of national environmental protection and environmental development policies and priorities, and to adopt or modify accordingly its environmental laws and policies" as a general condition for the State's obligation to protect the environment. No comparable affirmation of the right to regulate is found anywhere in the CCFTA investment chapter. Thus, States do not have an express right, for example, "to establish their own levels of investor protection and development policies in relation to private owners of assets". In this respect, the allocation of rights under the treaty – between foreign investors and the State in its regulatory role – is heavily skewed. The environmental side agreement also reveals that Canada and Colombia knew how to incorporate broad flexibility in the State's right to regulate, but did not to do so when it came to foreign investors' rights and protections. Among other things, this will undermine any future argument by Canada or Colombia in investor-State arbitration that any other language in the CCFTA investment chapter was meant to preserve their right to regulate in broad terms.

These limitations of the substantive obligations on labour rights and environmental protection are an important part of the CCFTA's imbalanced provision for Canadian investor rights but not investor responsibilities. A second major limitation of the side agreements is their relatively weak mechanisms for enforcement where a foreign investor has abused workers or damaged the environment and the relevant state fails to protect domestic victims. Thus, in a dispute about a State's compliance with its obligations under the labour side agreement, the procedure to resolve the dispute is as follows:[56]

- A State party (Canada or Colombia) may request consultations with the other state party at the ministerial level.
- Each State shall provide the other with sufficient information to allow a full examination of the matters raised.
- The States "shall make every effort to reach a mutually satisfactory agreement of the matter".
- Following consultations, a State may request that a panel of experts in labour matters or other appropriate matters be convened in the event that the matter is trade-related and that it involves "a persistent pattern of failure to effectively enforce its labour law" or failure to comply with certain obligations under the side agreement on the part of the other state.

- The panel must determine whether the matter is trade-related and, if it is not, cannot proceed.
- If the panel finds that the matter is trade-related and proceeds, it hears submissions from the two states and determines whether the state under review demonstrated a persistent pattern of failure to effectively enforce its labour law or comply with specified obligations under the labour side agreement.
- If the panel finds a failure to comply by the State, it can make recommendations to resolve the matter, "which normally shall be that the [state party] ... adopt and implement an action plan sufficient to remedy the pattern of non-compliance".[57]
- The panel then hears comments from the two states before issuing its final report. If the panel concludes that a state was in non-compliance, the two States have an opportunity "to reach agreement on an action plan" based on the panel's report and, failings this or in the face of a complaint by one state that the other has not observed the action plan, a State can request that the panel be reconvened to impose a monetary assessment on the other State.
- The reconvened panel may then impose a monetary assessment on the non-complying state which is to be paid into a fund and expended by a ministerial council of the two States on "appropriate labour initiatives" in the non-complying State.
- In determining the amount of the monetary assessment, a panel must take into account "the pervasiveness and duration" of a State's non-compliance, the reasons for the State's failure to comply, the level of compliance that could reasonably be expected of the State "given its resource constraints", the efforts made by the State to remedy the non-compliance after the panel's final report, and any other relevant factors.
- In any event, the amount of monetary assessment cannot exceed US$15 million.

Based on this process, if a Canadian investor violates workers' rights in Colombia, the labour side agreement provides only that the investor's home state, Canada, can initiate a process to review Colombia's conduct, that a panel can make recommendations after a review, that Canada and Colombia can then agree to resolve the dispute, that a remedy can be awarded by the panel only after a further request by Canada, and that the remedy has various limitations including a monetary cap of CAD$15 million. The review process does not allow any private party to initiate an enforcement process of any kind against a foreign investor or the State. There is no provision for a private party to receive any remedy due to misconduct of a foreign investor or government. Assuming that the Canadian government can be expected to lobby on behalf of Canadian investors abroad, this is a very weak arrangement if the aim was to ensure that Canadian investors respect workers' rights in Colombia.

Also, again, this set-up contrasts starkly with the CCFTA investment chapter where, through investor-State arbitration, a foreign investor can bring a claim directly against the State, the claim cannot be filtered by the investor's home State, the claim cannot be withdrawn through an agreement between the two

States, the investor plays a role in determining the make-up of the tribunal, and the tribunal can award a potentially-unlimited monetary compensation – in cases to date, hundreds of millions and even billions of dollars – against a State without the various limitations on monetary assessments in the labour side agreement.[58] This reveals the extent to which Canada and Colombia elevated foreign investor rights above labour rights in the CCFTA.

The enforcement structure is even weaker for the environmental side agreement. The side agreement has no procedure to resolve dispute and enforce obligations beyond a requirement for each State party to consult with the other. In summary:[59]

- A State party may request consultations with the other state party regarding any matter arising under the agreement with the purpose of seeking a mutually agreed solution. The other State must "respond expeditiously".
- Beyond this, there is no process to resolve an outstanding dispute about the agreement.

Obviously this approach to enforcement pales in comparison to investor-State arbitration. If the aim was to ensure that foreign investors meet any responsibilities in relation to labour rights and environmental protection, the side agreements are very weak in comparison to the CCFTA investment chapter. Moreover, the side agreements prohibit Colombia and Canada from providing a right of action in their domestic law for an affected person – such as a victim of labour rights violations or environmental contamination – to sue the other State for failing to abide by the relevant side agreement.[60] As such, the side agreements are not enforceable at all in domestic law. Overall, the environmental side agreement has no real enforcement mechanism and the labour side agreement relies entirely on inter-governmental adjudication to resolve disputes and limits enforcement to situations in which, for example, labour rights violations were "trade-related" and reflected a "persistent pattern" of non-compliance.

In these ways, the CCFTA and its side agreements establish a regime for the effective protection of investor rights but not investor responsibilities. They establish a structure in which investor responsibilities are actionable only based on action by the investor's home State and, even then, based on weak obligations of the host State for the investor. At no point would an investor have to respond to a claim of misconduct or face an enforcement process or remedy. It is hard to imagine a regime that was more favourable to an investor who violated labour rights or environmental standards. Viewed alongside investor-State arbitration, the side agreements are a hollow, almost satirical, reflection of the stated purposes of the CCFTA to protect workers' rights and the environment and to encourage Corporate Social Responsibility.

C Canada–Colombia Human Rights and Free Trade Agreement

A third aspect of the CCFTA is the Canada–Colombia Human Rights Agreement or, in full, the Agreement Concerning Annual Reports on Human Rights and Free Trade. This treaty was concluded alongside the CCFTA and purportedly responds to concerns in Canada that a trade agreement with Colombia should not proceed due to the country's record of systematic human rights violations.[61] Does this Agreement ensure that Canadian investors meet rigourous responsibilities to respect human rights in Colombia? The answer is clearly not.

The Human Rights Agreement is very brief and limited in its purpose. It requires simply that the Canadian and Colombian governments present an annual report to their respective national legislature "on the effect of the measures taken under the [Canada–Colombia] Free Trade Agreement ... on human rights in the territories of both Canada and the Republic of Colombia" and to make the report public.[62] There is also an obligation for consultation between Canada and Colombia on implementation of the treaty.[63] Beyond this, there are no obligations for anyone. The treaty does not: establish or affirm any human rights standards; it does not lay out any responsibilities for foreign investors; it does not provide for any process in the event of a dispute about the conduct of an investor; it does not lay out any modalities or requirements for the reports to national legislatures; it does not provide for any process to enforce each country's obligation to provide a report; and it does not provide for any independent assessment – other than by the Canadian or Colombia governments – of the human rights situation and the effect of the free trade agreement in, respectively, Canada or Colombia.

Thus, the Human Rights Agreement does not provide a means to ensure investor responsibilities that is comparable in any way to the CCFTA investment chapter and investor-State arbitration. At most, it might encourage one country's government to draw attention to the human rights situation in the other country as it relates to their trade and investment relationship. Yet even in this respect the Human Rights Agreements limit the role of human rights reports to the implications of "measures taken" by each State under the CCFTA and does not include, for example, the conduct of foreign investors who enjoy extensive protections under the CCFTA. In other words, Canada and Colombia did not even agree to mandate reports on the human rights implications of their own investors' conduct or of the CCFTA provisions on investment or the decisions of CCFTA investor-State arbitrators. This is an extraordinarily weak response to the stated objective of Canada and Colombia – in the preamble to the Human Rights Agreement – to affirm "the importance of respect for democracy and human rights" in the countries' relationship.[64]

Even if the Human Rights Agreement does little to provide for reporting on the interaction between human rights and the CCFTA, a government can nevertheless take a broader approach in its reports on human rights and the CCFTA. The Human Rights Agreement creates an obligation to provide an annual report; it does not preclude reporting or monitoring on broader subjects and it does not preclude action in Canada to enforce responsibilities of Canadian companies operating in Colombia. For example, one could expect a report on the conduct of Canadian investors in Colombia, on whether investors have respected international human rights standards, and on the degree to which the CCFTA's rights for foreign investors may contribute to misconduct of Canadian investors or toleration of such misconduct by the Colombia government. However, the federal government's reports under the Human Rights Agreement have not done any of these things. Indeed, they have been absurdly narrowly-focused if the intent was to report on how the CCFTA may impact on human rights and democracy.

Thus, in its first annual report under the Human Rights Agreement in 2012, the federal government stated that it was too early to make any findings on human rights and the CCFTA.[65] Instead, it provided general information on Canada–Colombia trade and investment flows and on the CCFTA and its side agreements. The government also used the report to outline a methodology "to analyze the impacts of the [Canada–Colombia CCFTA] on human rights" in future reports. The methodology was vague and narrowly conceived, as follows:[66]

- Measures taken under the CCFTA in the previous year would be reviewed.
- Specific provisions of the CCFTA that were negotiated to benefit particular economic sectors would be reviewed to identify sectors where an increase in trade or investment is expected.
- Information about trade, investment, and services would be clustered into significant sectors and sub-sectors to facilitate annual tracking.
- Once the significant economic sectors affected by the CCFTA were identified, a report would be prepared "on the effect of the measures."
- Stakeholders would be consulted on the report and its methodology.
- Activities taken under the CCFTA mechanisms (i.e., consultation, public communications, and dispute resolution) would be reviewed where they "refer to human rights".
- Activities taken under the labour and environmental side agreements would be reviewed.

This was an opaque and confounding statement of methodology. It does not explain why particular sectors are being identified, it does not indicate what types of measures are to be included in the review, and it does not specify what human rights impacts are to be assessed. It does not refer to any outside sources on human rights assessment.[67] It strangely limits any report on the activities of dispute resolution tribunals under the CCFTA to situations in which the tribunal has referred to human rights on the dubious assumption that a tribunal's decisions may impact human rights only where the tribunal mentions the term. Overall, the methodology seems designed to avoid any serious monitoring of the relationship between human rights and the CCFTA. Certainly, it does not provide a clear outline of how the reports on this relationship will be carried out.

More importantly, the outline of reporting methodology does not seek to go beyond the extremely narrow issue of how specific measures adopted under the CCFTA may relate to and affect significant economic sectors affected by the

CCFTA. The methodology does not provide for any reporting on the question of whether Canadian investors have engaged in conduct that violates or contributes to the violation of human rights and whether the CCFTA played a role in endorsing, facilitating, or sheltering such conduct. The methodology also does not seek to evaluate whether the Canadian or Colombian governments changed their approach to human rights protection in order to limit the risk of liability to foreign investors under the CCFTA. Thus, the Human Rights Agreement, as implemented by the Canadian government, does not take any steps to monitor the conduct of Canadian investors under the CCFTA.

The second[68] and third[69] reports issued by the Canadian government also support the conclusion that the government approaches the reporting exercise pursuant to the Human Rights Agreement as a bureaucratic avoidance exercise. Neither report provided any critical evaluation of the human rights situation in Colombia. Neither considered in a serious way how the CCFTA may have affected the human rights situation. Both reports laid out general descriptions of trade relations between Canada and Colombia and of activities undertaken by the governments under the CCFTA and its side agreements. They then limit any review of human rights impacts to actions taken to implement the CCFTA in the previous year. In the second report, for example, such actions were limited to tariff reductions on some imported products. Also, the report took a strict approach to the issue of causation regarding the connection between tariff reductions and the CCFTA.[70]

It is not possible to establish a direct link between the [CCFTA] and the human rights situation in Colombia. There is no evidence of a causal link *between reductions in tariffs* by Canada in accordance with the [CCFTA] *and changes in human rights* in Colombia.... Based on an examination of the actions taken under the [CCFTA], it is not possible to reach any conclusion on whether any changes in human rights in either country have occurred.

Similarly, the federal government affirmed its limited mandate "to outline the actions taken by Canada under the [CCFTA] and the related [labour and environmental side agreements] and any effects these actions may have had on human rights" and concluded that "*Issues such as foreign investment* and Canada–Colombia trade in sectors where tariffs were not affected by the [CCFTA] *fall outside the scope of this report* as no actions were taken by Canada in these actions".[71] By adopting a strict mandate to review the linkages only between tariff reductions and human rights in Colombia, a wide range of other potential findings of human rights impact arising from the CCFTA – including impacts of foreign investors' activities under the FIPA – were effectively precluded.

Further, under a sub-heading in the reports entitled "Human Rights under Consideration", one could expect the Canadian government to outline relevant human rights instruments and the rights they establish in order to frame an evaluation of human rights impacts of the CCFTA. Instead, the federal government's report provided this brief and self-serving statement:[72]

The promotion and protection of human rights is an integral part of Canadian foreign policy. Canada stands up for human rights and takes principled positions on important issues to ensure that freedom, democracy, human rights and the rule of law are enjoyed around the world.

In light of this narrow and evasive approach to the opportunity to report on Canadian investors, human rights, and the CCFTA, one may reasonably dismiss the reporting exercise as a conscious avoidance strategy. None of the government's reports under the Human Rights Agreement discussed activities of Canadian investors or the ways in which the CCFTA may facilitate misbehaviour by Canadian investors. As the case studies in this book illustrate, there is ample information to examine on the conduct of Canadian investors in relation to human rights. Yet none of these case studies would fall within the Canadian government's extremely narrow framing of its mandate to report on human rights and the CCFTA.

The only part of the Canadian government's reports that refers to actual human rights concerns in Colombia is the following summary of public submissions made to the government as part of the reporting process:[73]

Two submissions were received this year, compared with none in 2013. These submissions raise concerns about assassinations of trade union activists and repression of those who are viewed as obstacles to the development of Colombian oil, mining and agriculture resources. These submissions also claim that there has long been, and continues to be, a great deal of civil resistance to the [CCFTA], as well as other FTAs. Civil resistance, in their submission, includes the activities of labour unions, indigenous and Afro-Colombian groups, "campesino" farmers, and traditional artisanal miners. They also allege that these groups are the primary victims of human rights violations because they resist handing their local resources and access to their local markets over to foreign corporations.

The concerns expressed in these submissions are similar to concerns arising from the case studies in this book. In response to the concerns, the federal government in its third report concluded (in its entirety) on this point:[74]

None of the submissions this year provide an analysis of changes in the human rights situation during the past year, or were able to demonstrate any link between the enjoyment and respect of human rights and Canadian tariff reduction measures arising from the implementation of the [FTA].

Thus, the federal government responded to submissions about human rights concerns in Colombia by stating it would not review the substance of the submissions because (1) the government decided only to concern itself with *changes* in the human rights situation rather than the human rights situation itself and (2) the government decided to review human rights changes arising only from its tariff reductions and nothing else.

Worse, the government's report on these public submissions leave open the possibility that victims of human rights in Colombia – expecting a process to review their concerns – were brought by the Canadian government to the attention of business and State actors alleged to have been involved in human rights abuses. According to Canadian government in its third report:[75]

[The] submissions state that human rights violations are witnessed regularly in Colombia, namely unpunished crimes, and the re-victimization of internally displaced people. These submissions also argue that there are discrepancies in the application of victims' laws in Colombia.

The submissions claimed that human rights violations against these groups have weakened them and that successive Colombian governments, under the obligations of international trade agreements and tribunals, use security forces to protect the economic interests of corporate investors.

Notably, these particular submissions appear linked directly to the CCFTA's investment chapter including its provision for "full protection and security" for Canadian investors in Colombia. Investor-State tribunals have interpreted this investor right in similar treaties as requiring host governments to take steps to protect foreign investors from opposition to their activities by local communities including by providing police protection.[76]

In response to the submissions, the Canadian government indicated in its report that the Canadian embassy in Bogota made "outcalls" to business, local authorities, labour unions, civil society, and local and departmental governments. The outcalls "were focused on the textiles and the cosmetics and personal hygiene (hair products) industries" (because of the link to tariff reductions that year) and examined "whether there was a noticeable impact on the enjoyment and respect of human rights as a result of tariff reduction measures arising from the implementation of the [CCFTA]".[77] Information received in these outcalls led to the government's conclusion that:[78]

With regard to the impact on human rights in Colombia, outcalls with business, local authorities, labour unions, civil society and local and departmental governments in the textiles and cosmetics and personal hygiene sectors in Colombia indicated that *none could demonstrate that any of the factors impacting upon human rights and worker satisfaction are directly related to the implementation of the CCOFTA.* Additionally, complaints over labour conditions either pre-dated the entry into force of the CCOFTA or were related to the implementation of FTA with other economies…

At this time, it is not possible to establish a direct link between the CCOFTA and the human rights situation in Colombia. *There is no evidence of a causal link between reductions in tariffs by Canada in accordance with the CCOFTA, and changes in human rights in Colombia.*

Again, then, the Canadian government was concerned about the human rights situation in Colombia only to the extent that the CCFTA made the situation noticeably worse. So long as assassinations of labour activists or repression of communities opposed to activities of foreign investors had not worsened (in sectors where the Canadian government made tariff reductions in the previous year), the Canadian government would not review or consider any human rights impacts potentially linked to the CCFTA. It is difficult to see this as more than an avoidance exercise including for the potential connections between the activities of Canadian investors and the surrounding context of human rights violations in Colombia.

Overall, the Human Rights Agreement clearly does not provide for any actionable responsibilities for Canadian investors in Colombia alongside their rights under the CCFTA investment chapter. The Human Rights Agreement has been approached so restrictively by the Canadian government as to preclude the great bulk of concerns about human rights impacts of the CCFTA. Canadian investors' conduct in this respect is excluded from the scope of the government's review on the basis that it does not arise from implementing measures adopted directly by Canada under the CCFTA. The Canadian government simply does not consider in its human rights reporting how the CCFTA – including its provisions for investor rights and the corresponding reforms to Colombia government decision-making – may affect the human rights situation where investor rights or interests are in conflict with the human rights of other constituencies.

Conclusion

There is a stark contrast between the broadly-framed and powerful rights of Canadian investors in the CCFTA investment chapter and the abject failure to affirm and enforce investors' responsibilities in the CCFTA, its side agreements, or the Canada–Colombia Human Rights Agreement. As a result, it is reasonable to suspect that the CCFTA is more likely to worsen than to ameliorate the human rights situation in Colombia because of its potential to facilitate and shelter investors who behave poorly and because of the one-way liabilities it creates for the Colombian government when faced with investor demands that conflict with those of domestic constituencies. The Canadian government is responsible for this state of affairs via its approval of the CCFTA investment chapter, the lack of meaningful enforcement in the side agreements, and the remarkably narrow scope and weakness of the Human Rights Agreement and its implementation. One may infer from this that the Canadian government prefers to elevate and protect Canadian investors even where they engage in gross human rights violations, abuse of workers, or environmental contamination.

How then should one respond to the potential misconduct of Canadian investors in Colombia or other impacts of the CCFTA that may worsen the human rights situation in Colombia? I suggest three broad options. The first is to work toward a new treaty between Canada and Colombia that would modify the CCFTA in order to address the existing imbalances. Such an agreement could establish actionable responsibilities for foreign investors alongside their elaborate rights and could strengthen the obligations of Canada and Colombia to implement labour and environmental standards. A second option is to push Canadian investors to make binding commitments directly to affected communities or other constituencies in Colombia which could be enforced in domestic proceedings in Colombia and Canada. Presumably most Canadian investors do not arrive in Colombia intending to exploit the imbalances created by the CCFTA in order to violate workers' rights, ruin the environment, or otherwise worsen the human rights situation in Colombia. A third (and weak) option is to engage further with the Canadian government's reporting process under the Human Rights Agreement or otherwise, if only to document its narrow mandate and other limitations. In connection with this, it should be demanded that the process ensure rigourous protections for individuals and organizations in Colombia who come forward with human rights concerns. The Canadian government may contribute directly to human rights violations in Colombia where its reporting process holds out a false promise of meaningful review and, in doing so, exposes Colombian victims of human rights abuses to retribution by businesses or the Colombian government. In its third report, the Canadian government reported that it made "outcalls" at which alleged victims and perpetrators of human rights abuses were brought together – leading to the conclusion that none of the human rights concerns raised fell within the government's extraordinarily narrow mandate – but did not describe how alleged victims' identities were protected in a country afflicted by widespread violence and systematic human rights abuse. Even if the human rights reporting were turned into more than an avoidance exercise, at least it should not lure vulnerable persons into a situation of potentially heightened risk of murder, torture, or other abuse.

Notes

1 *Canada–Colombia Free Trade Agreement* (CCFTA) (signed November 21, 2008, entered into force August 15, 2011), last accessed October 2, 2014, www.international.gc.ca/trade-agreements-accords-commerciaux/agr-acc/colombia-colombie/can-colombia-toc-tdm-can-colombie.aspx?lang=eng.
2 *Canada–Colombia Agreement on Labour Cooperation* (labour side agreement) (signed November 21, 2008, entered into force August 15, 2011), last accessed October 2, 2014, www.labour.gc.ca/eng/relations/international/agreements/lca_colombia.shtml; *Agreement on the Environment between Canada and the Republic of Colombia* (environmental side agreement) (signed November 21, 2008, entered into force August 15, 2011), last accessed October 2, 2014, www.ec.gc.ca/caraib-carib/default.asp?lang=En&n=FFEF249E-1.
3 *Agreement concerning Annual Reports on Human Rights and Free Trade between Canada and the Republic of Colombia* (Canada–Colombia Human Rights Agreement) (signed May 27, 2010, entered into force August 15, 2011), last accessed October 2, 2014, www.treaty-accord.gc.ca/text-texte.aspx?id=105278.
4 CCFTA (note 1 above), Chapter 8, Section A.
5 CCFTA (note 1 above), Chapter 8, Section B.
6 CCFTA (note 1 above), Articles 803, 804, 807, and 811.
7 CCFTA (note 1 above), Article 805(1).
8 I say "purportedly" because of the prospect that most-favoured-nation treatment may be used by arbitrators to remove the effect of limiting language in Article 805(1) where another trade or investment treaty concluded by Canada does not contain the limiting language. Howard Mann, "The Canada–China investment treaty sleight of hand" *Embassy News*, January 9, 2013, last accessed October 2, 2014, www.embassynews.ca/opinion/2013/01/08/the-canada-china-investment-treaty-sleight-of-hand/43048.

9 Valentina Vadi, *Public Health in International Investment Arbitration* (London: Routledge, 2013), 185; Roland Kläger, *'Fair and Equitable Treatment' in International Investment Law* (Cambridge: CUP, 2011), 116–119.

10 United Nations Conference on Trade and Development (UNCTAD), *Recent Developments in Investor-State Dispute Settlement (ISDS)*, IIA Issues Note No. 1 (April 2014), 2.

11 This was due to decisions of the Colombian Constitutional Court which precluded such treaties as incompatible with the Colombian constitution; the position in Colombia was changed in 1999 via a constitutional amendment. David Schneiderman, *Constitutionalizing Economic Globalization* (Cambridge: CUP, 2008), chapter 6.

12 See UNCTAD, Investment Instruments Online (Bilateral Investment Treaties), last accessed September 1, 2014, www.unctadxi.org/templates/DocSearch____779.aspx; Organization of American States (OAS), Foreign Trade Information System (Trade Agreements in Force), last accessed October 2, 2014, www.sice.oas.org/agreements_e. asp.

13 As of May 2014, US claimants brought 116 (29%), and Canadian claimants 26 (7%), of the total 395 known investment treaty claims (with verifiable public documents) worldwide to May 2014. Numbers are approximate due to the confidentiality of documents in investor-state arbitration. Data collected by author.

14 A Latin American or Caribbean country (including Mexico) was the target of 82 (21%) of the total 395 known investment treaty claims (with verifiable public documents) worldwide to May 2014. Of these, 55 (14%) were against a South American country. Numbers are approximate due to the confidentiality of documents in investor-state arbitration. Data collected by author.

15 Between them, Mexico and Peru have been targeted in 30 known cases (with verifiable public documents) and ordered to pay compensation in at least nine cases with numerous cases ongoing. Numbers are approximate due to the confidentiality of documents in investor-state arbitration. Data collected by author.

16 In 196 cases to May 2010 with sufficient information to gauge the type of conflict to which they related, 40 were found to relate to public health or environmental protection and 34 were found to have involved conflicts over natural resources. Data collected by author. See Gus Van Harten, *Sovereign Choices and Sovereign Constraints* (Oxford: OUP, 2013), 85–9.

17 *Mobil Investments Canada Inc. and Murphy Oil Corporation v Canada* (Award, 22 May 2012), last accessed October 2, 2014, www.italaw.com/sites/default/files/case-documents/italaw1145.pdf.

18 *Occidental Exploration and Production Company v. Republic of Ecuador (Oxy v. Ecuador No 1)* (Award, July 1, 2004), last accessed October 2, 2014, www.italaw. com/sites/default/files/case-documents/ita0571.pdf; *Occidental Petroleum Corporation and Occidental Exploration and Production Company v. Republic of Ecuador (Oxy v. Ecuador No 2)* (Award, October 5, 2012), last accessed October 2, 2014, www.italaw.com/sites/default/files/case-documents/italaw1094.pdf.

19 *Metalclad Corporation v. United Mexican States* (Award, August 30, 2000), last accessed October 2, 2014, www.italaw.com/sites/default/files/case-documents/ita0510.pdf.

20 Suzanne M. Wilkinson, "NAFTA, Mexico & Metalclad: Understanding the Normative Framework of International Trade Law", LLM Thesis, University of British Columbia, 2002.

21 For example, the award in *Oxy v. Ecuador No 2*, note 17 above, generated an award of $2.37 billion (including pre-award interest).

22 e.g., Thomas Singer, Paul Orbuch, and Robert Stumberg, *Multilateral Agreement on Investment: potential effects on state and local governments* (Western Governors Association, 1998).

23 e.g., Van Harten, note 16 above.

24 e.g., Kyla Tienhaara, *The Expropriation of Environmental Governance* (Cambridge: CUP, 2009), 262–4.

25 Interview with anonymous source (January 29, 2014).

26 Republic of Colombia (Departmento Nacional de Planeación, Consejo Nacional de Político Económica y Social), *Fortalecimiento de la Estrategia del Estado para la Prevención y Atención de Controversias Internacionales de Inversión* (Conpes Strategy), Conpes Document No. 3684, October 19, 2010, 24–27.

27 Conpes Strategy (note 25 above), 24–25.

28 Conpes Strategy (note 25 above), 26.

29 Conpes Strategy (note 25 above), 27.

30 Maria Fernanda Sánchez Montenegro, MCIT Advisor, Email communication, September 10, 2014.

31 Gus Van Harten, *Investment Treaty Arbitration and Public Law* (Oxford: OUP, 2007), chapter 5.

32 Ibid.

33 CCFTA (note 1 above), Preamble.

34 Ibid.

35 e.g., Prime Minister of Canada Stephen Harper, "Improving Free Trade and Human Rights in Colombia," August 10, 2011 ("The [CCFTA] includes a separate agreement that will call for Canada and Colombia to produce annual reports on the impacts of free trade on human rights in both countries."); Justin Trudeau, "Free Trade With Colombia," last accessed October 2, 2014, http://justintrudeau.liberal.ca/en/free-trade-with-columbia/ ("Mr. Speaker, over the past year I have received many letters and emails regarding the free trade agreement between Canada and Colombia. It is undoubtedly an issue that many Canadians care about. It is an economic issue, sustaining jobs in Canada and Colombia, and it is a moral issue when we consider the human rights situation in Canada.... Human rights are at the root of our Liberal values, so in order for us to support [the CCFTA], we needed to ensure that the economic agreement with Colombia would have a component that protects the right of Colombian workers and keep our companies out of human rights conflicts.... That is why it was such a key element that our international trade critic ... negotiated an amendment compelling each country to monitor and publicly report on how this trade agreement impacted human rights both in Canada and Colombia. In fact, under this new Liberal deal, Canada and Colombia must publicly measure the impact of free trade on human rights in both countries..." (emphasis added).

36 CCFTA, note 1 above, Article 805(1).

37 CCFTA, note 1 above, Annex 811.

38 CCFTA, note 1 above, Article 809(1).

39 CCFTA, note 1 above, Articles 807(4)(c) and 2201(3).

40 For an elaboration of this point, see "Statement of Concern about Planned Provisions on Investment Protection and Investor-State Dispute Settlement (ISDS) in the Transatlantic Trade and Investment Partnership (TTIP) signed by over 100 academics, last accessed October 2, 2014, www.kent.ac.uk/law/isds_treaty_consultation.html; Gus Van Harten, *Comments on the European Commission's Approach to Investor-State Arbitration in TTIP and CETA*, Osgoode Hall Law School Research Paper No. 59 (2914), 11 and 25.

41 Van Harten, ibid, 11.

42 Van Harten, note 16 above, 66–8.

43 CCFTA, note 1 above, Article 815.

44 Compare e.g., CCFTA, note 1 above, Articles 803, 804, 805, and 811.

45 CCFTA, note 1 above, Article 819(1).

46 CCFTA, note 1 above, Article 815.

47 CCFTA, note 1 above, Article 816.

48 Labour side agreement, note 2 above; Environmental side agreement, note 2 above.

49 Labour side agreement, note 2 above, Article 1.

174   G. Van Harten

50 Labour side agreement, note 2 above, Article 2.
51 Labour side agreement, note 2 above, Article 4.
52 Labour side agreement, note 2 above, Articles 3 and 5.
53 Environmental side agreement, note 2 above, Article 2(1).
54 Environmental side agreement, note 2 above, Article 2(2), (4), and (5).
55 See notes 4 to 7 above.
56 Labour side agreement, note 2 above, Part 3 and Annex 4.
57 Labour side agreement, note 2 above, Article 17(2)(c).
58 Labour side agreement, note 2 above, Annex 4.
59 Environmental side agreement, note 2 above, Article 12.
60 Labour side agreement, note 2 above, Article 23 ("Neither Party may provide for a right of action under its domestic law against the other Party on the ground that the other Party has acted in a manner inconsistent with this Agreement"); Environmental side agreement, note 2 above, Article 12(6) ("Neither Party shall provide for a right of action under its law against the other Party on the ground that the other Party has acted in a manner inconsistent with this Agreement").
61 e.g., Dawn Paley, "Deadly dealings surround Canada–Colombia Free Trade Agreement" *This Magazine*, August 24, 2009. See also note 34 above.
62 Canada–Colombia Human Rights Agreement, note 3 above, Article 1.
63 Canada–Colombia Human Rights Agreement, note 3 above, Article 2.
64 CCFTA, note 1 above, Preamble.
65 Government of Canada, *Annual Report Pursuant to the Agreement concerning Annual Reports on Human Rights and Free Trade between Canada and the Republic of Canada* (First report), May 15, 2012, last accessed October 2, 2014, www.canadainternational.gc.ca/colombia-colombie/bilateral_relations_bilaterales/rep-hrft-co_2012-dple-rapp.aspx. The available version of the report does not contain page numbers.
66 Ibid, Methodology.
67 e.g., James Harrison, *Conducting a Human Rights Impact Assessment of the Canada–Colombia Free Trade Agreement: Key Issues*, Background Paper for the CCIC Americas Policy Group (February 2009).
68 Government of Canada, *Annual Report Pursuant to the Agreement concerning Annual Reports on Human Rights and Free Trade between Canada and the Republic of Canada* (Second report), June 14, 2013, last accessed October 2, 2014, www.canadainternational.gc.ca/colombia-colombie/bilateral_relations_bilaterales/rep-hrft-co_2013-dple-rapp.aspx?lang=eng; The available version of the report does not contain page numbers.
69 Government of Canada, *Annual Report Pursuant to the Agreement concerning Annual Reports on Human Rights and Free Trade between Canada and the Republic of Canada* (Third report), May 15, 2014, last accessed October 2, 2014, www.canada international.gc.ca/colombia-colombie/bilateral_relations_bilaterales/AnnualReport_RapportAnnuel-2013.aspx. The available version of the report does not contain page numbers.
70 Second report, note 67 above, Summary of Findings.
71 Second report, note 67 above, Canada's Reporting Requirement under the Canada–Colombia Free Trade Agreement Implementation Act – Scope and Limitations.
72 This statement should at least include the rider: "except where they involve a requirement to report on the conduct of Canadian investors in Colombia." Second report, note 67 above, Canada's Reporting Requirement under the Canada–Colombia Free Trade Agreement Implementation Act – Human Rights under Consideration; Third report, note 68 above, Canada's Reporting Requirement under the Canada–Colombia Free Trade Agreement Implementation Act – Human Rights under Consideration.
73 Third report, note 68 above, Consultations with Stakeholders – Public Call for Submissions.
74 Ibid.
75 Ibid.

76 e.g., *Tecnicas Medioambientales Tecmed, SA v United Mexican States* (Award, 29 May 2003), late accessed October 2, 2014, www.italaw.com/sites/default/files/case-documents/ita0854.pdf, 72.

77 Third report, note 68 above, Consultations with Stakeholders – Outcalls by the Embassy of Canada to Colombia in Bogotá in the Textiles and Cosmetics and Personal Hygiene (Hair Products) Industries.

78 Third report, note 68 above, Summary of Findings.

Bibliography

Canada Treaty Information. *Agreement Concerning Annual Reports on Human Rights and Free Trade Between Canada and the Republic of Colombia.* Treaty E105278. Signed May 27, 2010, entered into force August 15, 2011. Accessed October 2, 2014. www.treaty-accord.gc.ca/text-texte.aspx?id=105278.

Environment Canada. *Agreement on the Environment Between Canada and the Republic of Colombia.* Signed November 21, 2008, entered into force August 15, 2011. Accessed October 2, 2014. www.ec.gc.ca/caraib-carib/default.asp?lang=En&n=FFEF249E-1.

Foreign Affairs, Trade and Development Canada. *Canada–Colombia Free Trade Agreement (CCFTA).* Signed November 21, 2008, entered into force August 15, 2011. Accessed October 2, 2014. www.international.gc.ca/trade-agreements-accords-commerciaux/agr-acc/colombia-colombie/can-colombia-toc-tdm-can-colombie.aspx?lang=eng.

Government of Canada. *Annual Report Pursuant to the Agreement Concerning Annual Reports on Human Rights and Free Trade between Canada and the Republic of Canada.* May 15, 2012. Accessed October 2, 2014. www.canadainternational.gc.ca/colombia-colombie/bilateral_relations_bilaterales/rep-hrft-co_2012-dple-rapp.aspx.

Government of Canada. *Annual Report Pursuant to the Agreement concerning Annual Reports on Human Rights and Free Trade between Canada and the Republic of Canada.* June 14, 2013. Accessed October 2, 2014. www.canadainternational.gc.ca/colombia-colombie/bilateral_relations_bilaterales/rep-hrft-co_2013-dple-rapp.aspx?lang=eng.

Government of Canada. *Annual Report Pursuant to the Agreement concerning Annual Reports on Human Rights and Free Trade between Canada and the Republic of Canada.* May 15, 2014. Accessed October 2, 2014. www.canadainternational.gc.ca/colombia-colombie/bilateral_relations_bilaterales/AnnualReport_RapportAnnuel-2013.aspx.

Government of Canada Labour Program. *Canada–Colombia Agreement on Labour Cooperation.* Signed November 21, 2008, entered into force August 15, 2011. Accessed October 2, 2014. www.labour.gc.ca/eng/relations/international/agreements/lca_colombia.shtml.

Harrison, James. "Conducting a Human Rights Impact Assessment of the Canada–Colombia Free Trade Agreement: Key Issues." Background Paper for the CCIC (Canada's Coalition to End Global Poverty) Americas Policy Group. (February 2009): 1–17. Accessed October 2, 2014. www.ccic.ca/_files/en/working_groups/003_apg_2009-02_hr_assess_of_cfta.pdf.

Kent Law School. "Statement of Concern about Planned Provisions on Investment Protection and Investor-State Dispute Settlement (ISDS) in the Transatlantic Trade and Investment Partnership (TTIP)." University of Kent, n. d. Accessed October 2, 2014. www.kent.ac.uk/law/isds_treaty_consultation.html.

Kläger, Roland. *'Fair and Equitable Treatment' in International Investment Law.* Cambridge: Cambridge University Press, 2011.

Mann, Howard. "The Canada–China Investment Treaty Sleight of Hand." *Embassy News*, January 9, 2013. Accessed October 2, 2014. www.embassynews.ca/opinion/2013/01/08/ the-canada-china-investment-treaty-sleight-of-hand/43048.

Metalclad Corporation v. *United Mexican States*. [August 30, 2000]. Case No. ARB(AF)/97/1. Accessed October 2, 2014. www.italaw.com/sites/default/files/ case-documents/ita0510.pdf.

Mobil Investments Canada Inc. and Murphy Oil Corporation v. *Canada*. [May 22, 2012]. ICSID Case No. ARB(AF)/07/4. Accessed October 2, 2014. www.italaw.com/sites/ default/files/case-documents/italaw1145.pdf.

Occidental Exploration and Production Company v. *Republic of Ecuador*. [July 1, 2004]. Case No. UN 3467. Accessed October 2, 2014. www.italaw.com/sites/default/files/ case-documents/ita0571.pdf.

Occidental Petroleum Corporation and Occidental Exploration and Production Company v. *Republic of Ecuador*. [October 5, 2012]. ISCID Case No. ARB/06/11. Accessed October 2, 2014. www.italaw.com/sites/default/files/case-documents/italaw1094.pdf.

Organization of American States (OAS). Foreign Trade Information System (Trade Agreements in Force). Accessed October 2, 2014. www.sice.oas.org/agreements_e.asp.

Paley, Dawn. "Deadly Dealings Surround Canada–Colombia Free Trade Agreement." *This Magazine*, August 24, 2009. Accessed October 2, 2014. http://this.org/magazine/2009/08/24/canada-colombia-free-trade-agreement/.

Prime Minister of Canada Stephen Harper. "Improving Free Trade and Human Rights in Colombia." Bogota, August 10, 2011. Accessed October 2, 2014. www.pm.gc.ca/eng/ news/2011/08/10/improving-free-trade-and-human-rights-colombia.

Republic of Colombia (Departmento Nacional de Planeación, Consejo Nacional de Político Económica y Social). *Fortalecimiento de la estrategia del estado para la prevención y atención de controversias internacionales de inversion.* Conpes Document No. 3684. Bogota, October 19, 2010. https://colaboracion.dnp.gov.co/CDT/Conpes/ 3684.pdf.

Schneiderman, David. *Constitutionalizing Economic Globalization*. Cambridge: Cambridge University Press, 2008.

Singer, Thomas, Paul Orbuch, and Robert Stumberg. *Multilateral Agreement on Investment: Potential Effects on State and Local Governments*. Western Governors Association, 1998.

Tecnicas Medioambientales Tecmed, SA v. *United Mexican States*. [May 29, 2003]. Case No. ARB(AF)/00/2. Accessed October 2, 2014. www.italaw.com/sites/default/files/ case-documents/ita0854.pdf.

Tienhaara, Kyla. *The Expropriation of Environmental Governance*. Cambridge: Cambridge University Press, 2009.

Trudeau, Justin. "Free Trade With Colombia." Accessed October 2, 2014. http://justin trudeau.liberal.ca/en/free-trade-with-columbia/.

United Nations Conference on Trade and Development (UNCTAD). *Investment Instruments Online (Bilateral Investment Treaties)*. Accessed September 1, 2014. www. unctadxi.org/templates/DocSearch____779.aspx.

United Nations Conference on Trade and Development (UNCTAD). *Recent Developments in Investor-State Dispute Settlement (ISDS)*. IIA Issues Note, No. 1. United Nations, May 2013. http://unctad.org/en/PublicationsLibrary/webdiaepcb2013d3_en. pdf.

Vadi, Valentina. *Public Health in International Investment Arbitration*. London: Routledge, 2013.

Van Harten, Gus. "Comments on the European Commission's Approach to Investor-State Arbitration in TTIP and CETA." *Osgoode Hall Law School Research Paper* no. 59 (2014): 1–55.

Van Harten, Gus. *Investment Treaty Arbitration and Public Law*. Oxford: Oxford University Press, 2007.

Van Harten, Gus. *Sovereign Choices and Sovereign Constraints*. Oxford: Oxford University Press, 2013.

Wilkinson, Suzanne M. "NAFTA, Mexico & Metalclad: Understanding the Normative Framework of International Trade Law." LLM Thesis, University of British Columbia, 2002.

7 Analytical Conclusions

Claudia Donoso and James Rochlin

Development, security, and human rights for whom? The Critical Human Security (CHS) perspective poses those questions in a quest to empower communities
in the Global South whose interests are sometimes forgotten by States and TNCs
in their pursuit of lucrative megaprojects. It does so in a highly practical manner
that appreciates that politics is all about interests. The art of the "deal" as it were,
is to ensure that all players simultaneously derive gain. Local communities need
to have their voices heard when development is defined, and TNCs require a
secure and stable environment for their investments. Rather than exacerbating
polemics, the objective here has been to define a concentric space where communities benefit along with TNCs and the State with regard to extractive megaprojects. During the course of the case studies addressed in this volume, the
parameters of the discourse on extractive development have shifted. We are
faced with what some had hoped was unthinkable: what is left for the community, the State, and TNCs when a boom goes bust?

We shall begin by considering the synergy between the realms of security,
human rights, and development, and the global implications derived from the
cases in this volume. We shall also consider the fallout from an implosion in the
commodity sector. Finally, there will be an analysis of corporate and governmental HRIAs as tools to promote human security for host communities as well
as stability and security for TNCs. To succeed, they require tripartite consultation and secure mechanisms for the vulnerable to communicate their concerns.

Security

Violence and Impunity

CHS appreciates continuity and change in the landscape of security. This means
the endurance of some traditional themes lingering from Modernity, as well the
recognition of newfangled ones. In Colombia's case, internal warfare has been
almost constant since independence in 1821. In the current panorama, insurgents
and illegal armed groups can be viewed as traditional in terms of their origin.
Examples include the emergence of the FARC in the 1960s as peasant guerrillas,
and the paramilitaries in the 1980s as defenders of large landowners. More
recently, these groups have blended with transnational organized crime, especially

the drug trade. This helped fortify their economic independence and military power, and whet their tastes for further profitable endeavors.

Since the extractive boom commenced in Colombia in 2007, insurgents and illegal armed groups predictably have become involved in various ways with the mining and petroleum industries. This is a highly contested landscape. Throughout the country, the United States has rendered Colombia to be a postmodern theater of warfare for the global South, with its use of ultra-surveillance, all-terrain and all-time combat, flexible organization, privatized war, the discourse of terror, and so on.[1] The Colombian armed forces and police have been retrained, re-armed, and expanded. Thus, the country's security backdrop, in terms of both its traditional and postmodern dimensions, must be appreciated as an important context for proposed and existing corporate investment projects.

With regard to the case studies in this project, we have observed a clear involvement of insurgents and illegal armed groups vis-à-vis the operations of Pacific Rubiales Energy Corporation in Meta and Gran Colombia Gold Corporation in Antioquia. In terms of the threats posed to the community and workers, in the Rubiales case leftist insurgents violently attacked UTEN members (the right-wing union) while right-wing paramilitaries attacked members of USO (the leftist union) during their complex struggle with the corporation. Within a climate of fear and intimidation, and the assassination of at least one of its members in the region, USO closed its office in Puerto Gaitán. Beyond that, it was shown that clashes between the military and USO supporters were sharply rebuked by the community. At other points, the community blamed USO for using violence as a political tool during what could have been peaceful protests.

More broadly, a key and historically persistent security problem in Colombia is the tendency to use violence as a means to resolve conflict, and the subsequent emergence of the politics of fear. Related to this is the context of impunity for crimes committed against labour activists in Colombia, with the impunity rate for assassinations of union members topping 90 percent. Impunity for violence and threats of violence, not just against workers but with regard to the community at large, casts a pall of fear and silence that stifles political freedom and development.

With regard to Pacific Rubiales and threats to security, the key danger has been the conduct of business in an area rife with well-funded guerrillas and armed groups. Threats that were realized in this case include the involvement of leftist insurgents and right-wing paramilitaries in the company's labour dispute. Beyond that, an escalation of pipeline bombings by leftist insurgents has caused significant bottlenecks for the distribution of oil. For instance, according to statistics of the Colombian Ministry of Defense, in 2013 there were 147 attacks on oil pipelines, 18 percent more than the previous year.[2] In 2014, 26 attacks against pipeline infrastructures have been reported by mid-year, and while less frequent than the previous year, they resulted in far more damage.[3] There are a plethora of other security threats. These include damage to the company's infrastructure from armed groups and from violent protests by workers. Other potential problems include extortion and the kidnapping of corporate executives. In fact, a Canadian mining company, Braeval, had one of its key executives kidnapped by the leftist ELN guerrilla group for 221 days before being released in late August of 2013. As a result, the company announced the termination of its operations in Colombia.[4] Returning to the case of Rubiales, against such a backdrop it is clear that the company benefited from the increased Colombian military presence that accompanied the establishment of its operations in the region, as well as State-led tripartite negotiation that ultimately helped to resolve conflict peacefully.

With regard to the case involving Gran Colombia Gold Corporation in Segovia and Remedios, we notice a similar set of actors as in the Rubiales case with respect to security. While some of the manifestations of violence were similar in the two cases, in others ways they differed. From the community's perspective, the presence of an assortment of insurgents and armed groups feeding off gold production and ranging from the Right to the Left, has generated a climate of fear that has stymied political expression. Conflict has been resolved through force, rather than through the peaceful negotiation of voiced concerns. Union activists were assassinated, apparently by right-wing paramilitaries. Local miners have been extorted by insurgent and paramilitary forces that control precious mining contracts linked to GCG. While the provision of additional Colombian military forces that accompanied GCG's arrival to the community has improved the situation, illicit armed actors remain powerful in the region.

Because Pacific Rubiales Energy Corporation has been responsible for pumping about a quarter of the country's oil, which is a prime source of revenue for the government, the Colombian State made a strong commitment to help resolve the problem through its provision of armed forces and its leading role in tripartite negotiations. By contrast, given the much smaller economic stake of GCG to the country, Segovia and Remedios have not attracted much needed government intervention. Tripartite negotiation has been weak and largely absent there, and an ambience of violence as the arbiter of conflict prevails. The community has suffered as a result.

There are some important implications regarding Gran Colombia Gold Corporation and security matters. Beyond the expanded military presence in host communities, the corporation has required costly private security services to protect its employees and infrastructure. Most importantly, while there is no apparent evidence or allegations suggesting the corporation is directly linked to violence, its investment in the communities may have propelled the activity of armed groups that illicitly feed off of gold mining.

Let us zoom out from these cases and consider the global themes that emerge from them. First, when a corporation becomes involved in a community and a country with a legacy of violence, the company's presence may likely incite further violence even when the business itself is not directly linked to violence and abhors its use. Thus, the repercussions of investment projects in terms of potential violence for the host community and for the corporation need to be seriously assessed. Both the host community and the corporation share an interest in ensuring that violence does not escalate as well as an interest in promoting peaceful conflict resolution mechanisms to reduce existing levels of violence.

The question then becomes how an investment project can become part of the solution rather than the center of the problem. Real and potential problems need to be fully addressed, and negotiation must take place between government, businesses and host communities to ameliorate these. If the community is not part of the process, violence is likely to persist. That lesson is quite clear from the contrasting cases of Pacific Rubiales in Meta, which succeeded at reducing violence, and Gran Colombia Gold in Segovia and Remedios, a case that remains problematic. The Rubiales case demonstrates the significance of tripartite conflict resolution as a means of mediating a conflict in a manner that is best for the community and the corporation, thereby sharply reducing violence.

Economic Security

Critical Human Security highlights the significance of economic security of host communities in the Global South. Let us begin with a focus on particularities, and then step back for a global view. All the cases in this project demonstrate threats to the economic security of the community in relation to foreign investment in the extractive sector. With regard to both the Marmato and Antioquia cases, we observed that traditional gold miners in Colombia – whose legacy dates back five centuries – have recently been declared "illegal" by the government through a broad-brushed approach that fails to distinguish those with an historic claim to mining versus newcomers linked to criminal organizations. A national strike that included traditional miners shut Colombia's key roads in the summer of 2013, demonstrating their collective power to protest peacefully against a highly unpopular policy.

We saw that Gran Colombia Gold Corporation has been engaged in a pilot project of formalization for a relatively tiny number of the country's miners. It has generated significant controversy since these miners who have social benefits are paid less for gold, at least in terms of take-home pay, than their unformalized counterparts, who have no such benefits. Clearly the State should embark on a nation-wide process of formalization that is efficient and provides traditional miners with necessary training free of charge. While gold prices rose spectacularly between 2007 and late 2011, the government easily could have administered a relatively small tax on mining companies. They would have received the benefits of a better trained workforce, as well as a more politically friendly and secure environment in which to invest. But such a tax would be impractical in the context of the severe collapse of gold prices since late 2011, since mining companies are struggling to survive and might not be able to endure higher costs through taxes. Perhaps the lesson here concerns the lost opportunity for a government that believed the good times in the extractive sector would never end.

In the case of the La Caypa mine in La Guajira, some of the inhabitants of the traditional communities of Patilla and Chancleta have lost their traditional livelihood of agricultural subsistence as a result of coal mining in or near their communities. Those who were relocated to new communities had no access to land for subsistence, and those who remained in their original locale faced pollution from the mines that severely hindered agricultural production. Because mining is not labour intensive, the coal project does not have the capacity to hire all those from the community who seek work, and even less so since coal prices have fallen drastically and the company faces pressure to cut costs. Little has been done to address this breach of human security as of this writing.

The case of Pacific Rubiales in Meta demonstrated a threat to the economic security of the community of Puerto Gaitán, but the company has set in motion a variety of policies to address the problem. By the end of 2011, Pacific Rubiales Energy Corporation indicated that it would source labour and materials locally whenever feasible. It also agreed to raise the wages and improve the accommodations of workers in some cases, and to better monitor its contractors regarding working conditions. These achievements were the product of tripartite negotiation that followed the protracted and violent strikes of 2011.

Through the case studies in this volume we have observed a variety of threats to the economic security of host communities that may be common in the Global South. Rather than more problems, host communities rightfully expect social gains. Communities anticipate benefits from foreign investment projects through, for example, increased employment, spin-off opportunities for local businesses, and from improvements in public services derived from the royalties paid by the company to the State. The expectations of host communities are raised with the prospect of a major foreign investment project, and these expectations have been encouraged by a State that has deemed foreign investment in the extractive sector to be the economic locomotive of the country. Finally, it is worth emphasizing that rising social expectations that go unfulfilled represent a potential political powder-keg, a point observed by Ted Robert Gurr decades ago.[5]

Human Rights

Displacement

Earlier we posed the question of "Security for whom?" Now the spotlight is upon the question of "Whose rights?" We have seen that an investment climate can privilege foreign corporate rights over the human rights of its citizens. This is especially the case in the countryside, out of sight of the urban population that has disproportionately benefited from the extractive boom. With regard to the studies in this volume, we observe a number of major threats to human rights in the extractive sector that have been related to Canadian foreign investment.

We observed the issue of displacement, or its potential, in the cases of Marmato and La Guajira. In the Marmato case, the TNC had intended to relocate the community, but it never reached fruition. Importantly, the community established a global network of support that publicized its plight and added pressure on Gran Colombia Gold Corporation to retract its goal of an open pit mine. By contrast, the communities of Patilla and Chancleta were relocated in the case of Pacific Coal Resources Ltd., but the relocation was consensual, incomplete and yielded mixed results. Community members indicated that they received no mediation by the State to assist them in negotiations regarding relocation. Many were unhappy with results that included the eradication of their traditional means of subsistence and doubtful economic circumstances for those who chose to move. The communities are relatively small and have not organized in a manner that has enabled them to voice strongly their human rights concerns.

In terms of global implications, displacement is a major theme in the literature regarding human rights and foreign investment, especially in relation to the extractive sector. Displacement is an issue that can be particularly difficult to resolve in a way that benefits the community and the TNC. A number of complex issues can appear, as we have seen. These may involve ethnic rights, threats to traditional subsistence, spiritual ties to territory, threats to community integrity, and so on. For relocation to occur in a manner consistent with the Critical Human Security framework, careful tripartite negotiations need to occur in a manner where all community concerns are voiced and addressed, and whereby the community is fully informed and supported in the mediation process. We shall expand upon this topic in subsequent sections.

Workers' Rights

Workers' rights represent another key theme of CHS. A huge surplus of cheap labour in Colombia, coupled with a State with poor regulatory capacity, provide ample fodder to a business wishing to exploit a vulnerable workforce. In the cases under consideration here, we have observed serious threats to workers' rights. Some have been resolved while other abuses persist. In the case of Pacific Rubiales in Meta, labour rights themes included allegations of prevention of freedom of association, substandard working conditions, unpaid labour, abuse of authority by foremen, substandard pay, undue force on the part of the military to subdue strikers, the obscurity of corporate responsibility through the use of contractors, and so on. While an important law suit launched by the labour union USO regarding allegations of a breach of freedom of association remains unresolved as of this writing, there has been clear progress on other matters noted above due to a lengthy tripartite negotiation process led by the country's Vice Presidential office.

In the cases regarding gold mining in Marmato and in the communities of Segovia and Remedios, the chief threat to workers' rights has been an abrupt shift in the country's legal regime that has criminalized about 300,000 traditional miners. The national government promised to help resolve the problem during the nation-wide strike of 2013, but there are no clear results as of this writing.

The use of contract workers has created tension in the cases involving petroleum production in Meta, gold production in Antioquia, and coal production in La Guajira. In all these situations, workers complained that the prevalent use of contractors obscured the responsibility of the key corporation involved in the project. Regarding gold production, labour argued that contractors were used as a means to pay workers less, to diminish job security, and to discourage union formation. Regarding coal production, labour complained that contractors did not pay the industry standard in the region, among other grievances.

In terms of global implications, when workers are unhappy, trouble is likely to result for corporations. This is especially the case in areas of the Global South where violence is the preponderant means to deal with conflict. This may manifest as peaceful but costly strikes, violent work stoppages, damage to company infrastructure, and highly negative publicity for the corporation. Ultra-competition inherent in globalization understandably has led corporations to seek all feasible cost-cutting policies. But a line can easily be crossed when the harm done to labour backfires in a manner that is costly for the company.

Colombia has been among the most dangerous places on the planet for union members in terms of human security. The numbers in Tables 7.1–7.4 provide a chilling illustration of this. Organized labour operates within a landscape of intense fear. In general, labour in Colombia has been stigmatized as being sympathetic to the insurgent Left, which has yielded attacks from the paramilitary right in a climate of rampant impunity. While attacks against labour are diminishing, and this should be celebrated, numbers remain high by global standards. Despite improving statistics, the same game of the politics of fear remains in place through assassinations of high-profile victims and through threats.[6] Foreign investment projects must be considered against this backdrop. As we saw in the Rubiales case, labour violence can be explosive in a way that is costly for all involved. Overall, the CHS framework underscores the practical importance of labour rights and a harmonious relation between labour, the community, the corporation, and the State.

Ethnic and Epistemic Rights

The Marmato case vividly demonstrates the importance of ethnic rights with regard to foreign investment in the extractive sector. This community, which is predominantly Black and Indigenous, has an historical legacy dating back 500 years. It has organized in a spirited and sophisticated way to protest against the

Table 7.1 Number of homicides of Colombian union members: 1986–2012

1986	36	2000	138
1987	73	2001	193
1988	138	2002	191
1989	96	2003	101
1990	58	2004	95
1991	96	2005	72
1992	141	2006	78
1993	201	2007	39
1994	104	2008	51
1995	229	2009	47
1996	277	2010	51
1997	171	2011	29
1998	99	2012	20
1999	83		

Source: Escuela Nacional Sindical, *Cuaderno de Derechos Humanos*, #22, 2010, Medellín: Interview by author with Guillermo Correa, Director of Research, Escuela Nacional Sindical, February 16, 2011; International Trade Union Confederation, "Annual Survey of Violations of Trade Union Rights," 2012, www.ituc-csi-org, viewed July 21, 2013.

Table 7.2 Human Rights violations against Colombian union members during three Presidential Administrations

Type of violation	President Pastrana: 1998–2002	President Uribe: 2002–2006	President Uribe: 2006–2010	Total
Threats	1,272	1,298	1,215	3,785
Homicides	580	362	166	1,108
Forced Displacement	264	146	388	798
Arbitrary Detention	209	206	89	504
Harassment	57	138	93	288
Physical Attack	70	43	40	153
Kidnapping	108	29	0	137
Disappearance	46	22	11	79
Breaking and Entering – Home	3	17	10	30
Torture	4	8	12	24
Murder of Relatives	1	0	0	1
Total	2,614	2,269	2,024	6,907

Source: Escuela Nacional Sindical, *Cuaderno de Derechos Humanos*, #22, October 2010, Medellín, p. 30.

Table 7.3 Number of Human Rights abuses against Colombian union members January 1, 1986 to August 30, 2010

Threats	4,826
Homicides	2,842
Forced Displacement	1,696
Arbitrary Detention	632
Harassment	310
Physical Attack	274
Disappearance	217
Kidnapping	165
Torture	82
Home Break and Enter	49
Murder of Family Member	3

Source: Escuela Nacional Sindical, *Cuaderno de Derechos Humanos*, #22, October 2010, p. 46.

Table 7.4 Violations of life, liberty, and integrity, committed against union members by economic sector, between January 1, 2010 and November 12, 2014

Economic Sector	2010	2011	2012	2013	2014
	# Cases	# Cases	# Cases	# Cases	# Cases
Education	374	381	326	107	43
Extractive Sector	30	68	82	101	33
Agriculture and Fishing	43	65	79	65	93
Services	51	72	31	61	56
Manufacturing	29	35	68	58	32
Health	15	44	27	19	14
State Bureaucracy	12	24	16	20	7
Electricity, Gas, and Water	5	21	7	10	14
Transportation, Communication, and Storage	8	8	7	8	4
Sales	1	1	3	2	4
Construction	1	1	4		1
Judicial	1	3	1		
Finance	4			1	
Total	574	723	651	452	301

Source: Sistema de Información en Derechos Humanos, SINDERH. Provided to author by Daniel Hawkins, Director of Research, Escuela Nacional Sindical, Medellin, November 14, 2014.

relocation of the town. At stake is the ethnic community's attachment to territory, in both a spiritual and material way. Also at issue is the possible fracturing of this historic community through an unpopular relocation process. Epistemic themes are paramount here. The community of Marmato does not share the epistemic approach of TNCs, with their typical emphasis on mass production, ultra-speed, maximized profit, speculation, and a devaluation of territory though an approach that views it as disposable or of tentative significance.

With regard to global implications, the Marmato case illustrates that sometimes the interests of the community and the TNC are fundamentally incompatible.

It was shown that GCG, and its predecessors, appeared to wish away the profundity of the community's objections to relocation. The Marmato community has shown itself to be sufficiently organized and well-connected to challenge GCG. Whether it is due to community protest, and/or the crash of gold prices, the project remains halted indefinitely. The global implication, then, is that TNCs need to listen to the community and must be able to accept the possibility that their interests are irreconcilably at odds. Attempting to proceed under such circumstances could turn out badly for the corporation in terms of a costly cancellation of a project, emerging security problems, and a black eye to its public image.

Impunity

Impunity represents a major threat to political rights and freedoms in Colombia.[7] While the community at large is likely to receive the worst effects of a climate of impunity, this threat to human security is also highly deleterious for foreign investors. A panorama of unaddressed crime, violence, and fear raises the prospect of costly and dangerous security problems for corporations. The upshot is that TNCs need to assess the judicial climate of countries in which they plan to invest. If such an environment is unfavorable, corporations and their home governments should consider ways to bolster the host country's judicial system in a manner that is good for host communities and the TNC. When legal recourse is absent, violence is likely to prevail.

Development

Development for whom? There is no question that Colombia has had a TNC-friendly policy during the new millennium. Beyond its accommodating policy to foreign investors, the Colombian government has celebrated the extractive sector as the country's engine of development. In terms of 'development for whom?', then, the foreign extractive sector has been held in favor by the State.

Development and Equity

Whether this development model has been in the interests of the poor and the marginalized is more debatable. If one accepts the "trickle-down theory" – that what is good for foreign corporations is good for a nation's economy since the benefits will trickle down throughout society – then the policy has been a sound one. The government has indicated, as we observed in Chapter 1, that almost 82 percent of all foreign investment was in the extractive sector in 2013. Inequity, in terms of GINI coefficients, remains high but has decreased from 0.59 in 2008 to 0.54 in 2013. Government figures suggest poverty has decreased from 46 percent to 30.6 percent between 2008 and 2013, with extreme poverty rates falling from 17.8 percent to 9.1 percent. But those figures are based on a relatively new system of poverty calculation that the government admits has had the effect of lowering poverty rates. Moreover, the 2014 poverty lines of US$3.80 daily in the city and US$2.30 in rural areas appear to be impractically low.

Overall, we observed in Chapter 1 that even critics of government policy admit the poverty and equity rates in the country have improved significantly over the last decade, but the extent of this may be exaggerated by government figures. Improved social programs derived from mining and petroleum royalties, and more jobs, have helped reduce poverty and inequity.

Comparatively, other South American countries with a statist or socialist government that also depend heavily on the extractive sector, have done a better job at pushing the poverty rate below Colombia's 30.6 percent in the 2012–2013 period. For example, Bolivia's poverty rate declined from 42.4 percent in 2009 to 21.6 percent in 2012.[8] Ecuador's rate dropped from 38 percent in 2006 to 26 percent in 2013.[9] Venezuelan poverty rates dropped from over 50 percent when Chavez took office in 1999 to 23.9 percent in 2012.[10] Overall, in terms of benefiting the poorest sectors of society, Colombia's model has not kept pace with some of its neighbours.

Development and Sustainability

The political dimension is a crucial aspect of development. As the post-development literature reminds us,[11] development should be an inclusive political process whereby the majority poor population in the Global South have a strong voice in defining development. It should not represent a "now hear this" policy emanating from the country's capital in allegiance with transnational capital. Social inclusion is key to sustainable development.

In Colombia, the issue of sustainability is troublesome on two broad fronts. First, we have seen that each of the Colombian cases considered here suggests threats to the environment from the extractive sector. Petroleum production, for example, involves the proliferation of toxic tailing ponds, and oil pipelines increasingly have been bombed by leftist guerrillas leaving ecocide in affected regions. Gold mining is highly toxic, as we saw with regard to the communities of Segovia and Remedios that host the world's worst levels of mercury pollution. While switching to cyanide is claimed to be a better approach environmentally, it is also toxic to the land and waterways. In Marmato, this is combined with land erosion, an almost constant presence of particulate in the air from mine-related explosions, and with less toxic but still bothersome noise pollution. Any further gold mining will continue to erode the environmental health of those regions, the only question is to what degree.

Finally, in the case of coal mining, we noted that there is an omnipresent dust of carbon particulate in Patilla and Chancleta. This has limited agricultural production and has contaminated water in the region. The local hospital that serves those communities and the wider area reports that 15 percent of people seeking treatment claim they have pulmonary problems that they suspect are linked to air pollution. Overall, the extractive sector represents a major threat to environmental sustainability. The central questions remaining are how to manage this threat, and what further degree of environmental destruction is tolerable.

A second theme entails debates surrounding the sustainability of Colombia's economic model of development that has leaned so heavily on the extractive sector. Betting the economy of the country on the oil and mining industries may be imprudent given the boom and bust cycles the commodity sector has witnessed over the centuries, and there is a deservedly rich literature on this.[12] Beyond the mercurial markets for oil and minerals, recently we have witnessed the rise and fall of stock markets, of financial markets and currencies, of real estate markets, and so on. The speculative nature of the extractive sector, and of the postmodern economy more generally, provide a shaky foundation upon which to build a long term vision of development.

In Chapter 1 we noted that between 1995 and 2013 the agricultural sector has shrunk from 10.1 percent of total export value to 4.5 percent, while manufactured exports fell by nearly half from 65.1 percent to 36.9 percent during that period. However, according to Colombian government statistics, the mining and petroleum sector has risen from 24.7 percent of total exports in 1995 to 58 percent by 2013, with oil representing most of that. A representative of the United Nations Industrial Development Organization argued in late 2014 that Colombia's current economic model is harmed by a large environmental impact, and that "the agro-mining model has the great disadvantage of keeping economic productivity low. What we have to do is seek alternatives that increase these levels and remove the lag that exists in Colombia."[13]

As of early 2015, the mining and petroleum market in general appears to be midway through a crash. Production of petroleum in Colombia has fallen to its lowest level since 2005. A small part of this is a result of pipeline destruction by rebel forces which rely on such tactics as their central bargaining chip in "peace" negotiations with the government. But more important has been the falling price of oil. This has raised a nightmare scenario for Pacific Rubiales, Colombia's fifth largest corporation. It was reported in February 2015 that the company has dismissed 7,000 of its employees, and has retained only 3,150 due to plummeting oil prices and a high debt load. A respected newspaper in Colombia reported that an assortment of companies that supply Pacific Rubiales claimed that their contracts were abruptly dropped or that Rubiales demanded a renegotiation of terms, while others feared delays in payment from the oil giant. Leaders of Colombia's stock exchange, the Bolsa de Valores de Colombia, have requested assurances from Pacific Rubiales amidst the plummeting the value of its stock.[14] More broadly, the government loses US$3.6 million in annual revenue for every US$1 drop in the price of a barrel of oil. This is significant, since oil peaked at US$147 a barrel in 2008, and fell from over US$100 a barrel in July 2014 to under $60 by the end of that year. Petroleum royalties accounted for 31 percent of government revenue in 2014.[15] Colombia's finance Minister indicated in summer of 2014 that it "is essential for Colombia that oil prices will not fall much below US$100 per barrel,"[16] or that the country would confront serious fiscal problems.

Other cases in this volume deal with gold and coal. Gold prices also have declined significantly since their crescendo, falling from a peak of US$1,921 an ounce in 2011 to below the key US$1,200–$1,300 threshold that Gran Colombia Gold Corporation had established as its break-even price in 2013. GCG has seen the value of its stock crash from nearly CAD$60 in 2011 to about 50 cents a share by the end of 2014. The company reported that it had missed a payment on its outstanding in December 2014, but that payments were scheduled to resume in February 2015.[17] Reports in Canada's business pages indicate that gold producers are now desperately attempting to set the threshold of gold production even lower to below CAD$1,000. But in the context of all the fat that has already been cut, this will prove to be a difficult and painful task.

Coal prices have fallen 64 percent by the end of 2014 after peaking at about US$330 a metric ton in 2011. Much of that cascade has to do with declining Chinese imports of coal, resulting from both the slowdown of its economy and its attempt to rely on greener power sources of energy such as solar. We saw that Pacific Coal was already struggling for economic survival when research on that case was being conducted for this volume.

To imagine the best scenario from the Colombian government's perspective, the extractive sector would take a brief fall, and then bounce back. One could base such a view on the idea that although the economy of nations such as China and India have decelerated temporarily, they are fundamentally healthy emerging powers with billions of people and will soon require much more petroleum and metals. Thus, the argument is that the boom and bust commodity cycles of the past are no longer relevant in the context of emerging powerhouses such as China and India. Such a perspective would justify the government's almost singular focus on extraction as the motor of development.

On the other hand, this is more likely just another bust in the historic cycles of commodities. What is clear is that gold, coal and petroleum producers – and the extractive sector more broadly – have felt an economic pinch. This not only results in less royalties to the Colombian government, it means fewer jobs for Colombians in the extractive sector and weaker spending by these corporations on CSR programs. It may mean shuttered mines and project closures. Left behind would be the environmental damage caused by petroleum and mining extraction. Against that backdrop, Colombia's resilient illegal economy would likely assume even greater dominance.

Colombian Senator Jorge Robledo, like many critics, predicted the eventual collapse of the extractive economy. Commodity cycles ride boom and bust waves, he said. Robledo indicated that the most serious problem facing Colombia is that the last two Presidents have promoted the extractive sector while its traditional manufacturing and agricultural sectors have withered. "Once you lose those sectors, it's hard to get them back," he said, indicating that they would require decades to rebuild.[18]

The Road Ahead: Resolving Conflict Amidst Boom, Bust and Neoliberalism

Colombia, like most developing nations, never achieved the milestones associated with Modernity. Since independence in 1821, the country has failed to create a Leviathan in Hobbesian terms, that is, the State has not nearly achieved a monopoly on the use of force. Conflict resolution has not been sufficiently institutionalized, and force predominates as a means to settle scores. Judicial and policing mechanisms are anemic, and impunity prevails. The State's regulatory capacity is feeble. Further, as we noted in Chapter 1, the country remains politically fragmented, rather than united through a strong presence of the State throughout the country. Political exclusion has remained the norm until recently, and still persists in some important ways. The development model in place has privileged urban areas over the countryside. These are some of the constraints that frame the path ahead.

Given that the Colombian State is relatively weak and undeveloped, and that the country's context of insecurity and inequity remains particularly problematic, the resolution to the problems described in this volume necessitates significant capacity building for the State. This needs to occur in areas including corporate regulation, environmental regulation, judicial fortification, tax collection, formalization for about half the country's workers that remain in the informal sector, vast wealth redistribution, as well as institutionalized conflict resolution mechanisms such as tripartite negotiation. Thus, the central challenge is to build the capacity of an historically weak State that has chosen a decidedly neoliberal path. This model is designed to restrict State intervention and may deprive the government of needed resources, as exemplified by a relatively low government take on commodities.

State capacity building needs to occur not only to serve Colombians but to serve the interests of business, as well. This has become very clear as a result of a variety of interviews conducted for this book and the wider project of which it is part. TNCs have been attracted to Colombia's business friendly environment and have benefited by progress toward establishing peace with the FARC. But representatives from Pacific Rubiales Energy Corporation, Gran Colombia Gold Corporation, Cosigo Resources Ltd., Pacific Coal Resources Ltd., Canacol Energy Ltd. and others, all indicated that local communities in which they operate have expected them to fill enormous gaps left by a weak or absent State. At times, the lack of support from the national government and the elevated expectations of the host community have been both overwhelming and alarming for TNCs.

Leaders of a TNC for which Rochlin and Donoso delivered a course on human rights, as well as other representatives from corporations covered in this volume who wish to remain anonymous, indicated that corruption of local officials was sometimes a significant a problem in the field. They highlighted instances when it was clear that local authorities received funds from the central government for municipal development, but did not proceed to use the money for that purpose. This put even more pressure on TNCs to provide social programs demanded by the community.

A spokesperson for Pacific Rubiales emphasized that while the corporation has been very appreciative of support received by the national government, especially regarding the 2011–2012 struggle in Puerto Gaitán, much more needs be done. His suggestions include a clear post-conflict plan on the part of the government that would retain advances in security if a peace negotiation is reached with the FARC, but which would also work to reduce lingering security problems emanating from other illegal armed groups. Related to this, he indicated that a strong, country-wide government program to eliminate extortion is badly needed.[19] A representative from Cosigo Resources Ltd., a junior mining company, suggested that it would be better served by a more stream-lined national bureaucracy in Colombia. He observed that small companies often do not have the resources to wait for a protracted decision making processes, and have been hurt by this as metal prices fall.[20] Finally, representatives from all corporations interviewed for the project suggested the institutionalization of nation-wide tripartite negotiation processes to reduce conflict between corporations and host communities.

What is problematic for corporations, especially junior companies that lack the capital and durability of their larger counterparts, is the ability to weigh short term interests in a low government take versus a higher government tax that could benefit corporations in the medium and longer term. These benefits would appear through the fortification of State capacity in ways mentioned above. But in practical terms, a higher government take would prove especially untenable at time of collapsing commodity prices.

Interestingly the corporate representatives interviewed for this project indicated that they are not part of united group dedicated to lobbying the government for reform on their behalf. Though the TNCs are Canadian, they have adopted the corporate culture of 'individualismo' that is common in Colombia, whereby companies compete against one another without any significant cooperation. These TNCs, and others in the extractive sector, would do well to organize themselves and put forth a platform of ideas they share to improve human security in a manner that benefits businesses and host communities.

Despite profoundly challenging circumstances, progress can still be made on a number of fronts in some practical ways. These concern the resuscitation and remolding of the HRIA and side accords attached to the CCFTA as well as the proliferation of corporate HRIAs. Highly useful would be increased Canadian assistance for the capacity building of the Colombian State. Let us develop those points.

Governmental HRIAs: How to Improve a Flawed HRIA

Gus Van Harten in Chapter 6 provided a legal critique of the attachments to the CCFTA, which include an annual report on human rights and two separate side accords on labour and the environment. Professor Van Harten posed the question: legal rights for whom? He argued strongly that the trade agreement empowers Canadian corporations with vast legal rights, especially through the mechanism of international investor state arbitration. At the same time, he demonstrated the very constrained legal rights afforded to the Colombian government and host communities to regulate TNCs. The CCFTA and its side agreements have a weak enforcement mechanism for human rights, and this is confined to the labour side accord. But that mechanism focuses only on State policy, and not upon the behaviour of a corporation or even upon a preponderantly dominant sector of corporations. Further, it entails mediation only by State agencies. Individuals, NGOs and other groups cannot participate in the mediation process, and there is no remedy to victims of human rights abuse. Instead, a maximum fine of $15 million potentially can be brought against the government.

Thus, legal rights should be more equitably distributed among TNCs, the State and host communities than they currently are. Complaint and mediation mechanisms need to be more inclusive and involve civil society. Remedies must be delivered to victims of human rights abuses. The optic needs to shift from a singular focus on the effects of tariff reductions, to the social effects of Canadian investment in Colombia that has been encouraged by the FTA.

The CCFTA focuses on both trade, especially tariff reductions, and upon investment. This is crucial, because it is Canada's investment in Colombia's extractive sector that has attracted most of the controversy regarding human rights. For example, 80 percent of the entire country's human rights violations occur in areas where the extractive sector dominates. In 2012, these were the site of 87 percent of the country's population displacement, 78 percent of the crimes against labour, and 86 percent of the human rights abuses against the Indigenous.[21]

Chapter 8 of the FTA, which is approximately 28 single-spaced pages, is totally dedicated to the matter of investment. This Chapter of the free trade agreement is quite detailed, and notes matters including national treatment, most favored nation treatment, compensation for losses for investments hurt by internal conflict and civil strife, the avoidance of expropriation, and so on. Further, Chapter 8 notes that it is "inappropriate to encourage investment by relaxing domestic health, safety or environmental measures."[22] Importantly, Articles 815 and 816 call on Canadian investors in Colombia to "voluntarily incorporate internationally recognized standards of Corporate Social Responsibility in their internal policies ... these principles address issues such as labour, the environment, human rights, community relations and anti-corruption."[23] Not only is investment a significant part of the FTA, but the discussion of investment in the FTA is explicitly linked to human rights and sustainability.

Chapter 16 of the FTA concerns "Labour," and Articles 1604 and 1605 focus on "commitments concerning the internationally recognized labour principles and rights that are to be embodied in each Party's laws" and the objective of "raising the level of compliance with labour standards..." The HRIA produced in 2013 observes that the Labour Cooperation Agreement between the two countries surpasses the 1998 ILO's "Declaration on Fundamental Principles and Rights at Work" by focusing on issues such as occupational health and safety, hours of work, wages, etc.[24] Chapter 17 is devoted to Environmental standards and the general theme of sustainability. Once again, investment is an integral part of the FTA, and the agreement mentions investment in relation to human rights, labour rights and sustainability.

The Canadian Government certainly anticipated more investment in relation to the FTA, and Canadian corporations in the extractive sector were key and vocal supporters of the agreement. For example, one posting from the Department of Foreign Affairs, Trade and Development Canada noted that the Canada–Colombia FTA "provides a more predictable, transparent and rules-based trading environment for Canadian investors ... We look forward to building on our already-close trade and investment ties with Colombia for years to come."[25] This message was echoed from others from the Canadian Trade Commissioner

Service: "Canada has already positioned itself as a leader in the Colombian oil and gas industry, and the Canada–Colombia FTA, which came into force August 15, 2011, will increase trade and investment by eliminating tariffs of up to 20 percent in this important sector."[26] Indeed, beyond investment guarantees and clearer investment rules, the elimination of tariffs in sectors such as machinery has been a boom for Canada's extractive industry through the exportation from Canada of relevant machinery to their operations in Colombia. As the second Canadian HRIA shows, exports of machinery have benefited the most of any sector in terms of increased trade since the FTA was established – from \$3.807 billion US pre CCFTA to \$5.744 billion US in December 2012. Not only does mining and petroleum occupy two of the top three sectors for Canadian investment in Colombia, Canadian investment represents more than half of all such investment in the country's extractive sector.[27]

Further, according to Canada's first HRIA, which was incomplete, the issue of investment would indeed be included in subsequent, more developed annual reports. It noted that "The methodological steps intended to be used to analyze the impacts of the CCOFTA on human rights will be applied to merchandise, services *and investment flows* from Canada to Colombia and vice versa (italics added)."[28] Also regarding methodology, the first report suggests future HRIAs will "Cluster the information about trade, *investment*, and services into significant sectors and sub-sectors for the purposes of annual tracking (italics added)."[29] It also suggests 'screening,' whereby the Government would identify those sectors where "an increase in trade and/or investment is expected" and to devise means to examine its affects vis-à-vis human rights.[30]

Given the promise of analyzing Canadian investment in relation to human rights and labour rights, in both the original FTA and the initial HRIA, it is spectacularly noteworthy that the Canadian Government decided to ignore entirely the relation between investment and human rights in its second and third full HRIAs. This omission is even more striking given the steep rise in Canadian investment that correlates with the discussion and subsequent implementation of the FTA. While statistics vary depending on sources, what is clear is that Canadian direct investment has increased substantially since discussions of the FTA began in 2008. Canadian direct investment in Colombia was \$270 million in 2003, about \$1.7 billion by 2011 and \$1.8 billion the following year, according to information from Canada's first HRIA with Colombia and from the Export Development Corporation. The Canadian Embassy in Bogota, however, placed the level of direct foreign investment in Colombia at about \$3 billion by 2011, with petroleum and mining ranking first and third respectively. The discrepancy is that the larger and more accurate figure reflects investment flows through third countries that are Canadian in origin, while the smaller official government statistics reflect direct flows only.[31]

Thus, a strong and reasonable argument can be made that the FTA helped to sustain and to increase Canadian investment through the establishment of enticing foreign investment rules and regulations as well as though tariff reductions in related industries such as machinery linked to the operation of Canadian extractive companies in Colombia. One sector clearly dominates in this trade and investment agreement, and unquestionably that is the extractive sector. The agreement is meant to stimulate investment in components of the extractive industry when the economic environment is favorable, and encourages the sustenance of existing investment when challenging circumstances appear such as the relative decline of gold, coal and oil prices. Therefore the HRIA should examine the effect upon Colombian human rights of the dominant Canadian extractive sector in the country. It would be in the interest of both the extractive sector and the local communities in which they operate to strengthen the HRIA as a tool for improving human rights and human security. Certainly that would reflect the spirit in which the HRIA was included in the Canada–Colombia FTA at the insistence of the Liberal Party and a variety of progressive Canadian NGOs.

Colombia's Annual Reports on Human Rights have been consistently better than Canada's, but they, too, are insufficient. Thematically, the second HRIA from Colombia is far better than any of its Canadian counterparts. This Colombian HRIA takes note of the significance of Canadian investment. Comparative investment levels are discussed, and the Report includes an 11-page list of Canadian corporations investing and operating in Colombia. Key themes regarding the human rights and security context in the country are noted, including the armed conflict in Colombia, widespread impunity for perpetrators of crimes and human rights, ethnic discrimination, and a generally weak government that has a limited capacity to enforce the rule of law as well as respect for human rights.[32]

Key threats to human security and sustainability emanating from Canadian investment in the extractive sector are discussed in the Colombian Report, such as the dangers of mercury contamination associated with gold mining.[33] The horrific legacy of the human rights violations of Colombian labour is discussed and analyzed in relation to impunity.[34] Importantly, the security threats aimed at TNCs are analyzed in relation to a web of human rights problems, including issues such as extortion of corporations, kidnappings of corporate employees, and so on. This general theme is key, since an obvious reciprocal relation is observed in the Colombian HRIA between the human rights and security of workers and communities, on the one hand, and the security of transnational corporations, on the other.[35]

Colombia's third Report, instead of improving upon its predecessor, is quite weak and seems to indicate a lack of serious interest in the project. Except for a few statistics on Canadian trade and investment in the first 15 pages of the 40 page Report, the discussion is so vague that one would not know that it is about Canada–Colombia relations if the title page were not attached. The Colombian Government seems to use much of the Report as a propaganda piece to convey its view on general progress achieved in relation to human rights. It is a one-sided affair and none of it is specific to Canadian trade and investment.[36]

A Better Governmental HRIA

Overall, based on an analysis of the three Annual Reports on Human Rights from both Colombia and Canada, it is clear that these governments do not treat them as a serious tool to improve human rights in Colombia. Instead, they appear to view these Reports as a nuisance they must tolerate annually. The second Colombian Report showed promise, but the third was rote. Regarding Canada, the Harper Government apparently has attempted to clip the potential wings of the HRIA and the two related side agreements on Labour and Environment, to the point that it is doubtful whether the first three can really be called Human Rights Impact Assessments. That was the term that academics and the media assigned to it when it was hoped that the government would indeed assess in a serious and thoughtful way the human rights impact of the CCFTA, especially in the area of extractive investment.[37] The government itself does not use the term HRIA, but instead deems them to be "Annual Reports on Human Rights and Free Trade between Canada and the Republic of Colombia." Despite the colossal failure of these two governments regarding the achievement of a meaningful HRIA, the tool itself remains valuable. A sincere and thoughtful governmental HRIA is an excellent way to promote human security, by improving the rights and living conditions of the host community while simultaneously boosting the security and reputation of Canadian businesses.

We observed in Chapter 1 that the Ruggie Report argues that HRIAs are an excellent tool to promote human security, and that it is up to the State to create the appropriate mechanisms to protect and respect human rights, and to remedy the situation when lapses occur. A revised Canadian HRIA, or its replacement, needs to incorporate those goals in a practical manner. We also saw in Chapter 1 that there is a rich literature on how to develop and conduct HRIAs, both their governmental and corporate versions. Both require a series of common steps. These include an assessment of the existing context and panorama of human rights, or the so-called 'screening' stage. Scoping then needs to take place, involving the development of clear human rights indicators to be used in HRIAs. A baseline needs to be established to determine change. It is best if a third party conducts the impact assessment, to avoid government or corporate bias in reports. Case studies need to be included in the HRIAs to provide an in-depth and nuanced analysis of key human rights issues.

In the Canadian case, if one wishes to resuscitate the HRIA there are a number of points to consider, beyond the methodological aspects noted above. The first concerns a shift in governmental attitude to utilize HRIAs with sincerity in order to improve human security. As Professor Van Harten has shown, even a well-meaning government may find itself challenged to reinvigorate in a practical way the HRIA associated with the CCFTA. A serious revision or even replacement of the current system may be required.

Many issues need to be addressed when reviving or replacing the current HRIA framework. Canadian investment in the extractive sector needs to be evaluated in relation to human rights for reasons we have shown. Rather than just State policy, corporate behaviour needs to be assessed. Governmental HRIAs study the effects of the FTA on human rights, and so the effects of the FTA in terms of encouraging corporate investment in Colombia need to be examined. Indeed, the behaviour of the dominant Canadian extractive sector in Colombia needs to be evaluated in relation to human rights in the country. Complaint mechanisms need to be secure and accessible, so that groups in Colombia may raise human rights issues without threat. Mediation mechanisms need to be inclusive and involve civil society, and not just the State. Remedies need to be provided to victims in cases where human rights have been abused.

Finally, a governmental HRIA could also be used in a broader way to chronicle the general human rights conditions of Colombia in a balanced manner that is beneficial for host communities and investors. It could also mention cases where Canadian corporations fall short in terms of achieving respect for human security. Publicizing such cases could prod TNCs into improved behaviour that it beneficial for corporations and host communities. A sea change in the perspective of the Canadian government would need to occur to achieve a meaningful HRIA.

Corporate HRIAs

Corporate HRIAs can be highly beneficial for companies. They can be used by corporations to assess a situation prior to the actual investment stage to determine if there are any red flags that could impede the project. Such knowledge could determine if investment is wise under the circumstances, and could help chart a course to ameliorate existing human security problems in the region and to prevent new ones from appearing. Once the project is underway, an HRIA can be utilized in a manner that adapts to changing circumstances to promote human security and to prevent abuses.

It is important to emphasize that corporate HRIAs should not be viewed as public relations window-dressing. They can be highly practical mechanisms that save the corporation money by helping to improve the human security context in host communities. Reduced private security costs, reduced threats to corporate executives and infrastructure, and the diminished likelihood of violent work stoppages are some of the potential benefits of an HRIA. These impact assessments can help prevent the costly cancellation of projects due to human rights problems the corporation had not anticipated. Most of the problems addressed in the case studies of this volume would never had occurred if the corporation had administered a sound HRIA.

Dialogue and Security

While HRIAs can detect real and potential problems, their resolution depends on dialogue and a secure platform from which to raise concerns and make formal complaints. The authors of this volume are participants in a wider project that deals with those two objectives. The Rubiales case demonstrates a global lesson that boils down to basic common sense: the necessity of dialogue to resolve problems among all stakeholders, which includes the State, the corporation, the host community and labour. What is so astonishing is that basic dictum of common sense is a rarity in practice. In the cases of Marmato, Chancleta and Patilla, as well as Segovia and Remedios, tripartite negotiation was either absent or infrequent and incomplete. Protracted conflict has been the result, and this has occurred in a manner that is beneficial neither for the community nor for the corporation. Capacity building to assist the Colombian Government in taking the lead in tripartite negotiation on matters involving the Canadian extractive sector should be provided by Canada for that purpose. Such negotiations need to ensure that all participants, and especially the community and labour, are treated with rights and power equal to the State and corporations within such negotiations.

We have observed in the various cases of this book the role of the politics of fear. Given the legacy of violence in the country, and especially violence directed toward labour in Colombia, secure mechanisms need to be established that permit host communities and labour to freely voice concerns or formal complaints regarding the presence of the foreign extractive sector in their communities. There are three goals here. The first is to protect the identity of those who wish to voice a concern or complaint. Secondly, the objective is to ensure that the complaint reaches proper authorities in the State and the related corporation. Finally, it is important to ensure that dialogue and remedies occur that address the situation.

Benedict Anderson stimulated much thought about the politics of space and community though his book *Imagined Communities*.[36] Colombia has been in a process of re-imagining itself to propel all that is good in the country and to escape from preponderant violence, fear, inequity and political exclusion. There has been an attempt to amplify the magic of Colombia's embodiment of magical realism. Toward this end, we have tried to help locate that concentric space – an imagined but not yet achieved community – between the interests of TNCs in the extractive sector and those of host communities. Politics is based on interests, and to achieve social harmony the challenge is to discover paths for interests to coincide.

Notes

1 See James Rochlin, *Social Forces and the Revolution in Military Affairs: the Cases of Mexico and Colombia* (New York: Palgave Macmillan, 2007).
2 Colombia Reports. *Rebel attacks in Colombia drop 46% on year: Ministry*. November 26, 2013. http://colombiareports.co/rebel-attacks-colombia-drop-46-year/. Accessed on November 22, 2014.
3 Colombia Reports. *2nd guerrilla attack on oil pipeline in northeast Colombia in 5 days*. June 25, 2014. http://colombiareports.co/arauca-reports-second-oil-pipeline-attack-5-days/. Accessed on November 19, 2014.
4 CBC News, "Kidnapped Canadian Mining Executive freed by Colombian Rebels," 27 August 2013, www.cbc.ca/news/world/kidnapped-canadian-mining-exec-freed-by-colombian-rebels-1.1335014. Accessed 10 November 2014.
5 See Ted Robert Gurr, *Why Men Rebel* (Princeton: Princeton University Press, 1969).
6 See James Rochlin, "Colombia, Globalization and a Ray of Hope," *Global Labor Journal*, vol. 2, #3, 2011.
7 See, for example, Amnesty International, "Impunity," www.amnestyusa.org/our-work/countries/americas/colombia/impunity, 2013 (no specific date). Accessed November 21, 2014.
8 See, La Razón. *En cinco años, medio millón de bolivianos dejó de ser pobre*. www.la-razon.com/index.php?_url=/sociedad/anos-medio-millon-bolivianos-pobre_0_1556244432.html, March 3, 2012. Accessed November 10, 2014. Ministerio

de Economía y de Finanzas Públicas. Estado Plurinacional de Bolivia. *El Gobierno logra disminuir en 22% la tasa de pobreza extrema en el campo. Agosto 5, 2013.* www.economiayfinanzas.gob.bo/index.php?opcion=com_prensa&ver=prensa&id=29 31&categoria=5&seccion=306. Accessed 10 November 2014.

9 Banco de Desarrollo de América Latina y FLACSO. *Tendencias de las Políticas Sociales en América Latina y el Caribe.* II Boletín. Febrero-Septiembre 2014. www. flacso.org/sites/default/files/Documentos/libros/secretaria-general/Boletin%20Politi-cas%20Sociales%202%20v5%2019%20nov.pdf Accessed November 15, 2014.

10 Comisión Económica para América Latina y el Caribe (CEPAL), *Panorama Social de América Latina,* 2013, sobre la base de tabulaciones especiales de las encuestas de hogares de los respectivos países. www.asocamerlat.org/CEPAL_Panorama Social2013_AmericaLatina_diciembre2013.pdf, p. 13. Accessed November 20, 2014.

11 See, for example: Gustavo Esteva, "Regenerating People's Space," *Alternatives,* vol. 12, #198, 1987; Arturo Escobar, "Reflections on 'Development,'" *Futures,* vol. 24, June 1992; Jan Nederveen Pieterse, "My Paradigm or Yours? Alternative Development, Post-Development, Reflexive Development," *Development and Change,* vol. 29, 1998, pp. 343–373; Stuart Corbridge, "Beneath the Pavement Only Soil: the Poverty of Post Development," *Journal of Developmental Studies,* vol. 34, #6, 1998, pp. 138–148; Ray Kiley, "The Last Refuge of the Noble Savage? Critical Assessment of Post-Development Theory," *European Journal of Development Research,* vol. 11, #1, June 1999, pp. 30–55; Meera Nanda, "Who Needs Post-Development?" *Journal of Development Studies,* vol. 15, #1, 1999, pp. 5–31; Andrew McGregor, "Development, Foreign Aid and Post Development in Timor-Leste," *Third World Quarterly,* vol. 28, #1, 2007, pp. 155–170; and Chizu Sato, "Subjectivity, Enjoyment, and Development," *Rethinking Marxism,* vol. 18, #2, April 2006, pp. 273–288.

12 An excellent example of this literature is Terry Lynn Karl, *Paradox of Plenty* (Los Angeles: University of California Press, 1997). See also Harold Innis, *Essays in Canadian Economic History* (Toronto: University of Toronto Press, 1956).

13 Ibid.

14 Norbey Quevado Hernandez, "El Enigma de Pacific Rubiales." Accessed 7 February 2015, El Espectador, www.elespectador.com/noticias/investigacion/el-enigma-de-pacific-rubiales-articulo-542709.

15 "Colombia's Economic Activity Fails to Generate Jobs," no author, *Colombia Reports,* 17 November 2014. http://colombiareports.co/colombias-economic-activity-generating-employment-un-representative. Accessed November 20, 2014.

16 "Colombia's Mother of All Problems Overtaken by Oil's Drop," Bloomberg, 9 October 2014, www.bloomberg.com/news/2014–10–09/colombia-s-mother-of-all-problems-overtaken-by-oil-s-drop.html. Accessed November 12, 2014.

17 Gran Colombia Gold, Press Release, "Gran Colombia Gold Announces Delay in Paying Interest on Senior Debt," 9 January 2012. Accessed January 12, 2015, http:// grancolombiagold.com/investors/press-Releases/press-releases-details/2015/Gran-Colombia-Gold-Announces-Delay-in-Paying-Interest-on-Senior-Debt/default.aspx. See also: Gran Colombia Gold, Press Release, "Gran Colombia Gold funds February 27 2015 Interest Payments on Senior Debt," Press Release, 5 February 2015, accessed February 8, 2015. http://grancolombiagold.com/investors/press-Releases/ press-releases-details/2015/Gran-Colombia-Gold-funds-February-27–2015-interest-payments-on-senior-debt/default.aspx.

18 Interview by J. Rochlin, Senator Jorge Robledo, Polo Democrático, September 15, 2014, Bogotá.

19 Interview by J. Rochlin with Alejandro Ramirez, Corporate Social Responsibility Manager, Pacific Rubiales Energy Corporation, Bogotá, September 18, 2014.

20 Interview by J. Rochlin with Andres Rendle, Vice President, South American Resources, Cosigo Resources Ltd., telephone, August 5, 2014.

21 Luis Jorge Garay Salamanca, *Minera en Colombia,* Controlaría General de la República, Bogota, Abril 2013, p. 63.

22 Canada–Colombia Free Trade Agreement, Chapter 8, Article 15. www.international. gc.ca/trade-agreements-accords-commerciaux/agr-acc/colombia-colombie/index.aspx? lang=eng. Accessed September 15, 2014.

23 Canada–Colombia Free Trade Agreement, Chapter 8, "Investment," articles 815 and 816.

24 Government of Canada, *Annual Report Pursuant to the Agreement Concerning Annual Reports on Human Rights and Free Trade between Canada and the Republic of Colombia*, June 19, 2013, p. 13/31. www.canadainternational.gc.ca/colombia-colombie/bilateral_relations_bilaterales/rep-hrft-co_2013-dple-rapp.aspx?lang=eng. Accessed November 1, 2014.

25 Government of Canada, Foreign Affairs, Trade and Development Canada, "Minister Fast Marks Second Anniversary of Canada–Colombia Free Trade Agreement," 15 August 2013. www.international.gc.ca/media/comm/news-communiques/2013/08/15a. aspx?lang=eng. Accessed September 15, 2013.

26 Government of Canada, The Canadian Trade Commissioner Service, "Canada–Colombia Free Trade Agreement – Oil and Gas Sector Opportunities," no date, www.tradecommissioner.gc.ca/eng/document/jsp?did=133064 accessed October 20, 2013.

27 For a discussion of this point, see Canadian Council for International Cooperation, Americas Policy Group, Rachel Warden and Barbara Wood, *Embassy Magazine*, June 26, 2012. www.ccic.ca/_files/en/working_groups/2013_06_Colombia_HRA_Op_ed. pdf. Accessed August 30, 2013.

28 Government of Canada, "Annual Report Pursuant to the Agreement Concerning Annual Reports on Human Rights and Free Trade between Canada and the Republic of Colombia," June 19, 2013, op. cit., p. 2/12.

29 Ibid.

30 Ibid, p. 3/12.

31 Interview by J. Rochlin, and subsequent correspondence, with J P Hamel, Counsellor, Commercial, Canadian Embassy in Bogota, Interview August 17, 2011 and subsequent email October 14, 2011.

32 Gobierno de Colombia, Ministerio de Relaciones Exteriores. "Segundo Informe Anual del "Acuerdo en Matería de Informes Anuales Sobre Derechos Humanos y Libre Comercio Entre La República de Colombia y Canada," Bogotá, May 15, 2013, pp. 8–10, section three of the document. Mimeograph.

33 Ibid. p. 14, section 5 of document.

34 Ibid., section 6.

35 Gobierno de Colombia, Grupo Tecnico Interinstitucional sobre Acuerdos Comericales y Derechos Humanos, *Tercer Informe Annual del 'Acuerdo en Materia de Informes Anuales Sobre Derechos Humanos y Libre Comercio Entre la República de Colombia y Canada,'* Bogotá, Mayo 15, 2015. Mimeograph.

36 Much of that literature is covered thoroughly in Chapter 1 of this volume.

37 Benedict Anderson, *Imagined Communities* (London: Verso, 1983).

Bibliography

Amnesty International, no author. "Impunity," www.amnestyusa.org/our-work/countries/americas/colombia/impunity, 2013 (no specific date). Accessed November 21, 2014.

Anderson, Benedict. *Imagined Communities* (London: Verso, 1983).

Banco de Desarrollo de América Latina y FLACSO. *Tendencias de las Políticas Sociales en América Latina y el Caribe.* II Boletín. Febrero-Septiembre 2014. www.flacso.org/sites/default/files/Documentos/libros/secretaria-general/Boletin%20Politicas%20Sociales%202%20v5%2019%20nov.pdf. Accessed November 15, 2014.

Bloomberg news, "Colombia's Mother of All Problems Overtaken by Oil's Drop,"

October 9, 2014, www.bloomberg.com/news/2014-10-09/colombia-s-mother-of-all-problems-overtaken-by-oil-s-drop.html. Accessed November 12, 2014.

CBC News, no author. "Kidnapped Canadian Mining Executive freed by Colombian Rebels," 27 August 2013, www.cbc.ca/news/world/kidnapped-canadian-mining-exec-freed-by-colombian-rebels-1.1335014. Accessed November 10, 2014.

Colombia Reports, no author. "Colombia's Economic Activity Fails to Generate Jobs," 17 November 2014. http://colombiareports.co/colombias-economic-activity-generating-employment-un-representative. Accessed November 20, 2014.

Colombia Reports, no author. *Rebel attacks in Colombia drop 46% on year: Ministry.* November 26, 2013. http://colombiareports.co/rebel-attacks-colombia-drop-46-year/ Accessed November 22, 2014.

Colombia Reports, no author. *2nd guerrilla attack on oil pipeline in northeast Colombia in 5 days.* June 25, 2014. http://colombiareports.co/arauca-reports-second-oil-pipeline-attack-5-days. Accessed November 19, 2014.

Comisión Económica para América Latina y el Caribe (CEPAL), *Panorama Social de América Latina*, 2013, sobre la base de tabulaciones especiales de las encuestas de hogares de los respectivos países. www.asocamerlat.org/CEPAL_PanoramaSocial2013_AmericaLatina_diciembre2013.pdf. Accessed November 20, 2014.

Corbridge, Stuart. "Beneath the Pavement Only Soil: the Poverty of Post Development," *Journal of Developmental Studies*, vol. 34, #6, 1998, pp. 138–148.

Escobar, Arturo. "Reflections on 'Development,'" *Futures*, vol. 24, June 1992.

Esteva, Gustavo. "Regenerating People's Space," *Alternatives*, vol. 12, #198, 1987.

Garay Salamanca, Luis Jorge. *Minera en Colombia* (Bogotá: Controlaría General de la República, April 2013).

Gobierno de Bolivia. Ministerio de Economía y de Finanzas Públicas. Estado Plurinacional de Bolivia. *El Gobierno logra disminuir en 22% la tasa de pobreza extrema en el campo.* Agosto 5, 2013. www.economiayfinanzas.gob.bo/index.php?opcion=com_prensa&ver=prensa&id=2931&categoria=5&seccion=306. Accessed 10 November 2012.

Gobierno de Colombia, Ministerio de Relaciones Exteriores. "Segundo Informe Anual del "Acuerdo en Matería de Informes Anuales Sobre Derechos Humanos y Libre Comercio Entre La República de Colombia y Canada," Bogotá, May 15, 2013. Mimeograph.

Gobierno de Colombia, Grupo Tecnico Interinstitucional sobre Acuerdos Comericales y Derechos Humanos. *Tercer Informe Annual del 'Acuerdo en Materia de Informes Anuales Sobre Derechos Humanos y Libre Comercio Entre la República de Colombia y Canada,'* Bogotá, Mayo 15, 2015. Mimeograph.

Government of Canada. *Annual Report Pursuant to the Agreement Concerning Annual Reports on Human Rights and Free Trade between Canada and the Republic of Colombia*, 19 June 2013. www.canadainternational.gc.ca/colombia-colombie/bilateral_relations_bilaterales/rep-hrft-co_2013-dple-rapp.aspx?lang=eng. Accessed September 12, 2014.

Government of Canada. *Canada–Colombia Free Trade Agreement*, Chapter 8, Article 15. www.international.gc.ca/trade-agreements-accords-commerciaux/agr-acc/colombia-colombie/index.aspx?lang=eng. August 2011. Accessed June 15, 2012.

Government of Canada. The Canadian Trade Commissioner Service, "Canada–Colombia Free Trade Agreement – Oil and Gas Sector Opportunities," no date, www.tradecommissioner.gc.ca/eng/document/jsp?did=133064. Accessed October 20, 2013.

Government of Canada. Foreign Affairs, Trade and Development Canada, "Minister Fast Marks Second Anniversary of Canada–Colombia Free Trade Agreement," August 15, 2013. www.international.gc.ca/media/comm/news-communiques/2013/08/15a.aspx?lang=eng. Accessed 15 September 2013.

Gurr, Ted Robert. *Why Men Rebel* (Princeton: Princeton University Press, 1969).

Innis, Harold. *Essays in Canadian Economic History* (Toronto: University of Toronto Press, 1956).

Karl, Terry Lynn. *Paradox of Plenty* (Los Angeles: University of California Press, 1997).

Kiley, Ray. "The Last Refuge of the Noble Savage? Critical Assessment of Post-Development Theory," *European Journal of Development Research*, vol. 11, #1, June 1999, pp. 30–55.

La Razón. *En cinco años, medio millón de bolivianos dejó de ser pobre.* www.la-razon.com/index.php?_url=/sociedad/anos-medio-millon-bolivianos-pobre_0_1556244432.html, 3 March 2012. Accessed November 10, 2014.

McGregor, Andrew. "Development, Foreign Aid and Post Development in Timor-Leste," *Third World Quarterly*, vol 28, #1, 2007, pp. 155–170.

Nanda, Meera. "Who Needs Post-Development?" *Journal of Development Studies*, vol. 15, #1, 1999, pp. 5–31.

Nederveen Pieterse, Jan. "My Paradigm or Yours? Alternative Development, Post-Development, Reflexive Development," *Development and Change*, vol. 29, 1998, pp. 343–373.

Rochlin, James. "Colombia, Globalization and a Ray of Hope," *Global Labor Journal*, vol. 2, #3, 2011, pp. 180–207.

Rochlin, James. *Social Forces and the Revolution in Military Affairs: the Cases of Mexico and Colombia* (New York: Palgrave Macmillan, 2007).

Sato, Chizu. "Subjectivity, Enjoyment, and Development," *Rethinking Marxism*, vol. 18, #2, April 2006, pp. 273–288.

Warden, Rachel and Barbara Wood, "Embassy Magazine," June 26, 2012. www.ccic.ca/_files/en/working_groups/2013_06_Colombia_HRA_Op_ed.pdf. Accessed August 30, 2013.

Index

Page numbers in *italics* denote tables.

For Product Safety Concerns and Information please contact our EU representative GPSR@taylorandfrancis.com Taylor & Francis Verlag GmbH, Kaufingerstraße 24, 80331 München, Germany